Heerajee Eduljee

History of the medical art

Past and present

Heerajee Eduljee

History of the medical art
Past and present

ISBN/EAN: 9783741169908

Manufactured in Europe, USA, Canada, Australia, Japa

Cover: Foto ©ninafisch / pixelio.de

Manufactured and distributed by brebook publishing software (www.brebook.com)

Heerajee Eduljee

History of the medical art

HISTORY

OF THE

MEDICAL ART,

PAST AND PRESENT.

BY

HEERAJEE EDULJEE,

GRADUATE OF THE GRANT MEDICAL COLLEGE, MEDICAL OFFICER
TO THE MANOCKJEE NUSSERWANJEE PETIT'S
CHARITABLE DISPENSARY, BOMBAY.

TRUTH, LIKE A TORCH, THE MORE IT'S SHOOK IT SHINE

[*Registered under Act XXV. of 1867.*]

𝔅𝔬𝔪𝔟𝔞𝔶:
PRINTED AT THE
EDUCATION SOCIETY'S PRESS, BYCULLA.

1880.

[*The author reserves the right of translation of the whole, or of any part of this work.*]

PREFACE.

I AM not acquainted with any book in the English language which professes to give in a condensed form an account of the history and progress of medicine and its practitioners from the remotest ages down to the present time. It has often struck me that the absence of such a work is an existing want, and it is with a view to supply this, that I have endeavoured to bring together in one review the condition of the Art of Medicine, and to trace its gradual advancement at successive periods of history. From the above remark I except the admirable work of Dr. Rutherfurd Russell, entitled *History and Heroes of Medicine*. But neither Dr. Russell's work nor the present one has the slightest claim to be called a complete History of Medicine. The preparation of this volume has not been an easy task, however imperfectly I may have fulfilled it. It was impossible, even if it had been in my power, to complete a work of this kind in Bombay. However, I have neither spared trouble nor expense in rendering the work acceptable to the reader, and with a resolution to speak fairly, not flatteringly. Truth and impartiality are two important qualifications in an author. To these I have strictly adhered throughout the execution of this work, and with its many imperfections, of which I am conscious, I yet venture to hope that it may be useful both to the professional and general reader. I will only further add that, in contrasting the present work with that of Dr. Russell, the reader is the best judge of the

amount of work done, and the quantity of valuable ma
contained in each, or of any merits the one may poss
over the other. If my readers will look at Dr. Russ
work, they must be disappointed with the superficial manner in which the author disposes of the first four chapters on the condition of the Medical Art among the Greeks, Romans and Arabians. Strange to say, he has taken no notice of the labours of the ancient Egyptians, Hindoos, Persians, &c. But the remaining chapters of his work contain a large amount of valuable information. In conclusion, I entertain a hope that some allowance may be made for errors of composition and idiomatic inaccuracies, and ask my readers to remember that the author writes in a foreign language a book whose scope is so wide, and whose subjects are so varied. I have not, I trust, failed to acknowledge the sources whence my information is derived, but if any omissions exist, they are unintentional. Of the defects of this work I am painfully alive. Should it meet with a favourable reception, I shall derive no small gratification, and shall feel that my labours have not been altogether unprofitable.

CONTENTS.

CHAPTER I.

PAGE

The Origin of the Medical Art attributed by the Ancients to the Gods—Remedial means pointed out by Animals—Priests and Medicine—Assyria and Babylonia without Physicians—Egypt—Its Antiquity and Civilization—Hermetic Book of Medicaments—Practice of Medicine confined to the Priests—Medical Code—Charms and Amulets—Specialists—Midwives—Surgery—Embalmment—Abundance of Medicinal Herbs 1

CHAPTER II.

State of Medicine among the Greeks—Belief in Oracles—Malampus—He cures the daughters of king Proetus—Chiron—Æsculapius—His birth—Is worshipped after death—Surgeons in the siege of Troy—The Asclepiadæ and the Æsculapian Temples—Philosophy and Medicine—The Ionic, the Italic, and the Eleatic Schools of Philosophy 10

CHAPTER III.

Hippocrates—His birth and parentage—Records in the Temples of Æsculapius—Medical Gymnastics—The Plague in Athens—Nature cures Diseases—Contraries cure contraries—Similars cure similars—Elements and Humours—Dogmatists—Empirics—Methodists—True System—On the genuine works of Hippocrates—On works with or without additions by his followers—On his doubtful works 26

CHAPTER IV.

Draco—Thessalus—Aristotle—Theophrastus—Diocles—His letter to Antigonas—Praxagoras—Chrysippus—Foundation of Alexandria—Its Schools and Libraries—Herophilus and Erasistratus—Criminals dissected alive—Improvements in Anatomy—Love-sickness—Serapion—Lithotomy and Lithotrity 57

CHAPTER V.

Eminence of the ancient Hindoos in the healing art—Herbs highly prized—Ayurveda—Its knowledge imparted by Brahma—Surgeons divine—Charaka—Dhanwantari—Susruta—Origin of the Vaidya caste—Just estimate of a skilful physician—Moral discipline—Dissection of dead bodies—Chemistry—Surgical operations and instruments—Small-pox Inoculation—Materia Medica—Pharmacy—Pathology—Incurable Diseases supposed to be produced by sins—Influence of evil spirits and gods in producing diseases—Diagnosis and Prognosis.—The present Vaids and Hakims—Graduates of Medicine in India—The peculiar patients—European medical skill not acknowledged by the natives of India—The Indian Medical Service 66

CHAPTER VI.

Rise of the Buddhist Religion in India—Founder of Buddhism—Chandragupta—Asoka—Foundation of Hospitals—Inscriptions on the Rocks at Girnar and at Dhauli—Buddhadaso—His charitable acts—His extraordinary cures—Persecution and decline of the Buddhist religion in India—China—Its antiquity and civilization—Arts and sciences stationary—Barriers to improvements in practice—Medical sects—Treatment of the sick while under the influence of demons—Materia Medica—Complicated Prescriptions—*Yang* and *Yin*—Scheme of Physic—Contemptible treatment—The Pulse—Anatomy—Midwifery—Surgery—Moxa—Acupuncture—The Jews—Their knowledge of Medicine—Their superstitious practices—Leprosy—Surgery—Cæsarian section 118

CHAPTER VII.

Ancient Persia—Its power and extent—Its conquest by the Arabs—Persecution of Zoroastrians—Their Emigration to India—They regain their ancient prosperity—Their philanthropy and benevolence—Signs of degeneracy—The ancient Magi—Their learning and influence—Account of Thrita, the first Physician—Test of the capability of a person wishing to practise the healing art—Recompenses to be paid to successful physicians—Egyptian and Greek Physicians in the Persian Court—The Sassanian Kings—Their love of learning 136

CHAPTER VIII.

Zarathustra Spitaman—The age in which he lived—His birth and parentage—His early career—He communicates his Divine mission to King Gustasp—His persecutions—Gustasp becomes a zealous convert to the Zoroastrian faith—Rapid spread of the new religion—Assassination of Zarathustra—His monotheism—His sacred writings—His extant works—Avesta and Hygiene. 154

CONTENTS.

PAGE

CHAPTER IX.

Rome without Physicians throughout the Republic—Opposition to Greek Philosophy and Physic—Archagathus—Medicine practised by Slaves—Asclepiades—His simplicity of Treatment—His Inventions—His theory of Disease—His Death—Themison—State of Medicine during the Empire—Celsus—Survey of his treatise *De Medicina*—Pliny—Thessalus—Clinical instruction—Andromachus—Aretæus—Character of his writings—Dioscorides—Cælius Aurelianus—Galen—His wanderings—His knowledge of Anatomy—Of Physiology—Of Pathology—Active Treatment—Influence of his writings—Oribasius—Ætius—Alexander Trallianus—Paulus Ægineta 198

CHAPTER X.

Decline and fall of the Roman Empire in the West—Rise of the splendid Empire of the Saracens—Destruction of the Alexandrian Library—Accession of the house of Abbas—The Caliphs Almansur, Harun-al-Rashid, and Almamun—Their love of learning and patronage to Arts and Sciences—Empire of the Saracens in the West and of the Fatimites in Egypt—Library of Cordova—Foundation of a College at Bagdad—Magnificence of the Saracen Courts—Medical Schools—Addition of new drugs to the *Materia Medica*—Discoveries in Chemistry—Celebrated Arab Physicians 238

CHAPTER XI.

Christianity and Medicine—Medical Practice engrossed by Monks and Clergy—Their superstitious practices—Decrees of Popes and Councils—Praiseworthy efforts of Charlemagne—Relics of Saints—Astrology blended with Medicine—Charms and Amulets—Strange Prescriptions—Royal Touch for the cure of King's Evil—Proclamation—School of Salerno—Dissection of dead bodies—Mondini—Roger Bacon—His learning—Curious receipt—Arnoldus de Villa Nova—Linacre—Foundation of the Royal College of Physicians of London 255

CHAPTER XII.

Paracelsus—His Travels—Azoth and Arcanum—Professor at Basle—He burns the writings of Galen and Avicenna before his class—Rejects the doctrine of humours and the law of contraries—His eccentric behaviour and dissipated habits—His favourite sword—His death—Jerome Cardan—His early education—Magic and Astrology—Is consulted by Edward VI.—He dies by starvation—Vesalius—Servetus—Is burnt to death for improving Anatomy—Galenists and Chemists—Opposition to the use of chemical remedies 270

CHAPTER XIII.

Van Halmont—He studies Medicine—Rejects the writings of the ancients—His humility—His Archæus—Lord Bacon—His early career—His employment of the word *Idolæ*—Healing art uncertain and unprogressive—Remedies pointed out—Descartes—His early education—Studies medicine—His notions about the production of Motion and Animal Heat—Boyle—Imperfection of the curative branch of Medicine—Simple medication—Rationale of specifics 280

CHAPTER XIV.

Harvey—His medical career—Physician to Charles I.—Discovers the circulation of the blood—Is persecuted by his colleagues—Claim of Cesalpinus to the discovery—Sylvius de la Boe—Disease and Chemical Actions—His system of cure—Willis—Rise of the Mathematical School—Borelli—Bellini—Mechanical Theory—Sydenham—His early career—Specifics wanted—Fermentation and Depuration—Nature cures diseases—Rheumatism cured by Whey—Simplicity of Prescriptions—History of the Peruvian Bark—Prejudice against its use—Oliver Cromwell dies of an ague—Sydenham's testimony in favour of Bark and his mode of using it—Richard Talbot—His success in curing Agues 291

CHAPTER XV.

Stahl—His reputation as a teacher—Rejects the doctrines of the Chemical and Mechanical Physicians—His Anima—Expectant treatment—Hoffmann—Nervous fluid—Theory of Spasm—Flee doctors and drugs—Boerhaave—His reputation as a successful lecturer and practitioner—His system of cure—Power of Attenuated Medicines—Van Swieten—Haller—His early acquirements—Professor at Gottingen—His fame as a Physiologist—Doctrine of Irritability and Sensibility—Glisson—Whitt—His notions of the influence of Mind upon the Body 309

CHAPTER XVI.

Cullen—His early education—Visits Glasgow and Edinburgh—His fame as a Lecturer—His notion of Life—Experience without Reasoning fallacious—His theory of Fever—Cinchona Bark not a specific—Its action in curing fevers explained—Blood-letting in Pneumonia and Measles—Blisters in Small-pox—John Brown—His early career—Theory of Excitability—The Brunonians—Their fanaticism—Brown's disorderly behaviour and death 320

CHAPTER XVII.

Birth and education of Jenner—The peasantry of Gloucestershire, and the reputed power of Cow-pox—Jenner investigates the subject—Meets with various obstacles—True and Spurious Cow-pox—The *Grease* in Horses—Identity of Cow-pox and Small-pox—Birth-day of Vaccination—Small-pox after Cow-pox—Revaccination—Ravages of Small-pox—Honours paid to Jenner—Parliament votes him £30,000—India transmits a present of £7,383—The Peculiar People—History of Small-pox Inoculation 332

CHAPTER XVIII.

Abuse of drugs and wholesale destruction of life—Vulgar physicians—Recent advances of Medicine—Uncertainty of medical practice—Mischievous experiments on the sick—Allopathy—Homœopathy—Outline of the life and labours of Hahnemann—*Vis medicatrix Naturæ* 346

CHAPTER I.

The origin of the Medical Art attributed by the ancients to the Gods—Remedial means pointed out by Animals—Priests and Medicine—Assyria and Babylonia without Physicians—Egypt—Its Antiquity and Civilization—Hermetic Book of Medicaments—Practice of Medicine confined to the Priests—Medical Code—Charms and Amulets—Specialists—Midwives—Surgery—Embalmment—Abundance of Medicinal Herbs.

THE origin of the Medical Art was attributed by the ancients to their gods. It was referred by the Greeks to Apollo, and by the Egyptians to Thyoth or Thoth. In the very beginning of the famous Hippocratic oath the former is introduced by the author as a physician, "I swear by Apollo the physician." Ovid, speaking of him, says—

"Med'cine is mine, what herbs and simples grow
In fields and forests, all their powers I know,
And am the great physician call'd below."—*Dryden.*

Æsculapius, the supposed son of Apollo, was worshipped by the Greeks as their god of medicine. It is said in one of the oldest medical records of the Hindoos, "The judicious alleviation of human infirmities, the means of which were compassionately *revealed by the gods,* can only be effected from study and practice conjoined."* It is also stated

---
* Prof. H. H. Wilson's *Works*, vol. I., p. 381.

in some of the Hindoo medical Shastras that their gods, Brahma, Siva, Dacsha, Indra, Surya, and his two offsprings the Ashwins, were perfectly acquainted with the healing art, and performed extraordinary cures in heaven! The Hindoos believe that from these deities the Brahmins first derived their knowledge of medicine.

Later writers assert that animals drew the attention of man to the use of several means for the cure of disease. The ancients learned from the dog the use of purgatives; the bird called the ibis taught them the use of injections; the practice of bleeding was shown by the hippopotamus to the Egyptians; the value of the juice of chelidonium in ophthalmia was pointed out by the swallow; and dropsical cattle, by resorting to ferruginous waters, made man acquainted with their properties.

The art of medicine begins with the creation of the world. Hippocrates observes that "as soon as man began to distinguish the things which were good and bad in diseases, there was art." The first cry of pain, or a drop of blood from the first inflicted wound, must have compelled man to seek immediate relief. Every person in that age must have been his own physician. "It is sufficiently probable," says Dr. Cullen, "that very soon after the first beginnings of human society, some art of physic and some knowledge of remedies arose among men. And accordingly no country has been discovered among the people of which, however rude and uncultivated in other respects, an art of physic and the knowledge of a great number of remedies

and become acquainted with them. When medicines failed, they trusted exclusively to magical incantations, charms, and amulets. The superstitious practice of wearing amulets took its origin in ancient Egypt. We are told that the Egyptian king Nechepsus believed in the power of amulets, and had himself written that a green jasper cut into a certain form, if worn, possessed the power of strengthening the stomach.

Herodotus relates that the medical profession was sub-divided in Egypt, each physician treating disorders of a particular member of the body only. There were some for disorders of the eyes; others attended to diseases of the head; some practised dentistry; others confined themselves to the treatment of diseases of the abdomen. As the physicians were forbidden to practise two branches of the profession, there were a considerable number of them in Egypt. Homer calls each Egyptian a medical man.

There appears to have been a distinct class of midwives in Egypt, for not long after the death of Joseph, Pharaoh gave strict orders to the midwives to put to death all the sons of the Hebrews at their birth.

We learn from Celsus that the Egyptians had made great advances in surgery. He mentions Philoxenes as the author of many volumes on surgery. "From some observations made by the men of science who accompanied the French expedition to Egypt in 1798, it appears that there are documents fully proving that in very remote times this extraordinary people had made a degree of progress of which few of the moderns have any conception. Upon the ceilings and walls of the temples at

Tentyra, Karnac, Luxor, &c., basso-relievos are seen representing limbs that have been cut off with instruments very analogous to those which are employed at the present day for amputations. The same instruments are again observed in the hieroglyphics; and vestiges of other surgical operations may be traced which afford convincing proofs of the skill of the ancient Egyptians in this branch of medical science." (Larry, quoted in Cooper's *Surgical Dict.*)

The operation of bleeding from a vein was practised by the Egyptians at a very early date. Pliny the naturalist tells us that the Egyptians learnt the use of blood-letting from the hippopotamus, and styles it "The discoverer of the art of letting blood." "When the animal," says he, "has become too bulky by continued over-feeding, it goes down to the banks of the river, and examines the reeds which have been newly cut; as soon as it has found a stump that is very sharp, it presses its body against it, and so wounds one of the veins in the thigh; and by the flow of blood thus produced, the body, which would otherwise have fallen into a morbid state, is relieved; after which it covers up the wound with mud."*

The Egyptians were also acquainted with the mode of stopping decayed teeth with gold, as a few of those obtained from mummies were observed to have been stuffed with that metal.

That embalming of the dead was practised in Egypt at a very early period by the priests, who were also their physicians, appears from Genesis i. 2, "Joseph

---

* Pliny's *Natural History*, translated by J. Bostock and H. T. Riley, bk. VIII., ch. 40.

commanded his servants, the physicians, to embalm his father, and the physicians embalmed Israel." The Arabians brought myrrh, balm, and spicery into Egypt which the Egyptians made use of in embalming their dead. That the Arab merchants carried on their trade in drugs and spicery with the Egyptians is certain, for it is said in Genesis xxxvii. 25, "And they sat down to eat bread, and they lifted up their eyes, and looked, and beheld a company of Ishmaelites from Gilead, and their camels bearing spicery, and balm, and myrrh, going to carry it down to Egypt."

There was an abundance of medicinal herbs in Egypt which the natives of that country made use of. The book of Jeremiah (xlvi. 11) says: "Go up into Gilead, and take balm, O virgin, the daughter of Egypt; in vain hast thou multiplied medicines; for thou shalt not be cured." Helen while she stayed in Egypt learned from Polydamna, the wife of Thonis, the properties of several drugs:—

"Meantime with genial joy to warm the soul,
Bright Helen mix'd a mirth-inspiring bowl:
Temper'd with drugs of sovereign use t'assuage
The boiling bosom of tumultuous rage;
To clear the cloudy front of wrinkled care,
And dry the tearful sluices of despair:
These drugs, so friendly to the joys of life,
Bright Helen learned from Thone's imperial wife;
Who sway'd the sceptre where prolific Nile
With various simples clothes the fattened soil;
With wholesome herbage mix'd the direful bane
Of vegetable venom taints the plain."*

It is conjectured that opium was one of the ingredients that Helen mixed with wine.

---

* Pope's Homer's *Odyssey*, bk. IV.

CHAPTER II.

State of Medicine among the Greeks—Belief in Oracles—Melampus—He cures the daughters of King Proetus—Chiron—Æsculapius—His birth—Is worshipped after death—Surgeons in the Siege of Troy—The Asclepiadæ and the Æsculapian Temples—Philosophy and Medicine—The Ionic, the Italic, and the Eleatic Schools of Philosophy.

In the most remote period of Grecian history the art of Medicine was very little known to the Greeks. Before their intercourse with the Egyptians the Greeks were utterly superstitious and uncultivated, consulting their gods and demi-gods in calamity. Every disorder was attributed to the anger of one of their numerous gods and goddesses. As for instance, it is related that the three daughters of Proetus, named Lysippe, Iphinoe, and Iphianassa, were driven mad by the god Dionysus, as a just punishment for having despised his worship. According to another tradition, they were rash enough to boast that they were more handsome than the goddess Hera, who punished them with madness, in which state they wandered about naked in the jungles. This is not to be wondered at when we learn that in ancient times the gods and goddesses had the power and skill of metamorphosing a human being into an ass or an owl—even into a stone or a tree. Two out of the above named girls were pursued, overtaken, and cured by a physician named Melampus, as we shall presently see. According to others he effected a cure in all.

The Greeks, as well as the Egyptians, Lydians, &c. believed in the prophetic inspiration of the several oracles they consulted on particular occasions. We read in history of an instance in which an ancient king consulted the oracle of Delphi, because one of his sons was deaf and dumb. The following is the answer he received:—

"Lydian, wide-ruling monarch, thou wondrous simple Crœsus,
Wish not even to hear in thy palace the voice thou hast prayed for,
Uttering intelligent sounds. Far better thy son should be silent!
Oh! woe worth the day when thine ear shall first list to his accents."*

According to the credulity of the age, the following event happened after a lapse of time, as stated in the prophetic inspiration of the oracle. War broke out between the Persians and Lydians. King Cyrus, after having laid siege to Sardis, and taken it by surprise, gave up the town to plunder. One of his soldiers not recognizing king Crœsus, was about to slay him, when his son who, as mentioned above, was naturally dumb, alarmed at seeing the Persian rushing towards his father, uttered these words:—
"Man, do not kill Crœsus." Hearing this, the Persian spared the king's life, and made him a prisoner. Another person of great repute, named Battus, who stammered, went to Delphi to consult the oracle, when the Pythoness gave him the following reply:—

" Battus, thou comest to ask of thy voice, but Phœbus Apollo
Bids thee establish a city in Lybia, abounding in fleeces."†

* *History of Herodotus*, by G. Rawlinson, vol. I., p. 179.
† Ibid, vol. III., p. 106.

Even long after this period, when it was the practice to record the cures of diseases on tablets in the temples of Æsculapius, consulting the will of the gods was not neglected by some of the heathen nations of antiquity on occasions of illnesses. Four curious votive tablets have been discovered on an island in the Tiber. The following English translation of the inscriptions on them will elucidate the practice:—

I.—" In these days the oracle spake to a certain blind man of the name of Gajus; he was to go to the altar and to pray, then make a circuit from right to left, lay his five fingers upon the altar, raise his hand and place it upon his eyes. Thus, in the presence of the people, loudly rejoicing, he regained his health. This manifestation of omnipotence happened under the emperor Antoninus."

II.—" The oracle spake to the blind soldier Valerius Aper: he was to come and mix the blood of a white cock with honey, make an eye-salve, and smear his eyes with it for three days. He recovered his sight, and came and returned thanks to the god before all the people."

III.—" Julian appeared to be in a hopeless state after an attack of spitting of blood. The god, by means of the oracle, ordered him to come and take a pine-cone from the altar, and to eat this mixed with honey for three days. He was cured, and came and thanked the god before all the people."

IV.—" The son of Lucius, who lay hopelessly with a stitch in his side, was ordered by the god, in a night vision, to come and take ashes from the altar, to mix them with wine, and lay them on the side. He was rescued, and thanked the god before all the people, and the people wished him joy."*

The name of Melampus, who is said to have lived about the fourteenth century before Christ, is mentioned as the first who was in great repute

---

* *Vide* Smith's *Dictionary of Greek and Roman Antiquities*, and Russell's *History and Heroes of Medicine*.

amongst the Greeks for his medical skill. He spent the early part of his life in studying under the Egyptian priests, and was the first to introduce among the Greeks the ceremonies of Bacchus from Egypt; and had, according to Herodotus, acquired " the art of divination." We cannot at present do more than quote a few sentences from Hahnemann's *Dissertatio historico-medica de helleborismo veterum*, and Hempel's *Materia Medica* :—

"About the year 1,500 before our era, a certain Melampus, son of Amythaon, a most celebrated augur and physician, first at Pylos, then among the Argivans, is said to have cured the daughters of Proetus, king of the Argivans, who, in consequence of remaining unmarried, were seized with an amorous furor, and affected by a wandering mania; they were cured chiefly by means of *veratrum album* given in the milk of goats fed upon veratrum, which Melampus had observed to produce purgative effects on these animals. From this circumstance the great fame of this plant is derived."*

Let us now hear Dr. Hempel, who, in his lecture on Hellebore, gives a brief account of the cure performed by this physician :—

"In olden times, about the year 1,400 before Christ, there reigned a good and generous king Proetus, whose daughters were insane in consequence of menstrual suppression, or some other abnormal condition of the sexual sphere. The poor girls ran about the forests naked like beasts, and imitating the sound of animals. Proetus offered half his kingdom to any one who should cure his daughters. This tempted the good doctor Melampus to try the cure. He accomplished it with black hellebore, obtained half a kingdom, and he and his two brothers became the king's sons-in-law." †

On account of this, the black hellebore is also called Melampodium. We are also informed that

---

* Hahnemann's *Lesser Writings*, translated by R. E. Dudgeon, M.D.

† Hempel's *Materia Medica*, vol. I., p. 507.

Melampus succesfully used iron rust for the cure of sterility in one of the Argonauts.

About this period the Phœnicians and Egyptians, but chiefly the latter, led by their respective leaders, emigrated from their native countries, founded colonies in different parts of the Grecian Peninsula, built cities, and introduced civilization among the inhabitants. From them, the Greeks first derived their scanty knowledge of medicine. Others travelled in distant countries, chiefly Egypt, in search of knowledge.

The name of Chiron, " the wisest and justest of all the Centaurs," is mentioned in history as the first native who possessed a greater degree of medical knowledge than any of his predecessors. He is said to have lived 1300 years before Christ. Homer speaks of him in the *Iliad*, as the " Sire of Pharmacy," who taught the healing art to Æsculapius, and also to Achilles, one of the leaders of the Greek army in the Trojan war.

We have next to notice the history of an individual of considerable distinction among his countrymen—Æsculapius. According to the mythology of the Greeks, his mother's name was Koronis, who once "was beloved by Apollo, and became pregnant by him." She afterwards became unfaithful to the god by falling in love with one Ischys, an Arcadian, and was therefore mortally wounded with an arrow by Apollo, but Æsculapius, while an infant, was rescued from destruction by a shepherd, some say by Apollo himself. It is said that he was separated from his mother by an incision made into the abdomen before she was placed on the burning-pile. He was afterwards removed to a cave on Mount Pelion, and placed under the protection of Chiron, who instructed him in the art of medicine. Being possessed of superior talents, he assiduously cultivated medicine and became more famous than his preceptor. He was the first who studied medicine as a science, and acquired high celebrity by his successful practice. He devoted the greater part of his life to treating wounds and injuries, and was considered the best surgeon of his age. But among the fables of antiquity, we read that he at last invoked the anger of one of the gods, who killed him because he "even restored the dead to life." The god was Zeus, who " now found himself under the necessity of taking precautions lest mankind, thus unexpectedly protected against sickness and death, should no longer stand in need of the immortal gods: he smote Æsculapius with thunder and killed him."*

After his death, temples of health called Asclepia, were erected to his honour in various parts of Greece, such as Cos, Cnidos, Epidaurus, &c., where he was worshipped as a god with great reverence. It was in these temples that the descendants of Æsculapius first kept records of diseases and their remedies on marble. People loaded the temples with presents of great value, and offered sacrifices to the god. Kings showered rich gifts upon the temples to please the god of health and to avert his wrath. History tells us that Hephæstion, a favourite general and an intimate friend of Alexander the Great, of

---

* Grote's *History of Greece*, vol. I., p. 151.

Macedon, was carried off by a fever. The king was plunged into such grief for his loss that the physician who had prescribed for him was ordered to be crucified; and on one occasion, while making magnificent presents to the temple of Epidaurus to propitiate the god of health, reproached him in these words: "Æsculapius has shown me but very little indulgence in not preserving the life of a friend who was as dear to me as myself." This reproach offended the god, who became angry with the offender, and subsequently took away his life.

Æsculapius left two sons behind him—Machaon and Podalirius, the two eminent surgeons who joined Menelaus, king of Sparta, in the Trojan expedition, where they obtained high reputation for their practical skill in treating wounds and injuries, B.C. 1194. They were rulers of Æchalia, Ithome, and Tricca. They were not mere champions of the healing art; but fought at the head of their respective followers (men of Æchalia, Ithome and Tricca) in that memorable expedition. Mention is made of them in the Iliad as leaders and surgeons:—

"The Æchalian race, in those high towers contain'd,
Where once Eurytus in proud triumph reign'd,
Or where her humbler turrets Tricca rears,
Or where Ithome, rough with rocks, appears;
In thirty sail the sparkling waves divide,
Which Podalirius and Machaon guide.
To these his skill their parent-god imparts,
Divine professors of the healing arts.*

Agamemnon, the Commander-in-Chief of the Greek forces, is grieved to see his brother Menelaus

---

* Pope's *Homer's Iliad*, bk. II., p. 44.

wounded by an arrow, and orders the herald Talthybius to inform Machaon of the event, who instantly runs to the aid of the wounded.

> "'Now seek some skilful hand whose powerful art
> May staunch the effusion, and extract the dart,
> Herald, be swift, and bid Machaon bring
> His speedy succour to the Spartan king;
> Pierc'd with a winged shaft (the deed of Troy),
> The Grecian's sorrow and the Dardan's joy.'
> With hasty zeal the swift Talthybius flies;
> Through the thick files he darts his searching eyes,
> And finds Machaon where sublime he stands
> In arms encircled with his native bands.
> Then thus: 'Machaon to the king repair,
> His wounded brother claims thy timely care;
> Pierced by some Lycian or Dardanian bow,
> A grief to us, a triumph to the foe.'
> The heavy tidings grieved the god-like man;
> Swift to his succour through the ranks he ran;
> The dauntless king yet standing firm he found,
> And all the chiefs in deep concern around,
> Where to the steely point the reed was join'd,
> The shaft he drew, but left the head behind.
> Straight the broad belt with gay embroid'ry graced
> He loos'd; the corslet from his breast unbraced;
> Then suck'd the blood, and sovereign balm infus'd
> Which Chiron gave and Æsculapius used."*

When Machaon and Podalirius were once engaged at the head of their troops in a battle with the Trojans, the former was wounded by an arrow by Paris. Idomenes, the Cretan leader, requests Nestor to remove him from the field of battle, which he accordingly does:

> "'Glory of Greece, old Neleus' valiant son!
> Ascend thy chariot, haste with speed away,
> And great Machaon to the ships convey.

---

* Pope's *Homer's Iliad*, bk. IV., pp. 70, 71.

> A wise physician, skill'd our wounds to heal,
> Is more than armies to the public weal.'
> Old Nestor mounts the seat. Beside him rode
> The wounded offspring of the healing god,
> He lends the lash; the steeds with sounding feet
> Shake the dry field, and thunder towards the fleet."*

Achilles, who overlooked the engagement from his ship, is anxious to know the name of the person carried by Nestor from the field, and thus addresses Patrocles:—

> " Go now to Nestor, and from him be taught
> What wounded warrior late his chariot brought?
> For, seen at a distance, and but seen behind,
> His form recal'd Machaon to my mind;
> Nor could I, through yon cloud, discern the face,
> The coursers pass'd me with so swift a pace."†

Patrocles while carrying the sad news back to Achilles meets Eurypylus, also pierced by an arrow, who thus expresses his lamentations for the fate of the Grecian army, and piteously implores aid from the medical chief:—

> " .   .   .   .   No more my friend
> Greece is no more! this day her glories end,
> E'en to the ships victorious Troy pursues,
> Her force increasing as her toil renews.
> Those chiefs, that used her utmost rage to meet,
> Lie pierced with wounds, and bleeding in the fleet.
> But thou, Patrocles! act a friendly part,
> Lead to my ships, and draw the deadly dart,
> With lukewarm water wash the gore away,
> With healing balms the raging smart allay,
> Such as sage Chiron, 'sire of Pharmacy,'
> Once taught Achilles, and Achilles thee.

---

* Pope's *Homer's Iliad*, bk. XI., pp. 204, 205.
† Ibid., bk. XI., p. 207.

> Of two fam'd surgeons, Podalirius stands
> This hour surrounded by the Trojan bands;
> And great Machaon, wounded in his tent,
> Now wants that succour which so oft he lent."

The busy chief, like the knight in the time of the Crusades, instantly undertakes the office of a surgeon:—

> "'What then remains to do?
> The event of things the gods alone can view,
> Charg'd by Achilles' great command I fly,
> And bear with haste the Pylian king's reply:
> But thy distress this instant claims relief,'
> He said, and in his arms upheld the chief.
> The slaves their master's slow approach survey'd,
> And hides of oxen on the floor displayed:
> There stretch'd at length the wounded hero lay;
> Patrocles cut the forky steel away,
> Then in his hands a bitter root he bruised,
> The wound he washed, the styptic juice infus'd.
> The closing flesh that instant ceas'd to glow,
> The wound to torture, and the blood to flow."*

Machaon recovered, but was afterwards killed near Troy by Eurypylus. Podalirius on his return from Troy settled in Caria.

Venesection was known and practised by the Greeks in the earliest times, for we are told that Podalirius effected a cure by the employment of blood-letting on the daughter of Damethus who had received a severe fall. This cure is said to have obtained for him the sovereignty of the Chersonese. Scarifications were also practised by the Greek surgeons in the siege of Troy.

From the time of the Trojans until that of the

---

* Pope's *Homer's Iliad*, bk. XI., p. 212.

Peloponnesian war the art of medicine seems to have made very little or no progress. Its history, to say in the words of Pliny, remained "enveloped in the densest night." Its practice was solely confined to the Asclepiadæ or descendants of Æsculapius, who were the priests as well as guardians of the various temples dedicated to him. The temples of health may be regarded as so many hill sanitaria of our present day. They were erected on hilly situations which abounded in medicinal springs. The sick visited the temples from all parts of Greece, not only to obtain medical aid from the priests, but to pay devotion and make offerings to Æsculapius. The sick man had to undergo religious purification, bathing, friction, &c. before he was admitted into one of those temples for treatment. They laid down to sleep on the skins of sacrificed rams in the temples in hopes of receiving inspirations in their dreams for the relief of their sufferings. Change of air and scene, faith, imagination and diet, combined with water-cure, contributed more to the welfare of the sick than medicine alone. So much for the first period of Greek medicine.

We now come to an important epoch in the history of Greece, the second or grand period of Greek literature. Many important circumstances occurred about this period which contributed to the advancement of medical science. The Egyptians who for a long time bore hatred towards strangers, and lived sequestered from the rest of the world, soon found out the errors of their unwise policy, and much to the credit of Psammeticus, Egypt was opened without any restraints to the Greeks for the purposes of commerce 660 B.C. The Greeks who settled in Egypt were allowed pieces of land exempt from taxes, and enjoyed many other privileges. Numerous colonies were also established by the Greeks in Italy and Sicily. About this period some of the Asclepiadæ left their temples to practise as *travelling physicians*. Thus medical knowledge was no longer confined to the Æsculapian temples. About the same time also arose a few men of eminence who devoted their attention to the study of philosophy. This tended in some degree to the investigation of the medical art. The new set of men divorced superstition from science. The old religious feelings of the multitude were first opposed to the various doctrines of philosophy; at last science triumphed over superstition, and produced a powerful influence upon their minds. The second battle raged between the philosophers, who accused each other of impiety. The term philosophy was applied by the ancients to the knowledge of natural phenomena and the various departments of science, including medicine.

The most ancient school of philosophy first dawned in Ionia. It was founded by Thales of Miletus 640 B.C. As he was of Ionic origin the school was termed Ionic. He travelled in Egypt and Phœnicia, and visited the temples of Thebes and Memphis, the two large depositories of learning. Here he became acquainted with the priests, and from them obtained a knowledge of philosophy of which medicine formed a branch. He had some knowledge of geometry and astronomy. He is said to have been the first who foretold solar eclipse, and it was he who also believed in the immortality of the soul. He held water to be the principal element of all things, and asserted from the properties of magnet and amber that everything had a soul.

The most eminent followers of Thales were Anaximander, Anaximenes and Anaxagoras.

Anaximander studied astronomy, mathematics, and especially geography. He was the first person to prepare a map. The moon, he said, derived her light from the sun.

Anaximenes followed Anaximander. As Thales held water to be the principal element of all things, so Anaximenes asserted air to be the principle. "As the soul in us," said he, "which is air, holds us together, so breath and air surround the whole world."

Anaxagoras, the pupil of Anaximenes, applied himself chiefly to the study of astronomy and meteorology. He was the tutor of Socrates. He was tried for impiety and condemned to death. Some say that he was saved by a disciple of his, others say that he became a voluntary exile to escape the punishment.

> "Wise Anaxagoras did call the sun
> A mass of glowing iron, and for this
> Death was to be his fate. But Pericles
> Then saved his friend; but afterwards he died
> A victim of a weak philosophy."*

Soon after the Ionic, another school of philosophy was founded by Pythagoras, a native of Samos in

---

* Diogenes Laërtius, p. 62.

Græcia Magna (a portion of southern Italy, inhabited by Greek colonists). It was termed the Italic school of philosophy. Pythagoras, like Thales, also travelled in Egypt, Babylon, Chaldæa, Phœnicia, and other places for a period of twenty-two years, to acquire a knowledge of philosophy from the priests. He was the first who believed the earth to be round. Some say that Parmenides was the first who made known the earth to be a sphere. He is said to have discovered the 47th proposition of the Euclid. He believed in the transmigration of the soul.

> "They say that once, as passing by he saw
> A dog severely beaten, he did pity him,
> And spake as follows to the man who beat him :—
> 'Stop now and beat him not, since in his body
> Abides the soul of a dear friend of mine
> Whose voice I recognized as he was crying.'"*

Pythagoras was not only a profound philosopher, but a skilful physician.

After his death his pupil Empedocles, a philosopher of Agrigentum, rose to eminence. He applied himself chiefly to the study of medicine. He was not only renowned for his skill in curing diseases, but for preventing them by proper sanitation. "When a pestilence attacked the people of Selinus, by reason of the bad smells arising from the adjacent river, so that the men died, and the women bore dead children, Empedocles contrived a plan, and brought into the same channel two other rivers at his own expense; and so by mixing their waters with that of the other river, he sweetened the stream, and as the

---

* Diogenes Laërtius, p. 353.

pestilence was removed in this way, when the people of Selinus were on one occasion holding a festival on the bank of the river, Empedocles appeared among them; and they, rising up, offered him adoration, and prayed to him as to a god."*

In short, Empedocles had the power and skill of checking epidemics and pernicious winds. He was highly respected when he appeared at the Olympic games. He is said to have performed a most wonderful cure by restoring a dead woman to life after the lapse of seven days. From this time he was respected both as a physician and a prophet. In his medicinal discourse he says of himself:—

> " A doubtless god I am; mortal no more;
> Honour'd by all, with garlands cover'd o'er:
> Which, soon as e'er I come to any town
> Both men and women pay to me renown.
> Thousands of men enquire the way to wealth;
> Some wound divine, others restore to health."†

In another place he says in his poems:—

> "Med'cines to strengthen age and cure disease,
> Thou shalt be taught, for I am skill'd in these;
> The wrath of restless winds thou shalt assuage
> Which blast the corn in their pernicious rage."‡

As he called himself a god, "mortal no more," it is said of him that, to avoid disgrace at the approach of his death, and make the people believe that he was a divine being, he suddenly disappeared, threw himself from a height, and died in the crater of Mount Etna.

---

* Diogenes Laërtius, p. 366.
† Stanley's *History of Philosophy*, p. 491.
‡ Ibid.

THE MEDICAL ART.

Alcmæon of Crotona, one of the disciples of Pythagoras, was another philosopher and physician, who bestowed a great deal of attention to the dissection of animals and the study of medicine.

The next philosophers, supposed to be the followers of Pythagoras, were Democritus, Heraclitus, and Acron. The former travelled in foreign countries for the purpose of acquiring knowledge, studied anatomy in Egypt for several years, and was the author of atomic theory. The latter, it is stated, directed the lighting of large fires in the streets of Athens, for the purpose of destroying the epidemic constitution of the air when the great plague was fearfully raging in that city.

About 500 years before the Christian era, the Eleatic school of philosophy arose from the Italic. It was established in Elea by Xenophanes, assisted by Parmenides and Zeno.

CHAPTER III.

Hippocrates—His birth and parentage—Records in the Temples of Æsculapius—Medical Gymnastics—The Plague in Athens—Nature cures diseases—Contraries cure contraries—Similars cure similars—Elements and Humours—Dogmatists—Empirics—Methodists—True System—On the genuine works of Hippocrates—On works with or without additions by his followers—On his doubtful works.

We now come to Hippocrates, an individual of world-wide reputation, who laid a foundation to a system which has for centuries exercised a powerful influence on medicine. He was a linear descendant and the seventeenth from Æsculapius, and was born about the year 460 B.C. in the Asclepieum, or temple of Æsculapius, situated in the island of Cos. "That physic had been continually improving in one and the same family, by which one stood upon the other's shoulders." His first instructor was his own father, Heraclides. Being possessed of an inquisitive mind, he availed himself of all the clinical records which were preserved in the temple of Cos for several generations, travelled through different countries to obtain information, visited the other temples to examine the records of diseases and their remedies, and devoted some time to the prosecution of his medical studies in Selimbria (a town of Thrace) as a disciple of Herodicus, a physician. This Herodicus was the first to introduce gymnastic exercises for his patients. But the inventor of medical gymnastics sometimes abused them, by recommending his patients to walk several miles a day, which sometimes cost them their lives; for this he is reproached by Plato, and even by Hippocrates.

To Hippocrates is due the merit of separating medicine from philosophy and jugglery, and bringing it to its highest perfection. Yet he was not free from the superstitious belief that the position of stars had a great influence upon human disorders. He was an accurate observer of the phenomena of disease, and his practice was based on rational experience. His descriptions of diseases are given with such accuracy and acuteness, that they enjoy a degree of popularity and esteem, even to the present day. He was not only highly respected by his countrymen, from whom he had justly obtained the title of Father of Medicine, but was honoured by kings who sought his friendship and advice. He is reported to have cured Perdiccas, king of Macedon, of love-sickness. He received an invitation from Artaxerxes Longimanus, king of Persia, during a time of pestilence which was raging in that country, but he refused his request.

Hippocrates is said to have extinguished the plague in Athens by kindling large fires in different parts of the city. The symptoms of this disease are graphically described by Thucidydes, in his history of the Peloponnesian war; and as Hippocrates has not given an account of the epidemic in any of his works, it is conjectured by some that they were from his pen.

Hippocrates was the first to observe the fact that some diseases not necessarily fatal, when left to nature, terminate favourably. He therefore insisted that the chief duty of a physician is to follow nature. But he did not entirely rely upon nature in dangerous diseases, for he says, "To extreme diseases, extreme and exquisite remedies are best."* In another of his treatises he reproaches physicians of the Cnidian school for employing very few drugs, and observes : "All their therapeutics is limited to the administration of purgative remedies." Not content with employing desperate remedies in desperate diseases, he sometimes went a step further, and bled his patients *ad deliquium animi*, employed the most virulent drugs, and purged his patients to death. Thus he says in the aphorisms :—

"A convulsion caused by taking of hellebore is mortal."†
"A convulsion caused by a purging potion is mortal."‡
"Those who do not thirst while they are purged by a purging potion, must not cease purging till they do thirst."§

Hippocrates generally prescribed simple remedies on the principle of contraries. In one of his aphorisms he distinctly says :—

"All diseases which proceed from repletion are cured by evacuation, and those which proceed from evacuation are cured by repletion; and so on in the rest, contraries are the remedies of contraries."‖

He seems also to have, as will be seen elsewhere, some knowledge of the homœopathic law of similars,

---

* Sect. i. Aphorism 6. (Sprengeli's translation.)
† Sect. v. Aphorism 1.   ‡ Sect. vii. Aphorism 25.
§ Sect. iv. Aphorism 19.   ‖ Sect. ii. Aphorism 22.

for in a treatise attributed to him by a few the following passage is found :—

"Similar effects must by similar creating causes be treated, and not by opposite agencies."

Respecting this law Dr. Francis Adams, who has so ably translated the works of Hippocrates, remarks :— "It thus appears that the principles both of allopathy and homœopathy are recognised by the author of this treatise."

Hippocrates taught that the body was composed of four elements—air, fire, earth, and water, and that these when combined gave rise to the four humours. He fancied that there existed in the living body four fluids or humours—blood, phlegm, yellow bile, and black bile,—that a deviation or disturbance in the normal proportion of these humours gave rise to diseases,—that diseases when allowed to run a natural course had a tendency to a spontaneous cure after a certain time, which he called *crisis*, and to which he attached great importance; and that nature by removing the offending matter by critical evacuations and restoring the just proportion effected a cure. Hence his important line of practice consisted in assisting the evacuation of morbid humours by diuretics, diaphoretics, emetics, and especially by drastic purgatives.

Before closing the history of this "divine sage of Cos," we must not omit to mention that he did not belong or blindly attach himself to any of the then existing medical sects. His practice was based upon rationalism combined with experience, and to him we are indebted for the brief advice that the chief duty of a physician is "To do good, or at least to do no harm." These words deserve the attention of every true physician. It is impossible for any true and impartial observer to conceal his sentiments regarding the want of a guiding principle in therapeutics. From very early times up to the present day this want has given rise to various conflicting theories adopted by one sect and rejected by another. It has been the fate of many theories to appear in one age, and after temporary explosion re-appear in another. In ancient times the medical profession was divided into three principal sects. The founders and followers of these sects in opposition to each other professed and maintained their own doctrines, which have some influence over the practice of a few men even of the present day. The advocates of these sects were named the Dogmatists or Rationalists, the Empirics and the Methodists.

The Dogmatists maintained that practice must be deduced from theory, and that before attempting to cure a disease it was necessary to know its cause.

The Empirics, on the other hand, contended that this is unnecessary, that it is impossible to discover the occult causes of disease, and that we ought to be guided solely by experience.

The Methodists rejected the doctrines of both the Dogmatists and the Empirics, and took a middle course. They asserted that the best way of treating disease depended upon the observation of its symptoms. Hippocrates belonged to neither of these sects, but chose from each whatever was valuable, and, as said above, his system of treatment was founded upon reason and experience. To him true medicine was the science of observation, experience, and sound reasoning. This should be the aim of every true physician.

In his surgical practice, he was a bold and successful operator, and had a wonderfully accurate knowledge of treating dislocations and fractures.

In the practice of medicine, it must be however allowed that the "divine old man" was not wise in frequently resorting to bleeding, cauterizing, scarifying, and purging his patients. And yet he was one of the greatest physicians the world has ever seen.

His accurate description of the symptoms, causes, and prognosis of diseases, both medical and surgical, the influence of the atmosphere in creating them, together with his observations on climate, water, diet, and the different seasons of the year, have stood unshaken and unsurpassed for more than twenty centuries. What Herculean labour for a man who knew nothing of physiology, and in whose time the dissection of dead bodies was not allowed from religious prejudice! "If physicians that succeeded him had followed his steps, sure physic would have been long ago brought to its height of perfection, and we now might have exceeded Hippocrates as much in physic as Sir Isaac Newton did Aristotle in philosophy." There can be no doubt that his intellectual powers were of the first order. His brilliant and distinguished reputation naturally invited a spirit of envy, and he has been charged with the grave offence of setting fire to the Temple of Æsculapius at Cnidos, in order to destroy the ancient records after having copied out from them. This accusation in the absence of sufficient proof is totally groundless. We have in our own times a few jealous and unworthy members of the profession, who accuse others of the very practices of which they themselves are guilty. To admit such men, unworthy of their great function, to our societies would be to encourage them to carry on their dishonourable practices to the discredit of our profession.

After a glorious life spent in the pursuit of knowledge for the cause of suffering humanity, Hippocrates died in Thessaly at the advanced age of 109, full of respect, and the same honours were bestowed upon him by his countrymen as had been upon Hercules. He left behind him many writings as the true monuments of his greatness. They were supposed to be very numerous, but among his many genuine writings there were others which were falsely ascribed to him, but in reality were written in his name chiefly by his two sons Draco and Thessalus, his son-in-law Polybius, and his grandsons Hippocrates the third and fourth. The following are his generally acknowledged productions:

On the Epidemics i. iii.—These books contain the history of forty-two cases which came under his observation. His description of the four constitutions of certain seasons and the diseases which prevailed in them in an epidemic form, is clear and simple. In one of the books we find the following admirable lines, worthy of consideration by the physicians of the present day :—

"The physician must be able to tell the antecedents, know the present, and foretell the future—must meditate these things, and have two special objects in view with regard to diseases, namely, to do good or to do no harm. The art consists in three things—the disease, the patient, and the physician. The physician is the servant of the art, and the patient must combat the disease along with the physician."*

2. *Atmospheres, Waters, and Localities.*—In this treatise our author observes that a physician, in order to become successful, should possess a knowledge of the locality in which he practises. He should be also acquainted with the nature of the soil, the various kinds of waters, the different seasons of the year, and the winds which prevail in them.

"When one comes to a city its situation ought to be regarded—how it lies, to the north or south, to the rising or setting sun; and concerning the waters, whether they be marshy, or soft or hard, running from elevated or rocky situations; and the ground, whether it be barren and deficient in water, or wooded, or well watered, or whether it lies in a hollow confined situation, or is elevated or cold."

After quoting the above passage the *Lancet* remarks :—"In short, the ancients clearly recognised that different places were hurtful to different parts and members of the body," and then laments in the following terms :—"The influence that the physiological, geographical, and meteorological characters of a district have on its mortality from certain diseases, has however hitherto been imperfectly investigated by modern physicians."† Very discouraging indeed

---

* Adams' Hippocrates, vol. I., p. 360.
† The *Lancet*, March 24, 1877.

when we compare the age in which Hippocrates lived with our *age of progress!*

He then describes the seasons of the year and their influence on the health of the inhabitants, and also the different winds and their effects on persons exposed to their influence. A part of the treatise is devoted to the influence of climate and institutions of Europe and Asia on their respective inhabitants, in the formation of their different traits of character, and as producing men of various kinds of intellectual development.

3. *Regimen in acute Diseases.*—In this treatise Hippocrates not only blames the physicians of the Cnidian school for not distinguishing and classifying diseases in a systematic manner, but reproaches them as regards their rules of treatment and the use of few remedies in the following terms:—

"But when in addition to the diagnosis, they describe how each complaint should be treated in these cases, I entertain a still greater difference of opinion with them respecting the rules they have laid down; and not only do I not agree with them on this account, but also because the remedies they use are few in number; for with the exception of acute diseases, the only medicines which they gave are drastic purgatives, with whey and milk at certain intervals."*

In the same treatise the author treats at length on the use of barley-water, wine, hydromel, oxymel, baths, &c. in acute diseases.

4. *On the Prognostics.*—According to Dr. Adams and other authors this work is composed from the "Prorrhetics" and "Coan Prænotiones" of the Asclepiadæ, who kept records of diseases and their cures

---

* Adams' Hippocrates, vol. I., p. 282.

in the temple of Cos. In this work Hippocrates recommends the physician to become acquainted with prognosis for three reasons; first, for the confidence of his patients; second, by foretelling the fatal issue of a disorder he will free himself from censure; third, by having a foresight of the future changes he will be better prepared for prompt management of the case. Hippocrates drew his rules of prognosis by carefully observing and contrasting the differences between the phenomena in health and disease. Read his description of a dying face or *facies Hippocratica* given with such wonderful exactness in the following short passage :—

"A sharp nose, hollow eyes, collapsed temples; the ears cold, contracted, and their lobes turned out; the skin about the forehead being rough, distended and parched; the colour of the whole face being green, black, livid or lead-coloured."*

Hippocrates distinctly points out the importance of noting in the sick person the state of his countenance, such as the eye, the eye-lids, lips, &c.; the position of the sick when asleep and awake, the movements of the hands, the sleep, the respiration, the sweats, the excrements, the urine, the vomitings, the expectorations, &c. In giving his prognosis he attached great importance to the age, sex, and habit of his patient.

5. *On Wounds of the Head.*—In this work Hippocrates begins with a description of the cranial bones. Injuries of the head he divides into simple fractures, simple contusions without injury to the bones, fractures with depression, simple incision, in the outer

---

* Adams' Hippocrates, vol. I., p. 236.

table of the bone, and counter-fissure. After some observations upon the importance of ascertaining the situation and kind of injury, the author proceeds to the question of treatment. In the first two kinds, that is to say, in cases of simple fractures and contusions, his rule of practice was to perforate the skull when there was any danger of inflammation or effusion, but in cases of fractures attended with depression, in simple fractures in the outer table, and in the counter-fissure he did not operate. The operation of trepanning the skull is minutely described, and the treatment of erysipelas following wounds of the head either before or after the application of the trepan is next considered.

6. *On Fractures.*—This work treats both of fractures and dislocations. In the first place the author shows the importance of bandaging a fractured limb in the position in which it is intended to be kept during union, and says that neglect of this simple precaution on the part of a surgeon would result in a return of the displacement during the movement of the patient. The process of effecting reduction of a fracture, and keeping the fragments in apposition, together with proper bandaging, are distinctly described. Careful attention to position for their union is considered of great importance. Fractures of the forearm, arm, leg and thigh are considered at some length. The method of replacing them, the application of bandages, compresses and splints, and the position in which the limbs are to be placed after reduction are minutely explained. Injuries of the foot, and dislocations of the foot, elbow joint, and tarsal

bones are also treated of in this treatise. A very accurate description of compound fractures is given, and the various modes of treating them are correctly laid down. In compound fractures he condemns the practice of applying bandages to the parts on both sides of the wound, and leaving the wound itself exposed for dressings.

7. *On the Articulations.*—In this work the subject of dislocation is treated at length and with much clearness. It begins with a description of dislocations of the shoulder joint and the different modes of their reduction. Fracture of the clavicle is next taken into consideration. Dislocation of the wrist and fingers as well as dislocations and fractures of the lower jaw are next brought into notice. Curvature of the spine and congenital club-foot are described with much accuracy and precision. Compound dislocation of several joints and gangrene arising from fracture and other injuries are treated of. A full description is then given of dislocations of the hip-joint and the modes of their reduction. "Several sections of the work," says Dr. Adams, "are perfect masterpieces, such, for example, as the parts which relate to dislocations at the shoulder and the hip-joint, and more especially the latter, in which, as it appears to me, he has given a fuller and more complete history of everything relating to the subject than is to be found in any single work even at the present day."* And adds: "Now, I repeat, no systematic writer on surgery has given so comprehensive a view of the subject of dislocation in all its

---
* Adams' Hippocrates, vol. II., p. 557.

bearings as what is here given by Hippocrates . . . . . . The methods of reduction which our author describes are all based on the most correct principles, and some of them might perhaps be held preferable to those now in use."*

8. *Aphorisms.*—The work contains more than 400 short sentences, and is divided into seven sections.

Section i.—The first and most important aphorism of this section runs thus:—

" Life is short, and the art long; experience fallacious, and judgment difficult. The physician must not only be prepared to do what is right himself, but also to make the patient, the attendants, and externals co-operate."†

The others relate to diet and to purging:—

"A slender and restricted diet is always dangerous in chronic diseases, and also in acute diseases where it is not requisite."‡

" We must form a particular judgment of the patient whether he will support the diet until the acme of the disease, and whether he will sink previously and not support the diet, or the disease will give way previously and become less acute."§

A few aphorisms in this section as in others in regard to evacuations are founded upon his faulty notion of certain humours such as black-bile, yellow-bile, &c., and " obedience to them," in the words of Dr. Russell, " is a mark of ignorance, not of knowledge." The following 22nd aphorism is a specimen :

"We must evacuate such humours as are concocted, not such as are unconcocted, unless they are struggling to get out, which is not mostly the case."

---

* Adams' Hippocrates, vol. II., pp. 558, 559.
† Ibid., vol. II., Sec. i., p. 697.
‡ Ibid., vol. II., Sec. i., p. 698.
§ Ibid., vol. II., Sec. i., p. 700.

Section ii.—In this section a large portion of the aphorisms is devoted to the rules of prognosis. In the 22nd aphorism the author lays down the foundation of the therapeutic rule *contraria contrariis curantur*, which consists in curing diseases by their contraries:—

"Diseases which arise from repletion are cured by depletion, and those that arise from depletion are cured by repletion; and in general diseases are to be cured by their contraries."

The 46th contains the earliest announcement of the doctrine of revulsion:—

"Of two pains occurring together not in the same part of the body the stronger weakens the other."

The 52nd deserves to be mentioned in this place as showing the impropriety of frequently changing the plan of treatment when once based on a suitable indication:—

"When doing everything according to indication, although things may not turn out agreeable to indication, we should not change to another while the original appearances remain."

Section iii.—A portion of this section is devoted to the consideration of the various seasons of the year. The effects which the different seasons and the changes of the weather exercise upon the health, constitution, and age of the people, together with the diseases most prevalent in them, are clearly stated:—

"The changes of the seasons mostly engender diseases, and in the seasons great changes either of heat or cold, and the rest agreeably to the same rule."*

"Of the constitutions of the year the dry upon the whole are more healthy than the rainy, and attended with less mortality."†

---

* Adams' Hippocrates, vol. II., p. 715.
† Ibid., vol. II., p. 718.

"With regard to the seasons, in spring and in the commencement of summer, children and those next to them in age are most comfortable and enjoy best health; in summer and during a certain portion of autumn, old people; during the remainder of the autumn and in winter, those of the intermediate ages."*

The next enumerates the diseases incident in the different ages from the period of infancy to that of old age.

Section iv.—The first twenty-four aphorisms, which relate principally to purgings, hellebore, and black-bile are not deserving of notice. Others relating to fevers, their complications and prognosis, are worthy of consideration:—

"Sweat supervening in a case of fever without the fever ceasing is bad, for the disease is protracted."†

"In fevers frights after sleep or convulsions are a bad symptom."‡

Section v.—The danger of convulsions supervening in cases of wounds and excessive loss of blood is distinctly stated:—

"Spasm supervening on a wound is fatal."§

"A convulsion or hiccup supervening on a copious discharge of blood is bad."‖

The others relate to consumption, epilepsy, and empyema.

"Phthisis most commonly occurs between the ages of eighteen and thirty-five years."¶

"Phthisical persons, the hairs of whose head fall off, die if diarrhœa set in."**

---

* Adams' Hippocrates, vol. II., p. 719.
† Ibid., vol. II., p. 732.   ‡ Ibid., vol. II., p. 734.
§ Ibid., vol. II., p. 737.   ‖ Ibid.
¶ Ibid., vol. II., p. 738.   ** Ibid., vol. II., p. 739.

In another aphorism he enumerates the diseases induced by cold :—

"Cold induces convulsions, tetanus, mortification, and febrile rigors."*

The effects of heat and cold in certain diseases are briefly considered :—

"Such parts as have been congealed should be heated, except where there either is a hæmorrhage, or one is expected."*

The above aphorism is erroneously founded by the author on the law " *contraria contrariis curantur.*"

"In the case of a muscular youth having *tetanus* without a wound during the midst of summer, it sometimes happens that the effusion of a large quantity of cold water recalls the heat. Heat relieves these diseases."*

The remaining important aphorisms relate to pregnancy, danger of abortion, &c. :—

"It proves fatal to a woman in a state of pregnancy, if she be seized with any of the acute diseases."†

"If a woman with child be bled, she will have an abortion, and this will be the more likely to happen the larger the foetus."†

"In a pregnant woman if the breasts suddenly lose their fulness she has a miscarriage."‡

"If a woman with child have her courses, it is impossible that the child can be healthy."§

Section vi.—In this section a large portion of the aphorisms relates to prognostics founded on the appearance of a new disease, or symptoms coming on another. The first class contains cases in which a disease or symptom coming on another disease proves beneficial. Of these some furnish hints on

---
* Adams' Hippocrates, vol. II., p. 740. † Ibid., p. 743.
‡ Ibid., p. 744. § Ibid., p. 748.

which are founded the cure of certain diseases. We shall go over a few:—

"In a person having a painful spot in the head with intense cephalalgia, pus or water running from the nose, or by the mouth, or at the ears, removes the disease."*

"Hæmorrhoids appearing in melancholic and nephritic affections are favourable."*

"In a case of dropsy, when the water runs by the veins into the belly, it removes the disease."†

"In confirmed diarrhœa, vomiting when it comes on spontaneously removes the diarrhœa."†

"It is a good thing in ophthalmy for the patient to be seized with diarrhœa."†

The second class contains cases in which the supervention of another symptom or disease proves injurious:—

"A diarrhœa supervening in a confirmed case of pleurisy of pneumonia is bad."†

"Hiccup supervening in dropsical cases is bad."‡

"When persons having large spleens are seized with dysentery, and if the dysentery passes into a chronic state, either dropsy or lientery supervenes, and they die."§

In the same section there are other aphorisms which do not belong to the class of superventions:—

"When a person has been cured of chronic hæmorrhoids, unless one be left there is danger of dropsy or phthisis supervening."†

"It is not a good sign for an erysipelas spreading outwardly to be determined inwards; but for it to be determined outwards from within is good."‖

"A woman does not take the gout unless her menses be stopped."¶

"A young man does not take the gout unless he indulges in coition."¶

"Convulsions take place either from repletion or depletion."**

---

* Adams' Hippocrates, vol. II., p. 753.
† Ibid., p. 754.   ‡ Ibid., p. 758.   § Ibid., p. 759.
‖ Ibid., p. 756.   ¶ Ibid., p. 757.   ** Ibid., p. 758.

Section vii.—A large portion of the aphorisms contained in this section is devoted as in the last to the subject of superventions. The following are a few that deserve to be mentioned :—

"Delirium or convulsion from a flow of blood is bad."*
"Vomiting, or hiccup, or convulsion, or delirium in ileus is bad."*
"Pneumonia coming on pleurisy is bad."*
"Phrenites along with pneumonia is bad."*
"Convulsions or tetanus coming upon severe burning is bad."*
"Stupor or delirium from a blow on the head is bad."†
"Mortification or suppuration upon erysipelas is bad."†
"Convulsions upon severe purging is bad."‡
"Tenesmus coming on in a case of pregnancy causes abortion."‡

The following two aphorisms show that Hippocrates practised the operation of *paracentesis thoracis* in empyema either by a pointed instrument or cautery, and also knew the operation of opening an abscess of the liver :—

"When empyema is treated either by the cautery or incision, if pure and white pus flow from the wound, the patients recover ; but if mixed with blood, slimy and foetid, die."§
"When abscess of the liver is treated by the cautery or incision, if the pus which is discharged be pure and white, the patients recover (for in this case it is situated in the coats of the liver), but if it resemble the lees of oil as it flows, they die."||

9. *The Physician's Establishment or the Surgery.*—A considerable portion of the work treats of injuries and fractures. The author first lays down some general rules of diagnosis, the principal one, as for instance, being the comparison of the injured part with its sound neighbour. Next some general observations are made on surgical operations, and instruc-

---
* Adams' Hippocrates, vol. II., p. 763.   † Ibid., p. 764.
‡ Ibid., p. 765.   § Ibid., p. 768. || Ibid., p. 768.

tions are given to the operator with regard to the dexterity, nicety and firmness with which he should use his instruments. The author is not even silent in reference to the importance of attending to the position of both the patient and the surgeon during the performance of an operation. Directions are given that the surgeon himself must see that the surgical instruments are properly arranged to be readily handled when wanted. Even the arrangement of the dress of an operator is not neglected, for he says, "The robe is to be thrown in a neat and orderly manner over the elbows and shoulders, equally and symmetrically." The principal points to be attended to by the assistant are clearly laid down. Directions are given for the application of various kinds of splints and bandages. In applying the latter, the importance of regulating the amount of pressure is clearly shown. Directions are also given for the proper adjustment of a fractured limb, and careful attention to its position while setting it. The fore arm is to be kept bent, and the lower extremity straight. The treatment of atrophy of the muscles of the limb, owing to the pressure of tight bandages and long confinement to bed, during treatment for fracture, is clearly laid down.

10. *On the Instruments of Reduction, Mochlicus.*—The greater part of the work is devoted to dislocations and their treatment, the matter relating to fractures being brief. The author begins the work with a short description of the bones which constitute the human frame. Dislocations and the different modes of their reduction are correctly explained, and the

treatment of compound dislocations is distinctly laid down. The treatment of club-foot is briefly given as follows :—

"With regard to slight congenital dislocations, some of them can be rectified, especially club-foot. There is more than one variety of club-foot. The treatment consists in modelling the foot like a piece of wax; applying resinous cerate, and numerous bandages; or a sole or a piece of lead is to be bound on, but not upon the bare skin; the adjustment and the attitudes to correspond."*

The following observations are made on excision of articular bones :—

"Excision either of articular bones, or of pieces of bones when not high up in the body, but about the foot or the hand, is generally followed by recovery, unless the patient die at once from deliquium animi."†

Gangrene resulting from injury is next considered, and its treatment briefly given. The subject of displacement of the spine and fracture of the ribs is next taken up :—

"Displacement of the spine, if inwards, threatens immediate death attended with retention of urine, and loss of sensibility. Outwards, the accident is free from most of these bad effects, much more so than when there is merely concussion without displacement; the effects in the former case being confined to the spot affected, whereas in the latter, they are further communicated to the whole body, and are of a mortal character. In like manner, when the ribs are fractured, whether one or more, provided there be no splinters, there is rarely fever, spitting of blood and sphacelus, and ordinary treatment without evacuation will suffice, provided there be no fever; bandaging, according to rule; and the callus forms in twenty days, the bone being of a porous nature."‡

The subject of dislocations and fractures is so fully

---

* Adams' Hippocrates, vol. II., p. 674.
† Ibid., p. 675. ‡ Ibid., p. 676.

and accurately described by Hippocrates in his four treatises, namely, 'On the Surgery,' 'On the Articulations,' 'On Fractures,' and the 'Mochlicus,' that it has never been surpassed by any author even at the present day. The following passage expresses Dr. Adams' just estimate of Hippocrates and his four treatises:—" When we reflect on the admirable manner in which the whole subject is handled, and the many important truths which are evolved in the course of it, we cannot surely but regard with veneration the labours of our forefathers, nor can we miss to be impressed with the feeling that they have more cause to look down with contempt upon us their posterity, for not having prosecuted with more success the path of discovery which they had pointed out, than their posterity have to look back with scorn upon them because we have now made some little advances beyond their limits. In conclusion I do not hesitate to declare it as my decided opinion, that no other author has treated the same subject in so complete a manner as Hippocrates has done in these treatises."

11. *The Oath.*—This famous and historical document of antiquity, called also the " Hippocratic Oath," is generally believed to have been drawn up by Hippocrates. It binds the student of medicine to observe at all times rules of morality and good behaviour, in the practice of his profession. This interesting voucher is worth inserting in this place:—

" I swear by Apollo the physician, by Æsculapius, by Hygeia and Panaceia, and all the gods and goddesses, calling them to witness, that I will fulfil religiously and according to the best of my power and judgment, the solemn promise and the written bond which I now do make. I will honour as my parents, the master who has taught me this art, and endeavour to minister to all his necessities. I will consider his children as my own brothers, and will teach them my profession, should they express a desire to follow it, without remuneration or written bond. I will admit to my lessons, my discourses, and all my other methods of teaching, my own sons and those of my tutor, and those who have been inscribed as pupils and have taken the medical oath, but no one else. I will prescribe such a course of regimen as may be best suited to the condition of my patients, according to the best of my power and judgment, seeking to preserve them from anything that might prove injurious. No inducement shall ever lead me to administer poison, nor will I ever be the author of such advice; neither will I contribute to an abortion. I will maintain religiously the purity and integrity both of my conduct and of my art. I will not cut any one for the stone, but will leave that operation to those who cultivate it. Into whatever dwellings I may go, I will enter them with the sole view of succouring the sick, abstaining from all injurious views and corruption, especially from any immodest action, towards women or men, freemen or slaves. If during my attendance or even unprofessionally in common life, I happen to see or hear of any circumstances which should not be revealed, I will consider them a profound secret, and observe on the subject a religious silence. May I, if I rigidly observe this my oath and do not break it, enjoy good success in life and in [the practice of] my art, and obtain general esteem for ever; should I transgress and become a perjurer, may the reverse be my lot."*

If modern professors of the healing art, in addition to selecting a better class of aspirants to the noble profession of physic, had followed Hippocrates in exacting a somewhat similar vow, surely we should have never seen and heard of men of low breeding let loose upon a confiding public.

---

*Smith's *Dictionary of Greek and Roman Antiquities*, p. 747.

It appears from the above document that in ancient times no regular practitioner of medicine undertook to perform the operation for stone in the bladder, but left it to those who practised it specially. The practice of cutting for the stone was still more regarded by the Arabians as disreputable. Not only its practitioners, but those who witnessed it performed, were considered men of no respectable character.

12. *The Law.*—In the first paragraph of this little tract, the author says, " Medicine is of all the arts the most noble, but owing to the ignorance of those who practise it, and of those who inconsiderately form a judgment of them, it is at present far behind all the other arts."*

In the second paragraph some sensible remarks are made with regard to the advantages which the student of medicine ought to possess in order to acquire a perfect knowledge of the art of medicine:—

" Whosoever, is to acquire a competent knowledge of medicine, ought to be possessed of the following advantages—a natural disposition ; instruction ; a favourable position for the study ; early tuition ; love of labour ; leisure. First of all a natural talent is required ; for when nature opposes, everything else is vain."*

In other places of the same treatise the author remarks: " Instruction in medicine is like the culture of the productions of the earth," and "inexperience is a bad treasure and a bad fund to those who possess it, whether in opinion or reality, being devoid of self-reliance and contentedness, and the nurse both of timidity and audacity."

---

* Adams' Hippocrates, vol. II., p. 784.

The following may be accepted as the works of Hippocrates, with or without additions by his followers:—

1. *On Ancient Medicine.*—In this treatise an attack is directed by the author against some of his predecessors, who on vague hypothesis supposed dryness and moisture, heat and cold, as the causes of diseases. He expressly condemns those who founded their practice on theory, and rejects in striking terms the hypothesis of heat, cold, moisture, and dryness. " I wish," he says, " the discourse to revert to the new method of those who prosecute their inquiries in the art of hypothesis. For, if hot or cold, or moist or dry, be that which proves injurious to man, and if the person who would treat him properly must apply cold to the hot, hot to the cold, moist to the dry, and dry to the moist (on the principle of contraries), let me be presented with a man—not, indeed, one of a strong constitution, but one of the weaker— and let him eat wheat; such as it is supplied from the thrashing-floor, raw and unprepared, with raw meat, and let him drink water. By using such a diet, I know that he will suffer much and severely, for he will experience pains, his body will become weak, and his bowels deranged, and he will not subsist long. What remedy, then, is provided for one so situated— hot, or cold, or moist, or dry ? for it is clear it must be one of these. For according to this principle, if it is one of these which is injuring the patient, it is to be removed by its contrary. But the surest and most obvious remedy is to change the diet which the person used, and instead of wheat to give bread, and

instead of raw flesh, boiled, and to drink wine in addition to these; for by making these changes it is impossible but that he must get better unless completely disorganized by time and diet. What then shall we say ? whether that as he suffered from cold, these things being hot were of use to him, or the reverse; I should think this question must prove a puzzler to whomsoever it is put."*

The remaining portion of the treatise contains observations on fevers, inflammations, rheums, and defluxions, together with some remarks on the effects of the cold bath.

2. *On Ulcers.*—In this treatise the term ulcer is applied both to an open sore from any constitutional cause, and to a wound inflicted by violence. In the treatment of ulcers, and especially in fractures of the head, the author advocates a spare diet, when there is danger of gangrene or tetanus. He then advises rest and the prohibition of exercise to those suffering from ulcers:—

"In the case of an ulcer it is not expedient to stand, more especially if the ulcer be situated in the leg; but neither is it proper to sit nor walk. But quiet and rest are particularly expedient."†

In excised wounds inflicted by a sharp instrument, the object of the author appears to promote healing by the first intention, and in contused wound to excite suppuration. He distinctly states that when the surrounding parts of an ulcer are inflamed, or blackened by gangrene, or when there is a varix in the adjoining parts, the ulcer is difficult to heal. In

---

* Adams' Hippocrates, p. 169.
† Ibid., vol. II., p. 794.

another part of the treatise the author again reverts to his favourite practice of "purging upwards and downwards" when erysipelas supervenes, and makes an important remark that any piece of flesh which prevents a sore from healing is to be removed. For the treatment of ulcers he gives directions for the preparation of medicated poultices, consisting of leaves of several plants, with or without linseed, and also gives various prescriptions, of a corrosive, desiccative and emollient nature, containing carbonate of soda, alum, verdigris, flowers of copper, plumbago, flowers of silver, sulphur, arsenic, myrrh, pomegranate rind, galls, frankincense, saffron, hellebore, elaterium, horehound, sandarach, &c. Some of these he used in the form of powder, others in the shape of liniments and unguents. Wine, honey, vinegar, lees of oil, grease, white wax, resin oil, &c. chiefly entered into the composition of the latter two.

The last two paragraphs on the operations of venesection and cupping are foreign to the object of this treatise.

3. *On Fistulæ.*—The book opens with an enumeration of the causes which give rise to the formation of *fistula in ano.* The author recommends an early incision of the abscess to prevent its formation. When a fistula had already formed, his first method of cure consisted in introducing medicated tents into it. The operation with the ligature is next minutely described. In the first place he directs the operator to pass a bundle of threads through the eye of a director, which is then to be introduced into the fistula with one hand, at the same time the index finger of

the other hand is introduced per rectum. The end of the threads in it is then to be brought out of the anus, and both ends tied. The fistula is cut open by gradually drawing the ligature tighter, and pieces of sponge introduced into the wound so as to allow it to heal from the bottom, "when the fistula," he adds, "does not get eaten through, having first examined with a sound cut down as far as it passes." When the treatment by the ligature does not succeed, or is impossible, he advises the fistula to be syringed with injections, in which mode of treatment he appears however to have little faith, for he insists upon cutting the fistula in the following terms: "But it does not heal unless it be cut open."

4. *On Hæmorrhoids.*—In this treatise the treatment of piles by actual cautery and by the operation of excision is minutely described, along with the after-treatment. When the piles neither admit of cautery nor the excision, the author recommends their removal by caustic medicines.

5. *On the Sacred Disease.*—In this treatise the author emphatically scorns those ignorant physicians who, knowing nothing of the nature of epilepsy, attributed it to the gods, and called it " the sacred disease":—

"It is thus with regard to the disease called sacred: it appears to me to be nowise more divine nor more sacred than other diseases, but has a natural cause from which it originates like other affections. Men regard its nature and cause as divine from ignorance and wonder, because it is not at all like other diseases. And they who first referred this disease to the gods, appear to me to have been just such persons as the mountebanks, conjurors, purificators, and charletans now are who give themselves out for being excessively religious and as knowing more than other people. Such persons then using the divinity as a pretext and screen of their own inability to afford any assistance, have given out that this disease is sacred."*

He then explains the nature of epilepsy—that it arises from physical causes, not divine, and that it originates from the brain.

Doubts are entertained regarding the genuineness of the following works. According to some they were composed by Hippocrates himself:—

1. *On the Places in Man.*—In this treatise the author enters upon the important question of the homœopathic law of similars. For the treatment of suicidal mania he says:—" Give the patient a draught made from the root of mandrake in a smaller dose than will induce mania." The following are Dr. Adams' own words in reference to the subject:—" He (the author) then comments in strong terms that under certain circumstances purgatives will bind the bowels, and astringents loosen them, and he further makes the important remark that, although the general rule of treatment be ' contraria contrariis curantur,' the opposite rule also holds good in some cases—namely, ' similia similibus curantur.' It thus appears that the principles both of *allopathy* and *homœopathy* are recognized by the author of this treatise. In confirmation of the latter principle he remarks that the same substance which occasions strangury will also sometimes cure it, and so also with cough. And further, he acutely remarks that warm water, which, when drunk, generally excites vo-

---

* Adams' Hippocrates, vol. II., p. 843.

miting, will also sometimes put a stop to it by removing its cause."*

2. *On Diseases.*—This book of doubtful authenticity is supposed to have been written either by Hippocrates or his disciples. In it the causes, symptoms, diagnosis, and treatment of empyema and hydrothorax are given. The operation of *paracentesis thoracis*, that is of opening the chest to let out the confined fluid, is recommended in both these diseases. To ascertain the presence of fluid in the chest the author was acquainted with the method of succussion, which consists in abruptly shaking the patient quickly and gently by the shoulders, when a splashing sound may be heard. This mode of exploring the chest still goes by the name of "Hippocratic succussion." It is thus described by the author of the treatise:—" Having placed the patient in a firm seat, cause his hands to be held by an assistant, and then shake him by the shoulder in order to hear on which side the disease will produce a sound."† He also adds that " sometimes the thickness and quantity of the pus prevent us from hearing the fluctuation." It is also certain that the author was acquainted with mediate auscultation, in other words, he detected the existence of diseases in the chest by applying his ear to it. " You will know by this," he says, " that the chest contains water and not pus, if in applying the ear during a certain time on the side, you perceive a noise like boiling vinegar." Much

---

* Adams' Hippocrates, p. 77.

† Vide Laennec's *De l'auscultation mediate*, translated by Dr. J. Forbes.

more credit is therefore due to the author of this treatise for this important discovery than to Laennec, a celebrated French physician, who, it must be confessed, after a lapse of more than twenty centuries, carried it to its highest perfection, and invented the stethoscope. Laennec himself says in his work *De l'auscultation mediate* that long before his discovery of mediate auscultation he was acquainted with the writings of Hippocrates, and had read the above passage in the treatise *De Morbi.*

3. *The Epidemics.* i., iv., v., vi., vii.—These are the remaining five books of the treatise 'On Epidemic Affections' not recognized as genuine. In the fifth book is related a case of cholera treated successfully on the homœopathic principle, with hellebore. The following lines in the sixth express the writer's belief of the healing powers of nature over disease :— " Nature is the physician of diseases," and " nature although untaught and uninstructed, does what is proper."

In the seventh are related cases of consumption and empyema, and allusion is made to the morbid sounds heard within the chest. That the author did apply his ear to the chest to ascertain the presence of disease is obvious from the following short comments by Dr. Adams :—" Two cases of empyema would appear to have been phthisis with cavities in the lungs. In both mention is made of *rales*. A good many cases of phthisis are reported, in the last of these the pectoral *rales* are particularly noticed."

4. *On the Diseases of Women.*—According to Dr. Adams this treatise is devoted to midwifery

operations, and a few diseases of female organs of generation. In difficult delivery the author seems to have been acquainted with the operation of perforating the head or chest of the child, and extracting the body by a hook fixed on some convenient place. "The treatment of uterine hæmorrhage," remarks Dr. Adams, "which is recommended, can scarcely be improved upon even after the lapse of two thousand years."*

---

* Adams' Hippocrates, vol. I., p. 112.

CHAPTER IV.

Draco—Thessalus—Aristotle—Theophrastus—Diocles—His letter to Antigonas—Praxagoras—Chrysippus—Foundation of Alexandria—Its Schools and Libraries—Herophilus and Erasistratus—Criminals dissected alive—Improvements in Anatomy—Lovesickness—Serapion—Lithotomy and Lithotrity.

Hippocrates left two sons, Draco and Thessalus, who inherited their father's profession. They and their lineal descendants, satisfied with the vast improvement made by the Father of Medicine, accepted and adopted his theory of disease and method of practice. In fact, Hippocrates had brought the science to such a perfection, that nothing was left for them either in the way of new discoveries or substantial improvements. Thus medicine was allowed to remain stationary for some time. His two sons and his son-in-law Polybius, without making any alteration in his writings, made a few additions of their own, and it is supposed that some works, not considered to be the genuine productions of his, were written by them. M. Littre attributes the following two works to Polybius:—

1. On the Nature of Man.
2. Regimen of Persons in Health.

Thessalus was court physician to the Macedonian king Amyntas I. Galen frequently mentions him in high praise.

Another descendant of his, the fourth Hippocrates, was physician to Roxana, the Queen of Alexander the Great and daughter of King Darius Codomannus of Persia.

Another descendant of Æsculapius and a philosopher of great renown who understood medicine was Aristotle. His father named Nicomachus was for some time physician to the Macedonian king Amyntas II. Philip of Macedon, having heard of Aristotle's fame, invited him to his court, and appointed him tutor to his son Alexander. He wrote books on anatomy, midwifery, and medicine, and had some confused knowledge of the circulation of the blood. Whether he practised medicine or not is uncertain. "The philosopher," he says, "should end with medicine, the physician commence with philosophy."

Aristotle bequeathed his library to Theophrastus, one of his favourite pupils, and his successor in the academy. As an instructor, Theophrastus was so celebrated that he assembled round him scholars numbering about two thousand, the most renowned among whom were Erasistratus the physician, Nicomachus the son of Aristotle, Meander the comic poet, and Demetrius Phalereus. Hearing of his fame, Ptolemy invited him into Egypt. He was the first Greek author who wrote ten books on botany, which contained a description of five hundred plants.

Two other physicians who belonged to the family of the Asclepiadæ were Diocles of Carystius and Praxagoras of Cos. Both flourished in the fourth century B. C. Pliny says that Diocles was "second only in reputation as well as date to Hippocrates."

He belonged to the dogmatic sect, and was the author of several works, among which is the letter he wrote to Antigonas, one of the generals of Alexander, entitled "On the Preservation of Health." It appears from this epistle, that the author vulgarly followed Hippocrates as regards the doctrine of mischievous humours. "When a disease," he says, "is about to fix in the head . . . . the head ought to be purged; not indeed by any strong medicine, but taking the tops of hyssop and sweet marjoram, pound them and boil them in a pot with half a hemina of must or rob; rinse the mouth with this in the morning before eating, *and evacuate the humours by gargling.*" And again: "When some disease is about to fall upon the chest . . . . . procure vomiting after a moderate meal without medicine, vomiting also when the stomach is empty will answer well;—to produce which first swallow some radishes, cresses, rocket, mustard and purslain, and then by drinking warm water procure vomiting." Such were his notions about pathology and therapeutics.

Another renowned physician who lived in the fourth century before Christ was Praxagoras. Although belonging to the dogmatic sect, he adopted and defended the Hippocratic theory of disease, that is he maintained that diseases depended upon changes in the humours of the body. He paid especial attention to anatomy and physiology. He appears to have been bold in the use of the knife, for he was the first to perform the operation of gastrotomy (opening the abdomen) in order to restore the bowel to its proper place in intestinal obstruction occurring from intussusception.

Another physician of some eminence and a contemporary of Praxagoras was Chrysippus. We are told that he rejected the use of blood-letting and cathartics in his practice, and trusted to milder means.

We now come to the third period of Greek literature. The battle of Cheronæa, gained by Alexander over the Greeks, decided the fate of the latter. With the decline of the Greek power, literature and science, which were in danger of falling into neglect, found refuge in Alexandria. An important event after the death of Alexander, which very materially contributed to the progress of medical science, was the foundation of the famous library of Alexandria, and the school of philosophy which for many centuries maintained a high degree of reputation. The city of Alexandria, built by order of Alexander, and called after his name, became the centre of Greek literature and commerce, where many of the most literary men from every part of the world, and of all nations, whether Egyptians, Jews, Greeks, or others, resorted under royal patronage. Each and all the different sects had their separate schools and professors. The munificent Ptolemies, who were themselves the learned and most enlightened kings of Egypt, spared no expense to make Alexandria the common resort of learned men from various countries for the diffusion of knowledge. Ptolemy Sotor founded the library of Alexandria near his own palace. At the death of his son Ptolemy Philadelphus, it contained 100,000 volumes. When the volumes increased to 400,000, a branch was established at Serapion, which in lapse of time contained 300,000 volumes, making in all a total of 700,000.

Among the most celebrated physicians who settled in Alexandria were Herophilus, a pupil of Praxagoras and a contemporary of Ptolemy Sotor, and Erasistratus, the grandson of Aristotle. They were the first founders of the Alexandrian schools of anatomy and medicine. They obtained royal permission to dissect criminals alive. The rulers of Alexandria, though highly cultivated, were absolute and devoid of all genuine feelings. They allowed the most shocking cruelties to be practised on their subjects. Mercy was unknown at this period alike to kings and physicians. The latter to study anatomy amused themselves by dissecting human beings alive, and practised on them the most horrible barbarities. " They procured criminals," says Celsus, " out of prison by royal permission, and dissecting them alive, contemplated, while they were yet breathing, the parts which nature had before concealed—examining their position, colour, figure, size, order, hardness, softness, smoothness, and roughness."* Such abominable slaughter, says Celsus, is nothing but wickedness and dreadful cruelty, " *dira crudelitate.*"

We are not surprised at such shocking deeds of barbarity when we learn that some physicians of the

---

* Qui nocentes homines, a rigibus ex carcere acceptos, vivos inciderint, considerarintque, etiamnum spiritu remanente, ea, quæ natura ante clausisset, eorumque positum, colorem, figuram, magnitudinem, ordinem, duritiem, mollitiem, lævorem, contactum.

sixteenth century were not less cruel and savage than those who lived during the flourishing period of Alexandria. We are told that Mathiolus, in the year 1561, experimented upon two robbers by giving them large doses of aconite. Claud Richard is said to have tried the same upon another robber. Gabriel Fallopia procured criminals by permission to poison and dissect them. Of his barbarous practice he speaks thus:—" For, the prince ordered a man to be given us, whom we killed in our fashion, and dissected. I gave him two drachms of opium. He having a quartan ague had a paroxysm, which prevented the opium taking effect. The man in great exultation begged of us to try once more, and if he did not then die, to ask the prince to spare his life. We gave him other two drachms of opium, and he died."*

A Bill has been recently passed, we believe, in Parliament for the prevention of cruelty even to animals, as rabbits and frogs, in physiological laboratories and other places. Thus, if a surgeon in experimenting upon any vertebrata, causes tormenting pain or disease, he is liable to be punished by fine or imprisonment. What a striking contrast between human nature of the sixteenth and the nineteenth century!

The reputation which Herophilus and Erasistratus obtained in the department of anatomy was undoubtedly great. They wrote several works on anatomy and medicine, which were for a long time in great estimation. They are considered as having been the first Greek physicians who wrote treatises on anatomy from observations made by themselves

---

* Quoted by Russel, p. 148.

from dissection of human subjects. They were acquainted with the anatomy of the brain and nervous system, and had some notion of the circulation of the blood. The nerves were divided by them into two classes, first those of motion, and second those of sensation. The names "Torcular Herophili," the "Calamus Scriptorius," and the "Duodenum," given by Herophilus to different parts of the body, are retained in the anatomical works up to the present day. Erasistratus, like his instructor Chrysippus, protested against blood-letting and the administration of remedies compounded of several drugs, and trusted much to the healing power of nature aided by diet. He spent a few years of his life in the court of King Seleucus Nicator, where he obtained a high reputation by discovering the love of the king's eldest son for his step-mother.

King Seleucus had by his first wife a son named Antiochus. His second marriage was with Stratonice, the daughter of Demetrius. Antiochus was so charmed with the beauty of her person that he conceived a passion for her—

> "Alas! that fields and forests can afford
> No remedies to heal their love-sick lord!
> To cure the pains of love no plant avails;
> And his own physic the physician fails."

"His condition," says Plutarch, "was extremely unhappy. He made the greatest efforts to conquer his passion, but they were of no avail. At last, considering that his desires were of the most extravagant kind, that there was no prospect of satisfaction for them, and that the succours of reason entirely failed, he resolved in his despair to rid himself of life, and bring it gradually to a period, by neglecting all care of his person and abstaining from food; for this purpose he made sickness his pretence. His physician Erasistratus easily discovered that his distemper was love, but it was difficult to conjecture who was the object. In order to find it out he spent whole days in his chamber, and whenever any beautiful person of either sex entered it, he observed with great attention, not only his looks, but every part and motion of the body, which corresponds most with the passions of the soul. When others entered, he was entirely unaffected; but when Stratonice came in, as she often did, either alone or with Seleucus, he showed all the symptoms described by Sappho,—the faltering voice, the burning blush, the languid eye, the sudden sweat, the tumultuous pulse, and at length, the passion overcoming his spirits, a deliquium and mortal paleness.

"Erasistratus concluded from these tokens that the prince was in love with Stratonice, and perceived that he intended to carry the secret with him to the grave. He saw the difficulty of breaking the matter to Seleucus, yet depending upon the affection which the king had for his son, he ventured one day to tell him 'that the young man's disorder was love, but love for which there was no remedy.' The king, quite astonished, said: 'How! love for which there is no remedy?' 'It is certainly so,' answered Erasistratus, 'for he is in love with my wife.' 'What! Erasistratus,' said the king, 'would you, who are my friend, refuse to give your wife to my son, when you see us in danger of losing our only hope?' 'Nay, would you do such a thing,' answered the physician, 'though you are his father, if he were in love with Stratonice?' 'O! my friend,' replied Seleucus, 'how happy should I be, if either God or man could remove his affections thither! I would give up my kingdom, so I could but keep Antiochus.' He pronounced these words with so much emotion, and such a profusion of tears, that Erasistratus took him by the hand, and said, 'Then there is no need of Erasistratus; you, sir, who are a father, a husband, and a king, will be the best physician too for your family.'

"Upon this, Seleucus summoned the people to meet in full assembly, and told them—'It was his will and pleasure that Antiochus should intermarry with Stratonice, and that they should be declared King and Queen of the Upper Provinces. He believed,' he said, 'that Antiochus, who was such an obedient son, would not oppose his desire'; and if the princess should oppose the marriage, as an unprecedented thing, he hoped his friends would persuade her to think, that what was agreeable to the king, and advantageous to the kingdom, was both just and honourable.' Such is said to have been the cause of the marriage between Antiochus and Stratonice."*

Serapion was another Alexandrian physician. He was a pupil of Herophilus, and a professed empiric. He wrote in strong terms against the doctrines of Hippocrates.

Shortly after the foundation of the Alexandrian school of medicine, the medical profession was divided into the two important classes of physicians and surgeons. The operation of lithotomy, which was practised by a separate class of men from the time of Hippocrates, was now performed by the Alexandrian surgeons with great skill. Celsus and Paulus have minutely described the operation, and all the best Arab physicians were not ignorant of it. Ammonius, the renowned Alexandrian lithotomist, was the first to crush the stone in the bladder with a forceps introduced through the perineum when it was too large for safe extraction. On account of this he was surnamed the Lithotomos, meaning the stonecutter. Whether the operation of lithotrity was performed by the ancients is not exactly known, for neither in the Hippocratic treatises nor in the surgical book of Paulus Ægineta do we find any description of it. According to Dr. Adams, Aëtius is the only author who makes an allusion at lithotrity in the following brief passage:—" When the stone is large, neither lithotrity, or lithotripsy, nor lithotomy can be practised safely."

Plutarch's Lives. Translated by J. & W. Langhorne, pp. 958, 959.

CHAPTER V.

Eminence of the ancient Hindoos in the healing art—Herbs highly prized—Ayurveda—Its knowledge imparted by Brahma—Surgeons Divine—Charaka—Dhanwantari—Susruta—Origin of the Vaidya caste—Just estimate of a skilful physician—Moral discipline—Dissection of dead bodies—Chemistry—Surgical operations and instruments—Small-pox Inoculation—Materia Medica—Pharmacy—Pathology—Incurable Diseases supposed to be produced by sins—Influence of Evil Spirits and Gods in producing diseases—Diagnosis and Prognosis—The present Vaids and Hakims—Graduates of Medicine in India—The peculiar patients—European medical skill not acknowledged by the Natives of India—The Indian Medical Service.

The Hindoos profess the religion of Brahma. Their sacred Vedas—entitled Rig, Yajush, Saman, and Atharvan—were, according to Hindoo mythology, obtained from Brahma in the Satya-yuga, or the age of truth and happiness. They are revered by the Brahmans as having been issued from Brahma's four mouths. The Hindoos claim the highest antiquity for these sacred books, and pretend that they have existed from the creation of the world. The antiquity of the Vedas however is undeniable. They are ascribed by Colebrook to 1,400, and Sir William Jones to 1,600 years before Christ.

Brahma divided his people into four castes:—

1. The Brahmans or priests who pretend to have sprung from Brahma's mouth. They were the cultivators of the sciences.

2. The Khatryas, or warriors and sovereigns.
3. The Visa, cultivators, and merchants.
4. The Sudras, servants, labourers, and artizans.

The ancient Hindoos seem to have attained a considerable degree of civilization. There can be no doubt that their abilities in the arts and progress in the sciences were considerable. The Hindoos of former times were scarcely inferior in learning to any other nation on the earth. The practice of medicine was exclusively confined to the priests. The learned Professor Wilson remarks:—"In medicine as in astronomy and metaphysics, the Hindoos kept pace with the most enlightened nations of the world, and they attained as thorough a proficiency in medicine and surgery as any people whose requirements are recorded, and as indeed was practicable before anatomy was made known to us by the discoveries of modern enquirers."*

The medical art was held in high esteem by the Hindoos. One of their fourteen gems (ratnas) was a learned physician. Susruta says:—"Whoever studies this eternal (knowledge of medicine) first announced by the self-born and published (on earth) by the King of Kasi, that righteous man shall be adorned by kings while on earth, and after his death he will go to the region of Sakra."†

India in the remotest period of its history had excellent physicians. An Indian ruler offered to give up to Alexander the Great, among other things, a physician of extraordinary skill. On the ap-

---
* *Works*, vol. I., p. 269.
† *Susruta*, translated by Anna Moreswar Kunte, No. 2, p. 16.

proach of Alexander's army the Indians were alarmed for the fate of their country, and in order to avert a quarrel with Alexander entreated a peace. The Indian prince called Keyd, probably the Taxiles of the Greeks, with a conciliatory policy addressed the Greek ambassador as follows :—" I shall send to the great conqueror, your master, my beautiful daughter, a goblet made of a most splendid ruby, a philosopher of great science, and a physician who has such skill that he can restore the dead."* So great was the skill and fame of Hindoo physicians that Alexander, during his short stay in India, had invited them to his camp, and those of his followers who suffered from disease or were bitten by snakes, were carried to them for treatment by his express order.

Two Indian physicians named Manka and Saleh were physicians to Harun-al-Rashid, and their most ancient works, the Charaka and Susruta, were translated into Arabic. The former also translated a treatise on poison.

A general belief prevailed among the ancient Hindoos that " a person rejecting a Vaidya or physician will be punished in hell," and that " should a patient not pay his physician a price equivalent to the value of his soul, then all his holy virtues and good acts which he has performed during his lifetime will belong to the physician." The eminence of this people in the science of medicine is therefore unquestionable.

---

* Malcolm's *History of Persia*, vol. I., p. 77.

That medicinal herbs were highly prized by the ancient Hindoos there can be no doubt. We learn from the following passage in their Puranas, that among things to be saved from the Deluge medicines were not neglected :—

"Then shalt thou take all *medicinal herbs*, all the variety of the seeds, and accompanied by seven saints, enriched by pairs of all brute animals, thou shalt enter the spacious ark; and continue in it secure from the flood, on one immense ocean, without light; except the radiance of the holy companions."

Their earliest history of medicine is interwoven with fables. It is said in the Shastras that in the Kaliyug, or the fourth and present corrupt age, Brahma gave to the sinful man a commentary of the eternal Vedas in four treatises called Upavedas or minor Vedas, one of which was Ayurveda, meaning the knowledge of living, or the science of medicine. This was the most ancient work of the Hindoos on medicine, and has been almost lost. Some state that small fragments of the Ayurveda still exist. From their style of writing they are considered by some to be a part of the fourth or Atharvaveda, by others as an Upaveda of the Rigveda. It is stated in the most ancient medical works of the Hindoos that the Ayurveda consisted of 100,000 verses (slokas). This work was considered too voluminous to be learnt by men not possessing high intellectual power in the age of Kali-yug, and Brahma, pitying mankind for their sufferings, abridged and divided it into the following eight sections :—

1. *Salayam*, or surgery, which treated of surgical diseases and their treatment.

2. *Salakyam.*—This treated of external organic diseases of the eyes, nose, ears, &c.

3. *Kaya-Chikitsa.*—This division treated of all the affections of the human body.

4. *Bhutavidya.*—This division comprised the treatment of all the varieties of deranged mind, supposed to be caused by the entrance of offended gods and devils, and the spirits of the dead into the person of the sufferer.

5. *Kumarabhritya.*—In this division were described the diseases of infants and their treatment, also the treatment of puerperal diseases which were believed to be produced by angry devils.

6. *Agadatantram.*—This treated of the administration of antidotes in cases of poisoning.

7. *Rasayanatantram.*—In this division the therapeutic actions of medicines in general were considered, including the science of chemistry.

8. *Vajikaranatantram*, or the best means for the propagation of the human race.

We are told that the Ayurveda also contained an account of the human body.

We are informed by some of the medical shastras that the knowledge of Ayurveda was first imparted by Brahma to *Dacsha*, the *Prajapati* who according to some instructed the *Surja* (sun), according to others the Ashwins, or sons of Surja, who in their turn taught the thousand-eyed *Indra*, from whom Dhanwantari is said to have learnt it. These gods practised the healing art not on earth but in heaven among the gods! As the gods were immortal and never suffered from disease, they had no lives to be saved, but in their wars with giants they often received wounds, for the cure of which they were obliged to seek the aid of the surgical gods. The Ashwins were celebrated for their extraordinary skill in surgery. Brahma's fifth head, which was cut off in a battle between him and *Rudra*, was immediately reunited by the skilful Ashwins! When Ganesha's head, which was separated from the trunk, "flew away to the heaven of Krishna," the god Vishnu cut off the head of an elephant, and joined it to the trunk of Ganesha, who was thus restored to life!

Let us now pass from the practitioners in heaven to those on earth. Some time after this, human beings, in consequence of their vices, corruption, and wicked behaviour, becoming an easy prey to "the thousand ills that flesh is heir to," the holy sages of the period known by the name of *munis* were deeply affected at the sight of man's misery. Sincerely desirous of remedying the evil, a numerous body of them assembled in the Himalayan mountains. They found it absolutely necessary to solicit the aid of Indra, and unanimously decided to send one of their number to heaven to learn medicine from him. They chose Bharadwaja for the occasion, who with their consent went to heaven, and beheld Indra "resplendent with fire," and humbly prayed: "Oh! king of the gods! created for the salvation of mankind, I have been sent by the sages of the earth to ask your assistance. Take pity on the weakness and infirmities of man, and teach us the Ayurveda."* Indra complied with his wishes, and

---
* *Review of the History of Medicine*, by T. A. Wise, vol. I., p. 22.

instructed him in the knowledge of the Ayurveda. Bharadwaja returned, and communicated the knowledge thus acquired to the sages. One of these, *Atreya*, taught the healing art to several pupils, some of whom wrote books which were read before a meeting of the wise men with great applause, and the noise produced in praise of the authors reached to heaven! The work produced by *Agnibesa* was accepted as the best, and after a few corrections by the sage Charaka received his name. This work is the oldest medical record which has come down to us.

It would appear from a legend that Dhanwantari was the founder of the Hindoo school of medicine. One of the fourteen ratnas (gems) was "the health-bestowing Dhanwantari, the celestial physician,— who arose from the sea when churned for the beverage of immortality." He was instructed in Ayurveda by Indra, but afterwards came down upon earth to cure diseases and instruct men in the art of healing. In the Bhava-prakash it is stated that Indra requested him to descend to the earth for alleviating human sufferings, and addressed him as follows :—

"Oh! Dhanwantari, thou respected of gods, I have something to say to thee. Thou art the best person to do good to the world. Go to the earth, and become King of Benares, and for alleviating human sufferings publish the knowledge of the Ayurveda. He accordingly studied the Veda from Indra, and was born on earth in Benares in the family of the King."[*]

Anyhow he became ruler of Kasi or Benares. The sages having heard of his remarkable cures determined to implore his assistance, and learn from him

---

[*] See *Susruta*, translated by Anna Moreswar, No. 2, Note to p. 10.

the incomprehensible Ayurveda. For this purpose eight persons were chosen from among them to proceed to Kasi. When they reached that holy city they were informed that Dhanwantari had retired from the sovereignty to the forests, and had been leading the life of a hermit. Hearing this, they went thither in search of him. They at last came in sight of him, and, after bowing and saluting, addressed him as follows:—

"Deign Sovereign Ruler to bestow upon us the power of preventing and curing the many diseases under which mankind is suffering—affecting their bodies, tormenting their minds; and which with the numerous accidental and natural diseases distress them so much that they seem to be without friends. Their destitution grieves us much, and we pray that you will instruct us in the cause, the nature, and the cure of disease; the means for retaining health and for promoting the welfare of the soul in another world. Like scholars we come to receive this information from you."*

Dhanwantari replied: "You are welcome, my lads, all of you shall be taught in the Ayurveda."

Susruta, the son of *Visvamitra*, was selected by the sages to receive instructions from Dhanwantari, who said that it was impossible for man in that degenerate age to acquire an intimate knowledge of the Ayurveda, and advised him to abridge and divide it into parts. Susruta accordingly abridged it; and arranged the eight sections in the following six parts:—

1. *Sutra-sthana* (surgery).
2. *Midana-sthana* (pathology).
3. *Sarira-sthana* (anatomy).
4. *Chikitsa-sthana* (therapeutics).
5. *Kalpa-sthana* (antidotes).

---

*Hindoo System of Medicine, by T. A. Wise, vol. I., pp. 47, 48.

6. *Uttara-sthana* (supplementary section, including local diseases).

This work is still extant, and goes by the name of Susruta. The Charaka and Susruta are the two Hindoo medical works of the highest antiquity, and are mentioned in the Purans and Mahabharat. Their date is not quite certain. They are assigned by Prof. Wilson to the 9th or 10th century B. C. The former is chiefly celebrated as a medical, and the latter as a surgical and anatomical work. Those who received instructions from Charaka became physicians, and those from Susruta surgeons. The two works are the common basis of almost all the commentaries and compilations which have come down to us.

We have already stated that the practice of medicine was in ancient times exclusively confined to the priests. As the Brahmans on account of their multifarious duties could not devote their whole attention to the practice of medicine, the caste of the Vaidyas sprang up. The origin of the class of Vaidyas, whether legendary or true, is of some interest. A muni (sage) named Gulaba had in his service an unmarried female attendant of an inferior caste (Visa), named Amba. She gave him so much satisfaction that one day he blessed her, and previously apprised her that she would become the mother of a beautiful and esteemed son (perhaps an offspring of his own), who should be called by the name of Verabhadra (most fortunate), and added that he would become highly skilled and distinguished in the medical art. According to the predictions of the sage the female gave birth to a boy, who was called Verabhadra *alias* Vaidya (physician), and who was the first medical man of the mixed tribes. His thirteen sons received instructions in the Ayurveda from the sacred sages of the period, and became renowned physicians. The present Vaidyas of the mixed tribes are said to be their descendants. In later times, persons of all castes, even Sudras, were allowed to learn the ancient medical shastras, and to assume the name of a Vaidya. From a Brahmin and a Visa also arose the caste of the Gundhu-vuniks, or *druggists*. It is a melancholy fact that the mighty and learned Brahmans, who once exercised immense power, and " who placed themselves above kings in honour, and laid the whole nation prostrate at their feet," are at the present day degraded and sunk in dishonour. A number of them follow other trades and occupations. Some of them are even sunk to the level of menial servants.

In order to become a skilful physician the importance of practical study was not overlooked, but considered necessary in addition to the theoretical knowledge acquired from books, as appears from the following passage :—

" He who has merely learnt the principles (of medicine), and received no practical instructions, loses his presence of mind when he sees a patient, just as a coward gets confused in a battle. On the other hand, he who through mere rashness has obtained mere facility in practical work, and knows not the principles of medicine (as taught in books), does not deserve commendation of the learned, but punishment from the King. Both these are unaccomplished and unfit to become practitioners, just as a bird with a single wing is unable to fly."*

---

* *Susruta*, translated by Anna Moreswar, No. 3, p. 32.

It is also stated that both a theoretical and practical physician is fit to physic a raja, and goes on safely and successfully in saving lives, just as a war chariot with two wheels moves on easily. But to one who is imperfectly acquainted with his profession, medicines and surgical instruments are like poisons and swords. Surely such a practitioner is like a bird with but one wing, and is the murderer of his patients.

The following extracts given by Dr. Ainslie in his Materia Indica from the Tamil translation by Maharishi or Saint Aghastier of an ancient Sanscrit work will convey some idea of the character of a Hindoo physician of antiquity:—

"*What constitutes a good physician.*—The sages of antiquity (maharishies) have thus handed down to us the qualities which constitute a good physician. He must be a person of strict veracity, and of the greatest sobriety and decorum, holding sexual intercourse with no woman except his own wife. He ought to be thoroughly skilled in all the commentaries of the *Ayurveda*, and be otherwise a man of sense and benevolence, his heart must be charitable, his temper calm; and his constant study how to do good. Such an individual is properly called a good physician, and such a physician ought still daily to improve his mind by an attentive perusal of scientific books (vághádum).

"When a patient expresses himself peevishly or hastily, a *Vytian* (physician) so endowed, will not thereby be provoked to impatience; he remains mild yet courageous, and cherishes a cheerful hope of being able to save the sufferer's life; he is frank, communicative, impartial and liberal, yet ever rigid in exacting an adherence to whatever regimen or rules he may think it necessary to enjoin. Should death come upon us under the care of this earthly saint, it can only be considered as inevitable fate, and not the consequence of presumptuous ignorance."

This should be in fact the character of every man brought up in the modern schools of medicine. Yet how many "earthly saints" have been sent forth by the faculties into the world with a theoretical knowledge minus the qualities which constitute a good physician! Happily such men are, comparatively speaking, not numerous.

The ancient Hindoos seem to have had no prejudice against the dissection of human bodies. Sir W. Jones states that he had seen a portion of the Ayurveda, in which he found to his surprise a description of the structure of the human body. Charaka, their celebrated physician, says that a practitioner should become acquainted with the different parts of the human body. Susruta, another eminent physician, points out the necessity of learning the structure of the human frame. That the subject of anatomy was not omitted in Hindoo medical science, some conjecture may be formed from the following passage :—"Those men who in ignorance of the structure of the human frame venture to make it the subject of their experiments, are the murderers of their species."* The following two passages, quoted by Wise from Manu, their law-giver, show that the Hindoos were not prejudiced against *touching* a corpse or a fresh bone, but the law is not clear as to the dissection of dead bodies :—

"One who has touched a corpse is made pure by bathing."

"Should a Brahman touch a fresh human bone he is purified by bathing, and if there be not water, by stroking a cow, or by looking at the sun, having sprinkled his mouth duly with water."

There can be no doubt, however, that the ancient Hindoos could never have performed the most diffi-

---

* Wilson's *Works*, vol. I., p. 382.

cult operations described in their works without some knowledge of anatomy.

The knowledge of the Hindoos in physiology was imperfect and inaccurate. This branch of medicine as explained in the shastras is incomprehensible and full of absurdities.

We have already stated that the seventh division of the Ayurveda comprised the science of chemistry (*Rasayana*). The praise of originality is by some writers given to the Arabs for their investigation in this science; others, on the contrary, affirm that they borrowed mostly from the Hindoos. It is said that the celebrated Arabian chemist Geber himself confesses that he obtained his knowledge of chemistry from the books of ancient sages. Modern writers conjecture that the ancient sages were Hindoo philosophers, but this requires proof. " The Arabic name *sagimen*," writes Professor Royle, "indeed seems to have been derived from the Hindoo *sagi-noon*, that is saji or soda salt,"[*] and that sal-ammoniac is described both by the Sanscrit and Arabian authors under the name of *naosadur*.' From these and other instances Dr. Royle concludes that the Arabians had access to Hindoo medical works, and from this source derived their knowledge of chemistry and materia medica. It has therefore been inferred by some, that the Arabians must have borrowed from the Hindoos. We have no wish to discuss the differences of opinion, whether the Arabians derived their knowledge of chemistry from the Hindoos, or

---

[*] Royle *On the Arts and Manufactures of India*, Lecture XI., p. 463.

wrote independently of them on the subject; suffice it to say, that the claim of priority belongs to the Hindoos, who were acquainted with chemistry long before the foundation of the Saracen empire. The supposition that the Arabs borrowed from the Hindoos is, in the absence of better evidence, without foundation.

The Hindoos were familiar with the preparations of nitric, muriatic, sulphuric, oxalic and citric acids. They were also acquainted with the preparations of the oxides of copper, iron, lead, tin and zinc. They have long been familiar with nitre, sulphur, sal-ammoniac, borax and alum. The metallic salts such as blue, green, and white vitriol, the carbonates of lead and iron, and the sulphurets of copper, mercury, iron, antimony and arsenic were known to them.

Surgery *(salayam* or *sutrasthana)* was studied with great zeal by the ancient Hindoos. It was a favourite study of their gods, who were often required to cure wounds, as we have already stated. The first two divisions of the Ayurveda treated of surgery. Dhanwantari begins his lectures with surgery. It forms the first division of Susruta, who speaks of it as "the first and best of the medical sciences, less liable than any other to the fallacies of conjectural and inferential practice; pure in itself; perpetual in its applicability; the worthy produce of heaven and certain source of fame."*

The hand was considered "the first, best and most important of all instruments."

---

* See Royle's *Essay on the Antiquity of Hindoo Medicine*, p. 49.

The surgical operations were of eight kinds:—
Chhedana, cutting or excision as in fistula in ano; *Lekhana*, drawing lines by which means scarification and inoculation were produced; *Vyadhana*, puncturing parts, as in letting out the fluid confined in a cavity (this appears to be applied to tapping in hydrocele and dropsy); *Eschyam*, probing or sounding as in fistula and stone in the bladder; *Aharya*, extraction of solid bodies, as of stone, fœtus, teeth, &c.; *Visravana*, removal of fluids; *Sevana*, or sewing, as in wounds; and *Bhedana*, division or excision, as amputation of limbs, &c.

The Hindoos were familiar with the most difficult surgical operations, such as gastrotomy, or cutting open the abdomen; lithotomy, or cutting for the stone; and Cæsarian section, or cutting the abdominal parieties and womb to extract the child. They also couched for the cataract, performed amputations of the limbs, and operated for strangulated hernia. Tapping for hydrocele and abdominal dropsy was practised by them. Besides these they performed many minor operations too numerous to mention.

Before proceeding to operate for the stone the sanction of the raja was necessary, and the only instruments used on the occasion were a scalpel and an iron scoop. The method of operating described by Susruta is still practised by some learned vaidyas, as follows: The patient is placed on a table with his legs drawn up, and kept well aside by an assistant. They are then tied up to the wrists so as to expose the perineum to view. Two fingers of the one hand are introduced by the operator into the rectum, while with the other hand the abdomen is pressed down from above, and the stone brought down in the perineum, and made to project. An incision is then made an inch above the anus, avoiding the raphe, and carrying it downwards, until it reaches the stone. The aperture is enlarged, and the stone is withdrawn by means of an iron scoop. An incision in the perineum directly in the raphe is considered as destroying the generative powers.

To the Hindoos is due the credit of having first practised the rhinoplastic operations for the reparation of lost noses and ears by removing a flap of skin from the neighbourhood, and fixing it to the organ, to be repaired by means of sutures and bandages.

In difficult labour, when the child could not be expelled by the natural powers on account of some deformity of the pelvis, head, &c. the ancient Hindoos had recourse to craniotomy, or the operation of opening the head of the child. After the collapse and diminution of the size of the head, a hook was introduced, and inserted in a convenient place, and the fœtus brought down. In unnatural presentations they changed the position of the child.

The *Yantras*, or surgical instruments, employed by the ancient Hindoos were 127. The author of the Susruta enumerates one hundred and one implements. They were classed as follows:—

The *Sastras*, or cutting instruments. Twenty sorts are described by Susruta. They were lancets, knives, bistouries, trocars, saws, scissors, bone-nippers, needles, &c.

The *Swatikas* were pincers or forceps of twenty-four sorts. They were used for extracting extraneous substances lodged in the bones, and for removing teeth or splinters of bone.

The *Saudansas*, or tongs. They were employed for removing foreign bodies from the soft parts, such as skin, flesh, &c. They were of two kinds.

The *Talayantras* were also tongs, but smaller than the above. They were two in number, and were used for extracting foreign substances fixed in the ears, nose, &c.

The *Nadayantras*, tubular instruments shaped like catheters, canulæ, syringes, &c. They were used for removing obstructions from deep-seated canals as the intestines, urethra, &c., for examining and diagnosing diseases of deep-seated parts, and for drawing off fluids.

The *Salakas* were probes, sounds, rods, &c. They were twenty-eight in number, of various sizes and shapes, and were employed for examining foreign substances lodged in parts removed from inspection and difficult of access; for cleansing canals, particularly the urethra; for applying caustics and cautery; and for extracting nasal polypi (nakra).

The *Upayantras*, or minor yantras, were, as their name implies, accessory instruments, such as pins, tents, &c.

The Hindoos were acquainted with no less than fourteen kinds of bandages. *Kshara* or caustics, *agni* or the actual cautery, and *sringa* or cupping horns, were frequently employed by them. Blood-letting, scarifications, and the use of leeches were also long known to them.

Inoculation for the small-pox was practised by the Hindoos from time immemorial. It is said in the *Nidan*, an ancient medical work: " should woman bear inoculation on the left side, and man on the right, then there shall be no danger from bushunt" (small-pox). Before performing the operation, offerings were presented with prayers by the inoculating Brahmin to the *Sheetula-devi*, or goddess of small-pox, promising at the same time to present offerings to her if she was favourable. If the parents were able to bear further expenses, a Brahmin was employed to pray to the goddess every day till the recovery of the child. After recovery offerings were again presented with many prayers to the presiding goddess.

The Hindoos in ancient times were acquainted with the virtues of many plants. The materia medica (Dravyabhidhana) of Susruta is copious, and comprises 760 plants. The Hindoos were the first to administer minerals internally. Preparations of gold, silver, mercury, antimony, iron, copper, zinc, tin, lead and arsenic were administered internally from time immemorial. Arsenic as a remedy for intermittent fevers, and cinnabar fumigations for producing salivation were employed at a very early period. The Hindoos introduced into their materia medica several absurd remedies, such as pearls, diamonds, and other precious stones. They employed several medicines obtained from the animal kingdom, such as musk, castoreum, bile, bones of animals made into powder or reduced to ashes, &c. They also administered most disgusting things internally, such as cow's urine, the fresh juice of the dung of quadrupeds, &c. The poison of the snake cobra-de-capello as a therapeutic agent for the cure of several diseases has been employed by the Hindoos from a remote period, and its virtues highly extolled. When given in combination with other medicines it has been considered a very valuable remedy in serious disorders when ordinary remedies fail. It is said that cases given up as hopeless have been cured by its administration. Lately Dr. Hering, a well-known homœopathic physician of America, introduced the poisons of *Crotalus* and *Trigonocephalus Lachesis* into the homœopathic materia medica. The late Dr. Russell, who was one of the most eminent homœopathic practitioners of London, introduced the poison of *Naja Tripudians* into practice.*

Polypharmacy, or mixing a number of ingredients indiscriminately in a compound, was practised by the Hindoos at a very early date. It is not to be wondered that this practice has its licensed advocates in our own times.

The pharmacy or rasavidya of the Hindoos, though not unmixed with superstition, contains much that is valuable and important. In the *Kalpastanum* medicinal plants are arranged as follows :—Tuberous and bulbous roots, roots, bark of roots, bark of large trees, trees possessing a peculiar smell, leaves,

---

* For further information *vide* Hering *On the Poison of Serpents*, and the second clinical lecture delivered in the London Homœopathic Hospital by Dr. R. Russel, and published in the *Annals of the British Homœopathic Society*, No. VIII.

flowers, fruits, seeds, acrid and astringent vegetables, milky plants, gums and resins. In collecting medicinal plants the nature of the different kinds of soil, the climate and the seasons are considered at length. The proper period of their gathering is also insisted upon. Vegetable medicines procured from the Himalayan mountains are considered the best. The medicines should be gathered, prepared and administered on a lucky day and hour, and some ceremonies should be observed, and prayers offered up at the time. Medicines were used in the form of *Rasaha* or the fresh juice of plants; *Kalkaha*, the simple or compound powder of plants given either mixed with water or made into pills; *Sitaha*, cold infusions; *Srutaha*, *Pandaha*, and *Kashaiam*, decoctions. Syrup, honey, &c. added to the prepared decoction are called *Brativapam*. Decoctions prepared with oil are called *Tailam*; and strong decoctions of dry powdered ingredients, mixed with some oil or ghee, sugar or honey, and boiled for a very long time, *Leham* or electuary. "The place in which medicines are kept should be clean, dry, and not accessible to rats, white ants, or dust. . . . . . Fire, smoke, and water must be kept at a distance."* After a certain time medicines become useless. "Flowers, leaves, and fruits should never be older than one year. All kinds of wood and branches become useless after one year's keeping. Roots should never be used after they have been three years in store, several seeds and nuts will serve until the fifth year after their collection. Gums and resins may be employed for ten years."†

---

* Heyne's *Tracts*, p. 139.   † Ibid., p. 140.

Before administering medicines internally, the *Vaidya* should observe the motions of the stars, the increase and decrease of the moon's age, and the favourable and unfavourable days and hours. We learn from the *Kalpastanum* that "as patients are apt to grow worse in the night, double doses of medicine should be given them in the evening." Neither the god of medicine nor the remuneration of a physician is to be neglected by a sick person, for in the same work we are told:—"Before the patient takes the medicine, the god of physic is to be worshipped in the person of his deputy, the physician, who (it is seriously recommended for the good of the patient) must be paid well for his services."*

The importance and necessity of studying poisons and their antidotes (Kalpasthana) were impressed upon the minds of the Hindoos at a very early period.

The pathology of the Hindoos was based on the doctrine of humours. The Hindoo physicians believed that the three humours, viz., the wind (*vayu*), bile (*pitta*), and phlegm (*kofa*) were essential for the preservation both of health and life. They imagined that the humours when impure, deranged, or deviating from their due and healthy proportions, gave rise to disease. According to this notion they regulated their general treatment of disease (*Chikitsa*), and arranged their medicines into separate classes for purifying, evacuating, or restoring the just proportions of the superfluous or diseased humours; for example, errhines and various fumes were used to evacuate the diseased phlegm from the

---

* Hayne's *Tracts*, pp. 147, 148.

head, emetics to remove the superfluous bile from the stomach and phlegm, and purgatives to clear the bowels of excessive bile and other morbid humours. In fact, they relied chiefly on the use—or, properly speaking, the abuse—of blood-letting, purgatives, emetics, cautery, &c. for the cure as well as prevention of disease. These they seem to have carried to a very dangerous extent. Blood was drawn to the amount of 2 lbs. at a time, and the young aspirant to the medical profession is taught that if "all the bad blood is not discharged by the first bleeding, another is to be performed on the second or third day after the first." Drastic purgatives were made use of frequently, and to such an extent, that they sometimes produced fainting, frequent mucous and bloody stools, and protrusion of the lower portion of the bowels. Even when the disease yielded to treatment, purgatives were repeated daily to eject any remaining collection of the bad humours. Such a course was considered necessary to prevent a relapse. Not only this, but they recommended bloodletting, purgatives, and emetics to healthy persons. Blood-letting twice a year, the exhibition of purgatives once a month, and an emetic once a fortnight, were supposed to preserve health and prevent disease.

Diseases are divided into sthenic or *hot* and asthenic or *cold*. Hot diseases, according to the general belief of the Hindoos, require opposite or cooling remedies ; while cold diseases hot or stimulating remedies.

If the remedial means given in the *Shastras* failed to cure a particular disease, it was supposed to be produced by sins or bad deeds (karmas) committed by the sufferer. In such cases a course of penances, prayers and superstitious performances, gifts to the Brahmin and charity to the poor, were considered necessary to *wash off the sin,* and give the sufferer the last chance of cure.

The ancient Hindoos had other modes of preventing and curing diseases by many other practices equally ridiculous, which are still adopted by the modern *vaids*. They believe in the power of incantations over almost every disease. The physician having written a few verses from some religious book on a piece of paper repeats incantations, after which it is given to the sick to wear enclosed in a small case of metal. Diseases of children are sometimes attributed to the evil eye of an envious person. Tiger claws, coral, the hairs of certain animals enclosed in a metallic case, certain stones, &c. are supposed to have the power when worn of preventing diseases to which infants are liable, and of protecting them from the evil sight of malicious persons. The Hindoo physicians like their ancestors also call to their aid both astrology and magic, particularly when a disease is believed to have been produced by the entrance of a devil or some kind of evil spirit into the body. Some diseases are supposed to be produced by the entrance of living persons, generally old women known as witches, called by the Bengalee Hindoos *dainu,* and by the Guzeratees *dakin*. It is a fact that "when a person falls suddenly sick, or is seized with some new disorder, or behaves in an unaccountable manner, they immediately declare that he is possessed by a dainu. Sometimes the dainu is asked why she has entered this person. She replies that when she came to ask alms he reproached her." The friends and relations of the sufferer send for one of the men, who pretend to have the power of driving out the witch. On his arrival he asks her name, and the cause of her dwelling in the sufferer. He then reproaches her in the severest terms, and repeatedly threatens to destroy her by his art, or by inflicting cruelties on her. By these threats, it is generally believed by the superstitious that the pretender succeeds in forcing out the witch. If she continues obstinate and unwilling to return, he tries to persuade her by promises to present her the offering of sacrifices, such as goats, sheep, fowls, or rice, sweetmeats and fruits, or any other things she liked. It she consents to return, the promised offerings are presented with some ceremonies and mutterings, after which the individual recovers instantly, and the pretender gets his reward. This abominable superstition prevails not only among the Hindoos but among the Parsee females of the poor classes. The Mahomedans are worse than any other nation in this respect.

Mania, epilepsy, convulsions, and other disorders of a similar nature, have been sometimes supposed to be caused by one of their offended gods and goddesses. " Children in fits of epilepsy," says W. Ward in his History of the Hindoos, " are supposed to be seized by this god (Punchanunu), and thrown into a state of frenzy, till they foam at the mouth, tear their hair, &c. The mother asks the supposed

evil spirit his name, who answers through the child—
'I am Punchanunu, your child has cast dust on my image, kicked it, and is the ringleader of all the children of the village in this wickedness. I will certainly take away his life.' The dyasinee is now called, who comforts the weeping and alarmed family, and addresses the god thus : ' O Punchanunu ; I pray thee, restore the child : these are thy worshippers ; the offender is but a child, and it is not proper for thee to be angry with such paltry offenders. If thou restore the child, the parents will sacrifice a goat to thee, and present to thee many offerings.' If this should fail to render the god propitious, they take the child to the image, before which they sit down, and offer the most excessive flattery to the god, causing the child to beat its head on the ground. After using every contrivance, they retire, and at the close of the fit, believing that Punchanunu has cured the child, they present to him offerings according to their ability."*

The works which treat of hygiene (pathyapathya) are many. The ancient Hindoos successfully turned their attention to this important department of the medical science. The Hindoo physicians of remote ages seem to have been cautious and attentive in selecting the proper articles of diet for their patients. The author of a medical shastra justly remarks :—" If a patient did not attend to his diet a hundred good medicines would not remove the disease." In some cases they recommended the use of wine liberally. Among the articles of diet pre-

---

* Ward's *History of the Hindus*, vol. I., p. 234.

scribed to the sick by the ancient Hindoo physicians, the reader will be astonished to find meat, fish, sheep's marrow; the flesh and soup of deer, wild cat, mongoose, rats and porcupines; broth made of the flesh of wild birds, fowls, pigeons, crows, owls, turtles, shell-fish, earth worms, &c. Fish, cock's flesh, minced meat, &c. made warm were sometimes recommended to be applied as poultices to the diseased parts.

The Hindoos, notwithstanding their faulty knowledge of pathology, were sometimes very accurate in their diagnosis (Nidana). In finding out the nature of a disease they paid much attention to the pulse, temperature, tongue, countenance, speech, urine, perspiration, &c. These observations aided them a good deal in successfully foretelling and foreseeing the issue of a case. In forming their prognosis respecting the fate of their patients they also paid attention to crisis and critical days, and to the position of stars and other collateral circumstances. The prognosis of a disease is favourable when the following symptoms occur:—

"When the patient takes medicines without aversion; when his voice remains unaltered; when during his well days his pulse is clear and perceptible; when he keeps himself cleanly while asleep; when the hands and feet do not hang inertly from him; when the respiration is free and he does not expectorate too much phlegm; when he prostrates himself and adores his God in the morning, noon and evening; when his taste is natural, and especially when he can distinguish between sour, bitter, and sweet. Under these favourable circumstances we have no reason to be apprehensive of life, even if the patient should be very weak."*

---

* Heyne's *Tracts on India*, p. 164.

The following are the fatal symptoms:—

"1, Want of sleep; 2, a constant murmuring or unintelligible endeavours to speak; 3, want of memory; 4, deep groaning breath; 5, staring immovable eyes; 6, proneness to eat and to drink many improper things; 7, disquietude; 8, spasmodic contraction of the hands, feet and extremities; 9, failure of sight; 10, an unsteady pulse, that turns to the right or left when the finger is put upon it; 11, an intermittent pulse; 12, when the body becomes cold, and the eyes stare round; 13, dryness of the breast; 14, the protuberance of the veins, especially of that in the breast; 15, when the sides of the tongue, of the eyes, and of the joints become pale; 16, the swelling of the scrotum; 17, burned, dry excrements; 18, swelling of the feet and abdomen, especially of the navel; 19, total costiveness; 20, total want of appetite to eat or drink; 21, constant coughing and yawning; 22, extraordinary degree of thirst; 23, the sinking in of the eyes."*

Let us now turn to modern India. In the reign of Darius Hystaspes the Persians had subdued and annexed a part of India. It formed one of the twenty satrapies of that monarch. After him Alexander the Great defeated Porus, and ruled over nations inhabiting the other side of the Ganges. After his death the conquered provinces fell to the lot of one of his generals, Seleucus Nicator and his son Antiochus. In later times the rich and fertile plains of India attracted the hungry barbarians of Central Asia. Mahomed of Gazni, a Tartar, penetrated India as early as 1000 A.D., and laid the foundation of the Mahomedan Empire. After him torrents of barbarians under Gengiskhan, Tamerlane and Baber from central parts of Asia breaking down upon India devastated the most flourishing districts. The Mahomedan rule was one continual era of revolutions and bloodshed, and a serious drawback upon

---

* Heyne's *Tracts on India*, pp. 164, 165.

an．
to the
mense su．
and coloniza．
Company obtaine．
the East Indies, and obta......
princes to establish commercial factories ...
forts. Soon after it began to interfere in the internal affairs of India. "The adventurers," says Prof. A. F. Tytler, "were induced to enter into intrigues to dethrone princes, or advocate particular claims to a throne, always obtaining more advantage as the condition of their intervention." In short, India, exhausted by intestine struggles and misrule, fell an easy prey to the enterprizing British, who eventually became its rulers by force of arms. India rose from a state of miserable anarchy and darkness to that of peace and prosperity, and learning after many ages of darkness has once more shed her

                                    .irm
                                  ..seless.
                                ..e, and are
                              . Mahomedan
                           ...ng in the direction
                         ... culture of their children, and
                      ...ce and fanaticism shall bid farewell to India.
   Although the blessings of peace and justice have diffused themselves over India, and there is security to life and property never heard of before, yet much remains to be done. 1—It is of paramount importance to improve the industrial resources of India, for the double purpose of increasing the revenue of the country and of preventing much of the misery among the poor labouring classes. 2—To maintain the honour of the English name untarnished, those educated for the administration of India should be thoroughbred gentlemen, placing no reliance on cunning native subordinates, but always attentive

to the duties and responsibilities of their position.
3—To devise better means of training and developing the mental powers of the people, as education in India is deficient and defective, and no facilities exist for the higher training of the mind.

Dr. Macnamara, in his Introductory Lecture delivered at the Westminster Hospital on the 1st October 1878, justly remarks:—" The deep and growing conviction of many of them (natives) is that although England has in India preserved millions of human beings from the calamities of anarchy and chronic warfare, nevertheless under our rule native society is becoming rapidly disorganised. A vast number of the old families have disappeared; the mothers and wives of the rising generation see their educated sons and husbands given over to vices never heard of, utterly heedless of family or any other ties, and they contrast all this with times past when there was not so much law, education, or taxation, but then the greatest stain that could be cast on a man's name was that of being an undutiful son. It is a pity that some of our educational authorities could not be persuaded to go out to India, and study the working of purely secular education. In this country men are apt to forget how much they and society are influenced, if not by the belief, at any rate by the effect of their forefathers' confidence in the teaching of Christianity. But in India this influence is wanting; the rising generation of educated natives break away from the Hindoo faith, they entirely ignore even the existence of God, and live absolutely for self. The outcome of a purely secular education therefore in Bengal is precisely what any unbiased person might have supposed it would be—gross materialism and rank socialism."

In medicine as in other sciences and arts the Hindoos of the present day have not been celebrated for improvements; all the Vaids with few exceptions are ignorant and illiterate, and medicine is very little studied among them. In truth, the labours of their forefathers, who left nothing undone to enrich medical literature, have been lost or neglected. The Hindoo physicians of the remotest times were far superior to the Vaids who practise now-a-days. The present Vaid, who generally succeeds his father in office, follows and strongly adheres to the superstitious practices of the ancients in medicine, without possessing any of those scientific attainments which distinguished the Hindoo physician of yore. Most of them are astrologers, and place great reliance on charms and amulets. Midwifery is practised exclusively by a separate class of women, and surgery not unfrequently by barbers. At present there is not a single college for the instruction of youths in Sanscrit works of medicine. The few who are acquainted with the Sanscrit language learn from shastras on medicine, which have been preserved through generations. A considerable number of them learn from works translated from the Sanscrit in the dialects of the country. A Vaid generally teaches his son, brother, or any relation who wishes to learn and practise the healing art. The first task of the pupil is certainly an unpleasant one. For a few months he is directed to powder in an iron mortar roots, seeds, leaves, &c., to clean the bottles, funnels, infusion pots, and other utensils; to prepare and filter infusions and decoctions, and to spread a plaster. After this he is taught to compound medicines, make a pill, ointment, electuary, &c. Next to pharmacy he is taught the nature of medicines and diseases. Practical instructions are also given during the attendance of patients at the vaid's house, after which the student endeavours to obtain knowledge from books on practice of medicine. He is also taught to remove diseases by incantations. Astrology forms a part of his study. After having acquired an imperfect knowledge of medicine, the pupil styles himself a vaid, and practises medicine without a license.

The Hindoo practitioners of India are variously styled Vaid, Kaviraj, Vytian, Parikari, &c. Very few are acquainted with the original Sanscrit medical literature, others obtain their knowledge from commentaries. The works of Charaka and Susruta are held in high repute. Maharishi Aghastier was the first to translate Sanscrit medical works in the Tamil language, which are held in high estimation by the Tamil physicians of the present day. Dhanwantari (not the celestial physician mentioned before), under the patronage of Vikramaditya, wrote a work called Nighuntu, with which some of the Hindoo practitioners are familiar. The Ustanga Herudyem, a compilation by Vagbhutta, principally from Charaka and Susruta, is in much repute amongst Malayan physicians. In the twelfth century probably Ub'hatta wrote the Sutrasthana, a commentary on Susruta's work. The Nidana and Bhavaprakash are also works of great celebrity but of modern date.

The Mahomedan practitioners of India, called Hakims or Tabibs, are the followers of the Unani or Greek school of medicine. The principal medical works known to the learned amongst them are the Tib-i-Akbari, Karabadin-kabiri, Alfaz-ul-Adwia, Mizan-al-Tib, Tufatul-Momini, Magzan-ul-Adwia, &c.

The vaids and hakims are very numerous all over India, and the best among them are mere empirics. Their treatment, based upon an erroneous and absurd pathology, is in a majority of cases mischievous. Most of them carry on the grossest frauds on the miserable dupes who apply to them to the ruin of their health and purse. Yet an immense number successfully carry on a quack practice. To check the career of these dangerous quacks by legislation is at present out of the question. Although gigantic strides have been made during the last few years in medicine, yet its practice is unfortunately so defective, and in the best hands so uncertain, that it will be impossible to put in force such legislation until a distant time. His Excellency the Governor (Sir Richard Temple) was, we believe, misled by the statements of some heads of the Medical Department when he expressed a hope (in a speech delivered before the meeting held in the Grant College on the 7th February 1878 for presentation of scholarships and prizes to successful students) of the possibility of a law being introduced into this country prohibiting quacks to practise medicine, by raising up "a large body of cheaply remunerated men" and "men of second rate attainments" for the noble profession of physic. The "heads of the profession" should have advised His Excellency that such legislation will be permissible and practicable not by augmenting the number of cheap and yet qualified practitioners, but by raising a body of well educated general practitioners, and in the words of Sir James Simpson, " when our patients will be asked to breathe and inspire most of our drugs, instead of swallowing them; or at least when they will be changed into pleasant beverages, instead of disgusting draughts and powders, boluses and pills. But that day of revolution will not probably be fully realised until that distant time when physicians, a century or two hence, shall be intimate with the chemistry of most diseases, when they shall know the exact antidotes and eliminatories; when they shall look upon the cure of some maladies as simply a series of chemical problems and formulæ; when they shall melt down all calculi, necrosed bones, &c. by appropriate solvents, instead of removing them by surgical operations; when the bleeding in amputations and other wounds shall be stemmed, not by septic ligatures or stupid needles, but by the simple application of hæmostatic gases or washes; when the few wounds then required in surgery shall all be swiftly and immediately united by the first intention; when medical men shall be able to stay the ravages of tubercle, blot out fever and inflammation, dissolve or mummify morbid growths, cure cancer, destroy all morbific organic germs and ferments, annul the deadly influences of malaria and contagions, and by these and various other means markedly lengthen out the average duration of human life." There is no disgrace in acknowledging our shortcomings. It must not be supposed from this statement that we advocate quack practice. A true physician founds his practice on scientific pathology, of which the vaids and hakims are entirely ignorant. It must be apparent from the fearful destruction of life caused by the quacks who overflow all India that we need a body of well educated general practitioners, and not a lower grade of professional men, to check their abominable practices. Notwithstanding the existing state of things there are a very few learned and experienced among the vaids who practise their profession honestly. A few of the learned sometimes cut for the stone, couch skilfully for the cataract, and occasionally by the empirical use of some indigenous drug cure cases which are beyond the skill of duly qualified European and native practitioners.

The establishment of the several medical colleges at the different Presidencies in India has produced the most beneficent results. There can be no doubt that young men turned out of the colleges every year have, on the whole, an accurate acquaintance with medicine in all its branches. Their success in passing competitive examinations in England, and in obtaining commissions in the Indian Medical Service, is a sufficient proof of the superior nature of medical education imparted to them in India. Some of those who have been taught in the Indian medical colleges, though hardly earning sufficient to exist upon, render important services to the sick poor for a trifling remuneration. It is agreed on all hands that they are real friends to the poor; honest, humane, kind-hearted, and conscientious in the performance of their disagreeable duties; attentive to the sick even at the risk to which their lives are often exposed in the practice of their profession, and having more cause to complain of their thankless patients than their patients have to complain of them. Their claims to our admiration will appear the greater when we reflect for a moment how intolerable it is to practise among a superstitious and half-civilized people. It is an undisputed fact that the number sent out is insufficient to yield assistance to many hundreds of thousands of sick people in the course of a year, and to cope against the strong influences of prejudice and superstition of two hundred millions of people under British rule. It would be ungenerous not to admit the energy and influence several of the *alumni* of the medical colleges have brought to bear by their successful practice upon the gradual diminution of quacks throughout the length and breadth of the land. We notice, however, with regret that the conduct of some of them towards their professional brethren has not been characterised by that propriety and dignity which men in their position should feel a pride in displaying. It is much to be regretted that many who have obtained diplomas in the medical colleges and schools of India seem to be satisfied with their present possessions, and would never try to improve upon them. It is no wonder that young men admitted with imperfect preliminary education should, after obtaining certificates to practise, become presumptuous and show disregard for improvements. India is a wide field for investigation, and is fertile of drugs, but it is to be regretted there are no scientific labourers. When medical colleges were founded in India, the hopes entertained that young men, after obtaining their qualifications in this noble profession, would, by their incessant efforts, break the bonds of superstition and ignorance, and enlighten the people, have to our knowledge proved ineffectual. Blinded by the love of gold, some of these self-styled reformers, by not aiding their brethren in combating error and prejudice, have rather augmented the evil they were expected to mitigate. In other words, the remedy has proved worse than the disease. The disgraceful practice of visiting rich and influential persons when ill without being called, and of course without obtaining any remuneration except an occasional invitation to their table, is surely doing our profession a great deal of harm. We have known instances in which the rich and influential were treated *gratis*, while the poor were compelled to pay money. Had the unfortunate practitioners protected the poor sick people by demanding high fees from their wealthy patients, we should never have said a word against them in these pages. Again, almost all obtain their livelihood by compounding and charging for their own drugs with gratuitous medical advice. They place one or more large boards at their doors, on which are written their names, degrees, professional titles, and the names of diseases they profess to treat. They also make themselves known by advertising their skill, degrees and qualifications in the local papers. Surely something should be done to put a stop to such undignified courses. The root of all the evil is a want of healthy training before admission into colleges.

Of vulgar doctors in general we shall have to consider in the last chapter.

We trust not to be misunderstood. The above remarks are intended for the "scattered few." We write thus with a feeling of regret, and in no spirit of jealousy or malice, but with the most friendly sentiments. We have now only to desire that their example may not be followed by others. We write thus because we are fallen in the estimation of our countrymen, we are no longer respected, our profession is no longer appreciated, we are considered the employés of our patients, to attend at any hour of the day or night, or to compound and charge for our own medicines at our place of residence, including gratuitous medical advice, often for the handsome sum of four annas (6*d*.) ! A single case, incautiously pronounced by a qualified man as incurable, if cured under a quack, is noised abroad as if he had relieved the world of a pestilence, while our success in every-day practice is blindly slighted by unreasonable persons. A few wealthy young gentlemen of the Parsee community consider it below their dignity to consult us, while they allow their hysterical wives to consult quacks, Brahmins and Syads, for barrenness and imaginary complaints. Impudent and taunting remarks are not uncommon. The sneering nickname of *inferior doctors,* bestowed by our obliging patients even to the aged and experienced among us, in distinction to *superior doctors,* is a blot on our professional attainments. We have over-indulged our "peculiar patients," and we must suffer the consequences. "Let us not impute these evils," as Pliny says, " to the art, but to the men who practise it." A spirit of jealousy, low fees, submission and appeal to authority, routine practice, the frequent and indiscreet nod of the head, and the use of the words "Yes, sir," have seriously impaired our reputation. Want of union has brought our profession into disrepute. It is only necessary for the Graduates of Medicine in India to be united, in order to impress upon the minds of the stingy and ungrateful patients that we give more than we receive from them, that we are obliging them, and not they us; that we do not go to them without being called; that notwithstanding the strong fellow-feeling we possess we will never respect or give medical advice to those who will not respect or appreciate our profession; that the few who prefer to live or die under the care of "superior doctors" should be distinctly given to understand that we as well as they have spent the best years of our lives for one common cause, the cause of suffering humanity, and therefore both should command equal respect; that we have learnt to respect our worthy preceptors, seniors, superiors or consulting physicians, and our duty towards the sick, and therefore all interference and meddling on the part of the over-officious relations and friends of the latter are unnecessary and injurious. Thus only will our "peculiar patients" be brought to their right senses, and will prevent them from as frequently changing their doctors as they change their clothes. The habit of frequently changing doctors, so common in native society, should be discouraged by every conscientious practitioner. The effect of such a practice on the patient cannot be otherwise than mischievous. A Parsee child, aged 3, came under our observation in the stage of initiatory or eruptive fever of small-pox. Within a period of twelve hours no fewer than six medical practitioners were called in, who, without meeting each other in consultation, prescribed for the little patient. The grandmother distrusted the correct diagnosis of five, and adhered to the opinion of the sixth, by whom the case was diagnosed as one of worms, and treated accordingly. It merits notice that the fond grandmother, who, according to her own statement, had nearly suffocated the little creature by repeated dosing, abandoned the idea of worms on the first appearance of the characteristic eruption, and, getting alarmed, poured out the mixtures on the floor and the powders out of the window for fear of further offending the Shitulladevi (goddess of small-pox), showed repentance by putting out her tongue, and promised many offerings to conciliate her favour. Our credulous native patients, who are unable to distinguish between the true and the false, are often guided, while under our treatment, by their common clerks, nurses, ayahs, &c., who, for the sake of obtaining favour and promotion, boldly suggest a remedy, recommend a patent medicine, or a miserable quack. Such patients should never be countenanced, and their vulgar and meddling servants should always be condemned as usurpers.

A patient will come to you, and hold out his arm to have his pulse felt, and to test your skill will venture to question you regarding the nature of his malady, or the contents of the food swallowed by him.

Another will come and ask you whether he suffers from a *cold* or *hot* disease.

A third :—" I have been a sufferer for some years with elephantiasis. Is it from wind (vayu), bile (pitta), or phlegm (kofa) ?"

A fourth :—" I have been suffering for some years back from epileptic fits, so put into my nostrils some medicine having the quality of killing the worm in my brain. Is it a fact that epilepsy is also caused by the entrance of evil spirit ?"

Useless questions, not worth consideration. A consumptive patient will come and eagerly ask for an emetic " to clear away his phlegm," and a dropsical patient for a blister " to draw off the poisonous fluid from the intestines through the skin !"

You will meet with patients who will venture to advise you to give *hot remedy* in *cold disease,* and *cold remedy* in *hot disease*, or to open a vein " to draw off bad blood."

You will sometimes see men, suffering from extensive valvular disease of the heart, apply to you for an emetic in order " to throw up the accumulated bile in the chest."

Again, you will be urged by a patient to give a worm powder, when upon examination you will detect an enormously enlarged spleen.

This happens every day in the hospital, dispensary, or in private practice.

In such cases what should we do?

Do not take upon yourselves the responsibility of treating such vulgar patients according to their absurd pathology, but follow the dictates of your own conscience if you wish to be a successful practitioner. Look at nothing but the disease, and give an appropriate remedy according to your judgment and conscience.

We now come to the question of consultation. One says:—"All that a man hath will he give for his life." Another says:—"I am sure that I would not trust one paw of my great Newfoundland dog to a consultation of thirty or of three hundred of them." Both are right. There is nothing more humane than to save the life of a human being by the sacrifice of time, trouble, or money; on the other hand, there is nothing more cruel than to jeopardize a man's life by too much meddling, over-drugging, and over-feeding, which is generally the case when a multitude of physicians are called in, some of whom, notwithstanding their kind solicitude for the sick and dying, consent, against their own conscience, to the employment of a variety of remedies of doubtful efficacy for fear of offending the others, whose motives, it must be confessed, are praiseworthy, but whose presumption and self-conceit sometimes leads them in the wrong direction. The habit of frequently consulting a surgeon, so common with native graduates, to satisfy a patient suffering from slight or imaginary complaint, is derogatory to his professional reputation.

Listen to the words of a learned French doctor:—

"Every one in these days knows what value to put upon the custom of calling in several doctors in a dangerous case. These pretended consultations soothe the anxiety and flatter the vanity of the relatives, generally hasten the patient's preparation for his long journey, and send a little more grist to the mill of the medical gentlemen. These consultations have been such fruitful subjects for the satirists, that one may venture to speak very freely of them. One old writer said with truth—'He who has but one doctor, has *one*; he who has two, has but the *half* of one; but he who has three, has *none* at all.' It is much the same as when Napoleon I. said :—'I prefer one bad general to two good ones.' One might well say here: *tot capita, tot sensus*; which when freely translated is—so many doctors, so many opinions."

There has been of late a remarkable increase of students in the Indian medical colleges, not because there is an immense field for practice, as some imagine. The native youths enter them in the hope of a Government appointment, or of obtaining commissions in the Indian Medical Service after passing their examinations. We would venture to say that out of a few men turned out every year, there is hardly one who will not express a wish to accept Government service. The Indian youths learn not for the sake of learning; all have chosen the profession, not for the love of it. In the words of the *Bombay Gazette*, the Indian youths "flounder through a university course in the hope of being landed finally in some 'blissful Aiden' of a Government appointment, where they may scratch their heads and expectorate betel-nut during the remainder of their unnatural and useless lives." We do not agree with the latter remarks.

Those concerned in the cause of medical education in India are mistaken, we apprehend, in believing that the people of India are sensible of the benefits of English medicine. From what we know of the native character, we can confidently say that they are not rightly appreciated even by the upper classes of Hindoos and Mahomedans. We entirely agree with Dr. Smith, a member of the Bengal Medical Board, when he remarks:—"The rich and higher classes, unless when enlightened by European education and habits, invariably prefer the prescriptions of their own hukeems and byds to those of our physicians. The indigent, at least equally prejudiced and ignorant, would manifest the same predilections if they had the means of indulging them; in other words, if they could pay their own practitioners; but when under the pressure of pain, it is from necessity, and not choice, that they overcome their antipathies, and accept offers of gratuitous treatment and attendance from Europeans." A Hindoo gentleman of rank and wealth lamented when we called at his bungalow that, as he had been a member of the . . . . he had reluctantly put himself under the care of a European doctor to please the European members, who, he said, ridiculed him when he consulted a vaid. We were rather surprised to hear that he was sneered at even when he was under the treatment of an experienced native graduate. This statement shows that we are envied by men who, with an affectation of piety, make a boast, and deceive the world that they exert themselves on behalf of education.

The high-coloured reports of the heads of the medical colleges, and the noisy speeches of the Presidents, to the effect that the people of India resort to the benefits of European medicine, and that practice might be obtained throughout the whole of India by the Licentiates who always "hang about the large capitals of the different provinces," are, we believe, exaggerated. We affirm that in private practice even in large cities their prospects are not cheering. We must, however, admit that the benefits of English medicine are appreciated in Bombay by the Parsees, Khojas, and a certain number of the upper classes of educated and wealthy Hindoos and Mahomedans. Bombay contains, according to the last census, about 600,000 inhabitants. There are 46 native graduates of medicine in actual practice, excluding assistant surgeons and others employed in public dispensaries. Out of these, 34 practise chiefly among the Parsee residents in the Fort, Market, Khetwady and Dhobhee Talao Divisions, a very large number when we think for a moment that the Parsees form but about one-fifteenth of the total population of the island. The Khojas, an intelligent and enterprising sect of the Sheah Mahomedans, who number about 6,000 souls, have two practitioners among them. The remaining ten practise among the Hindoos and Mahomedans, who form four-fifths of the total population of the first and wealthiest city in the Presidency. Out of this small number some are fighting for their very maintenance. Medical practice in other cities is a very undignified and unprofitable affair.

There is in the United States of America one qualified doctor to every 600 inhabitants, in Austria and

Hungary one to 2,500, in Italy one to 3,500, in France one to 1,814, and in Great Britain one to 1,672. Northumberland, an English borough, for instance, with a population not exceeding 45,000, contains twenty-five duly qualified men in active practice. If we compute on an average only fifty practitioners to 100,000 souls, there should be in the whole of India, with its population of two hundred millions, 100,000 legally qualified practitioners, instead of a few hundred. Contrast this extraordinarily insignificant number with that of the United States, which, with a population of 45,000,000 (less than one-fourth that of India) contains 60,000 doctors. If the profession were really appreciated as in the United States, there would be in India more than 250,000 duly qualified medical men. The following will give an idea of the enormous number of doctors in the United States :—

"The number of medical schools in this country has increased out of all proportion to the extent of the population. Usually in the statistics of other countries—as France, England, Russia, Brazil, &c. —it has been found that one medical school for every 2,000,000 to 4,000,000 of population was an ample ratio, and it seems a matter of surprise that the United States should afford so notable an exception. Yet facts show that in a total population of 45,000,000, there are at least sixty-five regular schools of medicine, in addition to eleven of the homœopathic faith, four eclectic schools, fourteen colleges of pharmacy, and twelve dental colleges. As the druggists are frequently practitioners of medicine, it is safe to estimate that in this country there is one medical school for, at the most, every 500,000 inhabitants. The result is an enormous over-production of medical men, which has not been diminished, but rather increased by the depression of industrial interests driving new candidates for future medical honours from commerce to the profession. Probably 3,000 new graduates entered the ranks in 1875 alone. Dr. Pepper estimates that one thoroughly qualified man can minister efficiently to, and in turn be fairly supported by, a population of from 1,500 to 2,500 persons, but he states that the most reliable data show there are not less than 60,000 physicians in the United States, or one medical man to every 750 inhabitants. In some States the proportion rises as high as one to 400, and this too without making any allowance for the almost universal custom in America for druggists to prescribe over the counter, and thus to conduct a medical practice often of very considerable extent."*

At the time we were writing on this subject we received a hand-bill, signed by a Licentiate of Medicine and Surgery of the Grant Medical College, who, to get practice in a city like Bombay, expresses his readiness to give advice—medicine included—for two annas (3*d.*)! Thus our learned profession has been degraded even below that of the druggist, who for a single prescription charges from eight to twelve annas without advice. We write thus in no spirit of disparagement to the medical profession in India, but as a matter of fact. The statement of some who boast that people willingly resort to European and Indian graduates should be received with caution. We cannot refrain from quoting the following opinion in support of our statement. The editor of the *Medical Times and Gazette*, in reviewing a little book, observes:—"Candidates, he (the author) says, are misled as to the value of the Indian service; they go out to India expecting that, as soon as they pass the lower standard examination in Hindustani, they will receive never less than 450 Rupees per month, and that, in addition to this, there is no end of lucrative practice to be had among natives . . . . . Surgeons who have held charge of second-class civil

---

* Vide *Medical Times and Gazette* of February 23, 1878.

stations in India for eight or ten years assert that, in the whole course of that time, they have not received 1,000 Rupees in fees from natives."*

Edward Balfour, Surgeon General, Madras Medical Department, says:—" The people of India have no medical colleges of their own, and believe firmly in the views of their school; in the South of India they keep aloof from the science of Europe and from its practitioners, whose medical knowledge and skill they distrust, though fully acknowledging their great abilities as surgeons and accoucheurs."†

A cook or horse-keeper who earns 10 rupees (20s.) a month occasionally pays 2 Rupees for a visit to his medical adviser, and a Hindoo knight is content also to offer the same fee! We received lately from one of the wealthiest Hindoos, Sir . . . . . . a beggarly remuneration of two rupees (4s.) for a visit which detained us nearly an hour. The rich but stingy Hindoos value our professional worth at this rate! The fees paid by them are simply disgraceful.

When we reflect what numerous causes keep a young man fresh from an Indian medical college from the independent practice of his profession in his own country, what trouble, regret, disappointment and failure he experiences when he has already started in practice; what amount of labour is brought to bear against persons blinded by false and old prejudices; when we think of all this, we confidently say that the circumstances in which he is placed are exceedingly

---

* *Medical Times and Gazette*, March 23, 1878.
† *The Vydian and the Hakim, what do they know of Medicine?*

discouraging. The field is extensive, but it has not sufficient strength to support the crop.

In such a case what should he do? The best thing he can do is to quit the field where his exertions to reap a good harvest will meet only with failure, and to avail himself of the advantages of the Indian Medical Service open to him by the benevolence of our paternal Government. It is his misfortune if he does not. Listen to the present accomplished and worthy Principal of the Grant College, Dr. Cook:—" The Indian Medical Service has always stood high in public estimation. The advantages which it offers to the natives of this country in pay, position, and prospects, are unrivalled by any medical service in the world. They are, it seems to me, advantages without drawbacks. Working in their own country and climate, in the midst of their own relatives, and with none indeed of the contingent deprivations which attend the European members of the Service, they hold a most enviable position. It is not surprising, therefore, that the Service should offer attractions which, in all probability, will be promptly responded to, and that a large number of those educated here will eventually enter it."

The test required for the second licentiate examination in India is more rigid and severe than that of any London medical school. In a letter by Mr. William Gilbert that appeared in the pages of the *Fortnightly Review* for January 1879, that gentleman says:—" Having purposely dwelt somewhat minutely on the education of the native students of the medical school and college at Calcutta, with the intent of proving to the reader that the examinations are at least as severe as those of London, it may naturally be supposed that the number of candidates rejected would at least be equal to those of our metropolitan medical schools. Such, however, is very far from being the case, for, unflatteringly as it may appear to our national pride, the candidates rejected are, proportionate numbers taken into consideration, less than one-third of those of the London medical schools."

It is our unpleasant duty to notice the unworthy conduct of a few members of the profession, who, having no prospects in their own country, select the Indian Medical Department for their field of work. Imperfectly trained before entering upon their professional education, and forgetful of the dignity of their profession, they disregard the usual ethical proprieties of practice. Medical etiquette is little known in India, and the practice of reviling professional brethren is common. It is our opinion that to obtain better men (who are happily numerous) the Indian Medical Service should be remodelled. It is highly necessary to separate the military from the civil medical service. A certificate of moral character should be produced by every candidate of good birth and family, signed by at least three persons of standing in society, and the minimum age of admission should be twenty-six. The young man who is intended for the medical profession ought to receive a sound and liberal education. To prevent the admission of an inferior class of men into India, the standard of general education and sound mental and moral training should be raised. We need in India men of high general culture like Drs. McLennan, Don, Morehead, Peet, Ballingall, Arbuckle, Campbell, Carter, Cook, Hojell, Blanc, Weir, &c. of the Bombay Presidency, ornaments of their profession, whose high accomplishments and modesty have gained them the warm regard and respect of Europeans and natives who know them. In the Bengal and Madras Presidencies names are to be found equally eminent and honourable. It is needless to say that a majority of those who have entered the popular Indian Medical Service indisputably are, as a rule, well educated, active, intelligent, kind-hearted and polite gentlemen.

It is much to be regretted that a few, out of one or two scores of natives who have already entered the Indian Medical Service, or have gone to England to obtain an English qualification, have disappointed their parents and friends by their irregular and undignified conduct. As soon as they pass the necessary examinations they think too highly of their own competence or sufficiency, and rest satisfied with their present acquisition of knowledge. According to Dr. Macnamara, "utterly heedless of family or any other ties, they entirely ignore even the existence of God, and live absolutely for self." Shallow minds like these should in future be subjected to a more severe course of mental training than is at present afforded them, so that parents might not hesitate, as they do now, to send their children to England to give them the benefits of higher education. It is, however, desirable to state that, considering their small number, there are to be found among them young men who are honourable, and fully equal to the most eminent surgeons in India.

Since writing the above, we notice the prevalence of a report that the subject of amalgamating the British with the Indian Medical Service has been under consideration. Considerable dissatisfaction has arisen owing to rumours of this kind, which are disquieting to native candidates, who always stick to their own country No sane man would for a moment dream of asking for the abrogation of a warrant that does not exclude Indian youths from entering the Service. When preference is given without distinction of caste or creed only to the most deserving, the amalgamation system is no bar, and we fail to see why it should be the chief drawback to entrance in the Service.

CHAPTER VI.

Rise of the Buddhist Religion in India—Founder of Buddhism—Chandragupta—Asoka—Foundation of Hospitals—Inscriptions on the Rocks at Girnar and at Dhauli—Buddhadaso.—His charitable acts—His extraordinary cures—Persecution and decline of the Buddhist religion in India—China—Its antiquity and civilization—Arts and sciences stationary—Barriers to improvements in practice—Medical sects—Treatment of the sick while under the influence of demons—Materia Medica—Complicated Prescriptions—*Yang* and *Yin*—Scheme of Physic—Contemptible treatment—The Pulse—Anatomy—Midwifery—Surgery—Moxa—Acupuncture—The Jews—Their knowledge of Medicine—Their superstitious practices—Leprosy—Surgery—Cæsarian section.

The superstitious practices and arrogant pretensions of the Brahmins gave rise in the sixth century B. C. to the rival Buddhist religion in India, which for centuries had an extensive influence. The new religion founded and promulgated by Buddha, Sakya, or Gotama is Buddhism. To him is attributed the authorship of their sacred scriptures. The Buddhists despised the Hindoo priests, and rejected their sacred Vedas. They declared that the real Vedas were altered and corrupted by the Brahmins, and were not to be relied on as divine. The Buddhist priests did not pretend like the Brahmins that they received their instructions directly from the deity, but professed that the saintly Sakya or Buddha was their only instructor. The ancient Buddhists professed the belief of one Supreme Being named Buddha, or, properly speaking, Adi-Buddha, whom they revered as the immediate creator of all things, the self-created, eternal, self-existent, the creator of the world, and of all the Buddhas. "Adi-Buddha," they say, "was never seen. He is merely light." The ideas of the ancient Buddhists as to Adi-Buddha and other Buddhas may be learned from the following extract:—

"Buddha means in Sanscrit the wise, also, that which is known by wisdom, and it is one of the names which we give to God, whom we also call Adi-Buddha, because he was before all, and is not created but is the creator, and the *Pancha-Buddha* were created by him and are in the heavens. Sakya and the rest of the seven human Buddhas are earth-born or human. These latter by worship of Buddha arrived at the highest eminence, and attained *Nirvana Pad* (*i. e.* were absorbed into Adi-Buddha.)"*

According to the Buddhist scriptures seven persons gifted with divine wisdom instructed mankind in the *Buddha marga*, and became *manushi* or mortal Buddhas. Three were born in the *satya-yuga*, two in the *treta-yuga*, one in the *dwarpa-yuga*, and one in present *kali-yuga*. The seventh and last Buddha, also named Sakya, who founded and propagated the religion of Buddha, was the first of the present sinful age (*kali-yuga*). Little or nothing is known of Sakya's six predecessors. The Buddhist writings are silent as to their doings.

Sakya was born either at *Gunga Saugor* or in Oudh in the sixth century before the Christian era. His father was a sovereign of *Magadha* or Behar. At the age of twenty he separated himself from the

---

* Hodgson's *Literature and Religion of the Buddhists*, p. 67.

world, and retired to a solitary place to practise penances, mortifications, &c. For these meditations he received inspiration from the Divine Spirit, and became a Buddha. He first taught his doctrines to ten faithful disciples, and then travelled over different parts of India to preach his doctrine, and died in Assam at an advanced age. The Buddhist faith rapidly spread over India, and from thence extended to the neighbouring countries. The charitable and benevolent spirit of the new religion was very favourable to its progress, and contributed to explode the influence of Brahminical worship. The Buddhist doctrine was accepted by some of the rulers of India, among whom was the celebrated Vikramaditya, and the Buddhist missionaries propagated their faith in distant countries, as China, Japan, Burma, Thibet, Siam and Ceylon, where it still prevails, although not in its primitive pure state.

Chandragupta or Sandracottus, the celebrated Buddhist monarch, was contemporary with Alexander and Seleucus Nicator. The latter became an ally of the Indian king, and gave him his daughter in marriage. He also sent Megasthenes as an ambassador to Palibothra or Pataliputra, a city on the Ganges, and the capital of Chandragupta, from whom Arrian and Strabo derived their information about India." Chandragupta was of mean and obscure origin. He was the son of Nanda or Mahapadma Nanda by his second wife of *Sudra* extraction. According to other writers, Nanda's queen fell in love with a handsome barber, and gave birth to Chandragupta. He was the ruler of *Prasii*, and

Gangaridæ or *Gandhari* nations in the neighbourhood of the Ganges. He was a powerful king, having an army of 20,000 horses, 200,000 foot, 2,000 chariots, and 4,000 elephants.

He was succeeded by his son Bindusaro, who had, by his sixteen wives, one hundred and one sons. Among all the brothers, Asoka, otherwise called Pryadasi, " the beloved of the gods," was most distinguished for his piety, wisdom and acts of charity. This great and renowned Buddhist monarch of India flourished about the third century B. C. Devoted to his people, religion, and acts of charity, this benefactor of mankind caused to be erected numerous charitable institutions. He provided asylums for the blind, crippled, and destitute, and hospitals for the sick. It was in the city of Patna, probably, that the first hospital was built by this pious monarch. Once Asoka, hearing of the death of one Tisso, inquired of what disease he died. " Having heard of the particulars of the afflictions created in him, he caused to be constructed at each of the four gates of the city a reservoir made of white chunam, and filled it with medicinal beverage, saying—' Let there not be a scarcity of medicines to be provided daily for the priesthood.' "*

Inscriptions on the rocks at Girnar near Junaghur, and at Dhauli in Katak, are the living monuments showing the benevolence of Asoka's paternal government. The following is Prinsep's translation of the medical edicts promulgated by

---

* Turnour's *Translation of the Mahawanso*, vol. I., p. 38.

Asoka, and preserved on the rocks of Girnar and Dhauli :—

"Everywhere within the conquered provinces of Raja Pryadasi the beloved of the gods, as well as in the parts occupied by the faithful such as Chola, Pida, Satiyaputra, and Ketalaputra, even as far as Tambapanni (Ceylon)—and moreover, within the dominions of Antiochus the Greek (of which Antiochus' generals are the rulers)—everywhere the heaven-beloved Pryadasi's double system of medical aid is established, both medical aid for men and medical aid for animals: together with medicaments of all sorts, which are suitable for men and suitable for animals. And wherever there is not (such provision), in all such places they are to be prepared, and to be planted; both root-drugs and herbs, wheresoever there is not (a provision of them), in all such places shall they be planted."*

In this proclamation of a Buddhist sovereign there is an allusion to the Greek king Antiochus, *Antiyako Yona raja*. From this it seems likely that Antiochus was a contemporary of Asoka, and had formed alliance with him.

Buddhadaso was another Buddhist monarch, who was celebrated for his munificent acts of charity. "He was a mine of virtues and an ocean of riches." Among other charitable institutions, hospitals for the sick were erected by his commands, where physicians skilled in medicine received appointments. "Out of benevolence entertained towards the inhabitants of the island (Ceylon), the sovereign provided hospitals, and appointed medical practitioners thereto, for all villages. The raja, having composed the work 'Saratthasangaho,'† containing the whole medical

---

* Prinsep's *Indian Antiquities*, vol. II., pp. 14, 15.

† This work, which is composed in the Sanscrit language, is still extant. Native medical practitioners profess to consult it.

science, ordained that there should be a physician for every twice five (ten) villages. He set aside twenty royal villages for the maintenance of these physicians, and appointed medical practitioners to attend his elephants, his horses, and his army. On the main road for the reception of the crippled, deformed and destitute, he built asylums in various places, and provided with the means of subsisting (those objects)."*

He himself was perfectly skilled in the art of medicine. On a certain occasion the benevolent monarch, seeing a cobra de capello (*mahanaga*) stretched out on a hill, found out the nature of his malady, and cured him by performing a surgical operation. The snake recovered, and presented him a "superlatively valuable gem." A certain priest suffering from pains in his belly resorted to the raja for medical advice. The monarch enquired of him what food he had taken. The priest replied—"Rice, mixed with milk." Being convinced that the cause of his illness was worms in the milk, he bled a horse whose illness required a vein to be opened, and gave the blood to the priest as medicine, which he swallowed. After a while the raja informed him that what he had swallowed was horse's blood. The priest immediately threw it up, and with it some worms, and was soon free from his complaint. The raja then exclaimed—"By one puncture of my own surgical instrument both the priest afflicted with worms and the horse have been cured; surely this medical

---

* Turnour's *Mahawanso*, vol. I., p 245.

science is a wonderful one!" Other extraordinary cures performed by the benevolent monarch are described in the Mahawanso.

His eldest son Upatisso founded hospitals for pregnant women, for the blind and the diseased; and constructed alms-houses for the destitute and asylums for the crippled.

The monarch Dhátuséno built hospitals, and provided physicians for the sick and crippled.

The vast empire of the Buddhist began to decline with the death of Asoka. "In the third century the birthplace of Sakya was a wilderness." In the sixth century the Buddhists were cruelly persecuted, their places of worship defiled and destroyed, and they themselves were dispersed aud driven out of India by the adherents of Brahma, who were chiefly instigated by Cumavilla Bhatta. In the same century the last persecution was raised against the Buddhists under the King Sudhanvan, who issued a proclamation "to put to death the old men and children of the Buddhas from the bridge of Rama to the snowy mountain: let he who slays not be slain." Although the bigoted worshippers of Brahma succeeded in destroying the worship of Buddha in India, they failed in their attempts to totally destroy the Buddha scriptures. The persecuted Buddhists left their homes, and took refuge in neighbouring countries, where they received every protection, and taught to the uncivilized inhabitants the docrines of Buddha. Medical works written in the original Sanscrit, but afterwards translated into other languages with some modifications, were attributed by the followers of Buddha to their saintly Sakya, and not to the Hindoo Dhanwantari.

Let us now cast a rapid glance over the Chinese system of medicine.

The vast empire of China is said to have existed for four thousand years. Its inhabitants were among the earliest civilized nations of antiquity. In some arts the Chinese had excelled their contemporary nations. They invented the compass and the art of printing, and manufactured glass and gunpowder at a very early period. The study of astronomy seems to have been attended to in the remotest ages.

The Chinese always follow in the footsteps of their ancestors, and cling to their manners, customs, laws, literature, &c. "The student of the present day is poring over not the same letters merely, but the same books, the same maxims and laws, the same precepts and history in the very same expressions which the scholar of 2000 years ago studied. Here phrases of ceremony and maxims of life are stereotyped, government is stereotyped, and thought itself is *stereotyped,* and passes down from age to age unchanged. An original thought in their antiquated literature would be like a foreigner on their forbidden soil—a suspected object, and interdicted by law." Their boasted antiquity, their contempt for foreigners, and for their arts and sciences, and their national vanity, are great obstacles to improvement. In fact, they have neither retrograded nor advanced, but have remained stationary for upwards of two thousand years.

Confucius, or, properly speaking, Koong-foo-tse,

the chief of the Chinese philosophers, was the founder of the Chinese religion and philosophy. He was a contemporary of Pythagoras, and was born about the year 550 B.C. His numerous works are highly revered by the Chinese. The religion founded and promulgated by him is accepted as the state religion. The doctrine of Buddha, called by the Chinese *Fo*, and that of *Taou*, has also many followers.

Like all the other sciences and arts among the Chinese, the healing art has, without any alteration, remained stationary for several centuries. Its cultivation seems to have been very little attended to, and the profession itself is not held in high estimation by the Chinese. We are not indebted to them for a single good invention or improvement in the science and art of medicine. There are no medical schools in this extensive empire, with the exception of one at Pekin for the instruction of youths. The number of practitioners is large, yet we scarcely hear of a single individual of eminence or skill in his profession. They are said to have written volumes which contain nothing interesting but much that is worthless, obscure, and unintelligible. After having received instructions from those already in practice, or after having obtained a superficial knowledge from books, they assume for themselves the title of doctor, and practise the healing art without undergoing any examination.

In drawing up prescriptions every physician is obliged to adhere and follow the prescribed forms. If, however, he departs from them by neglect, or prescribes conscientiously according to his own judgment, and the patient dies, he is liable to punishment. Such an unjust law is a strong barrier to improvement in practice. There are distinct physicians for different diseases. Some diseases are treated by barber-surgeons, others by the priests of *Fo* and *Taou*, who pretend to cure supernatural diseases. All are allowed to practise unless they do not deviate from the prescribed rules.

In China, as in Greece and Rome, the medical profession was divided into sects that went by the name of their founders Chang-chung-king, Lew-show-chin, Le-tung, and Choo-tan-ke. The first declared that medicines should be always given in large doses; the second chiefly employed bitters and refrigerants; the third, like the followers of the Todd school, principally used stimulants and tonics; and the fourth, like some of the old-fashioned doctors of the present day, was never sparing in the use of purgatives, bleeding-lancet, red-hot iron, blisters, &c.

The Chinese, like the Hindoos and Mahomedans, attribute several diseases to the entrance of evil spirits into the body of the sufferer, for the cure of which the priests of *Fo* and *Taou* are chiefly consulted. " Persons under the influence of demons, and exhausted with excessive pain, should have their noses twisted, their face spat upon, their feet bitten, and their elbows burnt to awaken them from their state of stupor."

According to the Chinese mythology the Emperor Ching-nong was the first to discover the virtues of medicinal herbs, B.C. 3216. Houangty was another person who cultivated medicine B.C. 2637. The celebrated Shinnung, who was most skilled in medicine, is considered by the Chinese as their prince of physicians. But Chang-ke was probably the first who cultivated and improved the art in a systematic way, A.D. 229. Hwa-to was their most skilful surgeon. He is said to have " removed the eye-ball of a young prince, and having cut away the diseased part, replaced it."* On account of this and other wonderful cures he was deified after death. Chin-kwei was another famous surgeon and skilful operator. He is said to have been acquainted with the operation of gastrotomy. He practised it to remove diseased parts from the abdomen.

The Proceedings of the Asiatic Society, part VII., contains a notice of the celebrated work on Chinese medicine in forty volumes, entitled Chin-che-chun-ching, meaning " an approved marking line of medical practice." Of this seven volumes treat of nosology, *Tsu-ching*; eight of pharmacology, *Luy-fang*; five of pathology, *Shang-han*; six of surgery, *Waeka*; and the remaining volumes are devoted to the diseases of women and children. This is their principal work of reference in difficult cases.

The materia medica of the Chinese is said to be very copious. Medicinal drugs are divided into heating, cooling, temperate, and refreshing. For hot diseases cold remedies are recommended, and for cold diseases hot remedies. The most extensive work of their materia medica is called *Pentsao-cang-mou*, consisting of fifty-two volumes. Its distinguished author was Lishechen. The work contains not only the

---

* *China opened*, vol. II., p. 173.

names of almost every shrub, root, leaf, flower, fruit, and creeper, but also those of minerals, stones, insects, reptiles, fishes, the different parts and secretions and excretions of quadrupeds and birds, and many other disgusting things. The therapeutic virtues of no fewer than sixty-eight different kinds of fish are given. The properties and uses of every drug are also described, and their dose given. The work also contains 2935 different recipes. Of all the drugs ginseng root is considered by the Chinese as the universal remedy, " the wonder of the world, and dose of immortality." It is one of the ingredients in almost all their prescriptions. Many virtues are ascribed to it, but it is much used as a tonic and aphrodisiac. It is sold in China at an exorbitant price. Bathing, shampooing and rubbing the diseased part with embrocations and ointments are frequently resorted to by the Chinese. The sick and invalid also take advantage of mineral waters, which are numerous in their country.

The prescriptions of the Chinese are very complicated, each containing from twenty to forty or a hundred ingredients. They do this on the supposition that one or more of the multifarious ingredients may act and produce a favourable effect. The Chinese practitioners divide their prescriptions into the great prescription, the little prescription, the slow prescription, the prompt prescription, the odd prescription, the even prescription, and the double prescription. One of these he applies according to his fancy to the cure of a particular disorder.

They imagine that the upper part of the body belongs to *yang*, and the lower to *yin*, therefore the tops and upper parts of the plants operate best on diseases of the upper half and the roots on those of the lower half of the body. The bark is suited to diseases of the skin and flesh, and the pith of the tree to those of the viscera.

Mr. Davis, in his History of China, gives the following as "the scheme of Chinese physic on which is based all their medical as well as other theories":—

Five Planets.	Five Viscera.	Five Elements.	Five Colours.	Five Tastes.
Saturn	Stomach.	Earth	Yellow	Sweet.
Jupiter	Liver	Wood	Green	Sour.
Mars	Heart	Fire	Red	Bitter.
Venus	Lungs	Metal	White	Pungent.
Mercury	Kidneys	Water	Black	Salt.

According to the fanciful speculations of the Chinese, *sweet* and *yellow* medicines belong to earth, and act on the stomach; *sour* and *green* belong to the element wood, and they affect the liver, &c.

As a specimen of Chinese remedies nothing can be more absurd and contemptible than the following:—" In case of nightmare do not at once bring a light, or, going near, call out loudly to the sleeper, but bite his heel or his big toe, and gently utter his name; also spit in his face, and give him some ginger-tea to drink. He will then come round; or blow into the patient's ears through small tubes, pull out fourteen hairs from his head, make them into a twist, and thrust them into his nose."

The Chinese surgeon makes a minute and careful examination of the pulse in order to enable him to judge of the nature of a disease. In some cases he examines the pulse for hours before writing a prescription. A whole volume is sometimes devoted to their mysterious doctrine of pulse.

Of the internal structure of the human body the Chinese know nothing. They are totally ignorant of the position of the internal viscera, and do not even know the distinction between an artery and a vein. Reverence for the dead, religious prejudice, and dread of punishment prevent them from dissecting a human subject. As the Chinese preserve the bones of their ancestors, they avail themselves of the opportunity of acquiring a knowledge of the skeleton. Their knowledge of physiology is poor and meagre. Like the ancients they suppose that the arteries contain air and not blood.

Midwifery is practised by females in China. Male practitioners are seldom or never called in difficult delivery. When called, the practitioner, who is ignorant of midwifery operations, trusts to nature, and the administration of medicines internally. Thus many females are allowed to die without operative assistance.

Their knowledge of surgery is extremely low. In many cases persons are left to die without surgical aid. Like cowards they shrink at the very sight of blood. Their ignorance and cowardice, fear of losing reputation, and prosecution for manslaughter if the patient die, deter them from performing the simplest surgical operation. The Chinese physician will never venture to bleed or to remove a carious tooth. Surgical diseases are generally treated by barber-surgeons.

The Chinese frequently make use of the actual cautery or *moxa* for the alleviation or removal of many painful affections. The Chinese moxa is the most downy fibre obtained from the stems of *Artemesia moxa* rolled into conical-shaped masses. The base is firmly applied to the seat of disease, and the apex set on fire, when the whole consumes rapidly. It causes some pain, which however does not last long. From China it was introduced into Europe. At present it is rarely employed on many parts of the Continent.

Acupuncture is also freely employed by the Chinese for the removal of local pain. Fine metallic needles are deeply introduced in the muscles near or through the seat of the disease, and left there for a few minutes, hours or days, according to the severity or duration of the disease. Should their insertion cause excruciating pain and irritation, they are immediately dislodged.

Inoculation for the small-pox was practised by the Chinese from an early period. Their method consisted in inserting in one of the nostrils cotton wool containing dried crusts of pustules, either reduced to powder or rubbed down with a little water. Since the introduction of vaccination in China by Dr. Alexander Pearson, this mode is abandoned by the Chinese.

We now come to Palestine, the land of prophets and miracles. The Jews were a people little advanced in general literature, sciences and fine arts. Although these alternately beloved and despised people of God had justly acquired for themselves the reputation of teachers of religion, yet we meet with the names of very few men of high literary or scientific attainments; in fact "they were men in religion, and children in everything else." Some authors assert that Moses and Solomon were perfect in all the sciences and arts, including medicine. They have even ventured to say that Hippocrates, the physician, and Pythagoras, Plato, and Aristotle, the philosophers, pilfered from the writings of Moses and Solomon. But these charges, in the absence of clear proofs, appear to be without foundation. Like most other nations of antiquity, the Hebrew priests or Levites (so named from having been chosen from the warlike tribe of Levi) were the physicians. All the learned professions were hereditary in that sacred tribe. Like the Egytian priests, they exercised many functions, and were the sole masters of literature and science. They acted as judges, lawyers, physicians, &c. They received a certain portion from the produce of the land, and also derived their income from the sacrifices of the Hebrews. Thus maintained, they gave medical advice gratis to the poor. The Jews first received their scanty knowledge of medicine and surgery from the Egyptians. At first their practice consisted of surgical manipulations, external applications, and aiding women at child-birth, but by degrees they became more acquainted with the science and art of medicine, though not to any great extent. The minor operations of venesection and circumcision were practised by them at a very early period. They also employed issues and setons, and splints for keeping a fractured limb in position. Confident that too much drugging was injurious, they trusted more to diet and hygienic means. Their strict sanitary laws obliged them to bestow greater attention to the preservation of health than the cure of disease. The priests pretended to cure the sick by prayers, enchantments, and supernatural means. Besides these, they had recourse to amulets, the superstitious practice of wearing which was borrowed from the Egyptians. As physicians the priests had to enforce sanitation. The Jews were a "people of lepers." On the first appearance of leprosy in a person he was taken before the priest for examination. If upon inspection he detected signs of leprosy, the poor sufferer was instantly put under his care and supervision in a secluded quarter, shunned and despised by the community, and "whenever he went forth into the abodes of men, he had to appear with his clothes rent, his head bared, and his chin covered, and to utter the doleful warning 'Unclean, Unclean!' If the plague left him, he was cleansed by various and significant purifications, and restored again to all his rights as a member of the chosen community."

Under the protection and patronage of the Ptolemies a considerable number of Jews, who had taken refuge in Alexandria and other parts of Egypt, were not inferior to other nations either in medicine or the sciences. Amputation of limbs, excision of tumours, and other difficult surgical operations were performed by them. Mention is made in the Talmud of artificial teeth—"a tooth that was put in," "a tooth covered with gold so as to stop and hide the decay." The operation in midwifery called the Cæsarian section, or hysterotomy, which consists in opening the parieties of the abdomen and womb to extract the child alive, was performed by the Jews. The following passage occurs in one of their most ancient books called the *Mishna*:—"In the case of twins, neither the first child, which shall be brought into the world by the cut into the abdomen, nor the second, can receive the rights of primogeniture either as regards the office of priest or succession to property." The success of the operation in saving the life of the child must have been great, for a law had been passed by Numa Pompillius, king of Rome, "forbidding the body of any female far advanced in pregnancy to be burnt until the operation had been performed." The following passage from the Nidda, an appendix to the Talmud of the Jews, shows that the operation was also performed on the living mother:—"It is not necessary for women to observe the days of purification after the removal of the child through the parieties of the abdomen." The use of narcotics in surgery was long known to the Jews, in proof of which we find in the Talmud the following passage—"They gave him to drink a potion which cast him into a profound sleep, so that they were enabled to perform the operation of gastrotomy."

CHAPTER VII.

Ancient Persia—Its power and extent—Its conquest by the Arabs—Persecution of Zoroastrians—Their Emigration to India—They regain their ancient prosperity—Their philanthropy and benevolence—Signs of degeneracy—The ancient Magi—Their learning and influence—Account of Thrita, the first Physician—Test of the capability of a person wishing to practise the healing art—Recompenses to be paid to successful physicians—Egyptian and Greek Physicians in the Persian Court—The Sassanian Kings—Their love of learning.

We now turn to Persia, once the great, magnificent and mighty empire; its throne once adorned by the illustrious Jamshed, Kaikhosroo, Shiavax, Gustasp, Ardashir, Baharam and Noshirvan; its enterprising monarchs, by their brilliant conquests and formidable power threw the whole world into confusion, and threatened powerful Greece and Rome; its brave kings Baharam and Sapor defeated and captured the Emperor or Khakan of China and the Roman Emperor Valerian; its extent reached "from Thrace, and Cyrenaïca on the West to the Indus on the East, and from the Euxine, the Caucasus (or rather a little below it), the Caspian and the Oxus and Jaxartes on the North to Æthiopia, Arabia, and the Erythræan Sea on the South, and it embraced, in Europe, Thrace and some of the Greek cities north of the Euxine; in Africa Egypt and Cyrenaïca; in Asia, on the west Palestine, Phœnicia, Syria, the several districts of Asia Minor,

Armenia, Mesopotamia, Assyria, Babylonia, Susiana, Atropatene, Great Media; on the north, Hyrcania, Margiana, Bactriana, and Sogdiana; on the east, Paropamisus, Arachosia and India (*i. e.*, part of the Punjab and Scinde); on the south, Persis, Carmania, and Gedrosia; and in the centre of the east part, Parthia, Aria, and Drangiana."*

" My father's kingdom," says the younger Cyrus to Zenophon, " is so large, that people perish with cold at one extremity, while they are suffocated with heat at the other."

Such was ancient Persia: and what do we see now? A petty kingdom in a state of weakness and degeneracy, sunk in ignominy and infamy, and its modern rulers the despicable slaves of Russia.

The last king of the Sassanian family of Persia, and of the Zoroastrian faith, was Yezdigard Sheryar, who was crowned A. D. 632. About this time Mahomedanism was making rapid progress, and the Arabs who were pushing their conquests on all sides lost no time in invading Persia, and after many severe struggles completely subdued its inhabitants. The battle of Nahavand decided the fate of Persia and the splendour of the religion of Zoroaster—the sun set in the dominions of the unfortunate Yezdigard Sheryar A. D. 651. Torrents of barbarians from the sunny deserts of Arabia poured down upon the rich provinces, ravaging and desolating the country, and spreading Mahomedanism by the sword. Cruel persecution continued. Zoroastrianism was not toler-

---

* Smith's *Classical Dictionary*.

ated; there was no other alternative but to accept the Koran or death by the swords of their fanatical conquerors. Thousands of Zoroastrians daily deserted the religion of their forefathers, and embraced Islamism. In fact, Persia was forced to receive the religion of Mahomed. The faith was promoted, but not without an inhuman waste of blood. But there were many thousand devoted followers of the Zoroastrian faith, who accepted neither the so-called religion of Allah, nor preferred death by the hands of their ferocious conquerors. Devoted to their religion, they abandoned their dear fatherland, and, after suffering many hardships, landed in India, and there became known as the Parsees. They settled down chiefly as cultivators of the soil, and maintained friendly relations with the natives of the country. They were a people simple in their habits and celebrated for loyalty towards their rulers and devotedness to their religion which requires them to be faithful— "All the wicked are corporeal Drujas who heed not the Faith. All those heed not the Faith who do not hear it. All those hear it not who are unclean. All those are unclean who are sinners." Ven. F. XVI. They also did not neglect Zoroaster's great axiom— *homuté, hukhté, vurusté,* which means purity in thought, word and deed. "I lay hold on all good thoughts, words, and works. I abandon all evil thoughts, words, and works." "All good thoughts, words and works lead to Paradise. All evil thoughts, words and works lead to hell." "I praise the thought which is good, I praise the word which is good, I praise the work which is good." This is the very foundation upon which the whole structure of their religion rests. It was by observing this true and guiding principle that their ancestors in India rose from obscurity to fame. After undergoing many vicissitudes they distinguished themselves above the Hindoos and Mahomedans by their industry and civilization. Even under Mahomedan and Hindoo rule they reached to great eminence and rose to honour, and under the protection of British power in India they recovered their ancient prosperity. By their commercial enterprises they soon acquired wealth and influence, which they applied to charitable purposes. To provide food and shelter for the indigent, to minister to the wants of the sick, and to soothe the pains of a dying man are deeds considered highly meritorious. The impulse of philanthropy to help the poor and distressed is remarkable. In fact, their prophet enjoins on them the duty of benevolence. " Keep ready feet, hands, and understanding, O Mazdayaçnians, Zarathustrians, for the performance of good works according to the law and the commandment; for the avoidance of unlawful, forbidden, wicked works. Accomplish here good deeds; afford help to the helpless." Vis. XVIII., VV. 1 to 5. " With purity and good-mindedness will I support your poor." Yas. XXXIV., V. 5. "Let the wicked riches be extinguished through their badness." Yas. XLVIII., V. 10. " And the kingdom (we give) to Ahura when we offer succour to the poor." K. A. II., p. I., V. 3. " Charity which feeds the poor, praise we." K. A. VIII. p. 26, V. 7.* If we compare a Parsee with a Hindoo or a Mahomedan equally

---

* Spiegel's *Avesta*, translated by Bleek.

wealthy, we shall find the one the prince of liberality and munificence, and the other the covetous miser who amasses a good deal, and uses but little. The crying wants of the poor of all castes and creeds have always met with a warm response from the former. The relief unostentatiously given to distressed Parsee families, chiefly by men in the upper ranks of life, is highly creditable to them. Sir Jamsetjee Jejeebhoy, the first Parsee Baronet, has rendered his name immortal by his princely munificence, amounting to Rs. 25,00,000. Other members of the venerable family of Sir Jamsetjee are also renowned for their public benefactions. The late Sir Cowasjee Jehangir Readymoney, whose ancestors were celebrated for acts of purest charity, was always ready with his purse in responding to the various appeals made on behalf of charity. Dinshaw Manockjee Petit, Esq., and Nusserwanjee Manockjee Petit, Esq., the worthy and respected sons of the late Manockjee Petit, are not less renowned for their good qualities, their private charity, and their true liberality in aiding the poor and distressed. Their contributions to charitable purposes are discriminate and unostentatious, and are never made merely to please certain classes of people. It would be foreign to our present object to mention the names of many others who enjoyed great celebrity down to a late period. We regret to notice, however, that a few members of well known Parsee families, not possessing the good qualities and lacking the mercantile spirit of their forefathers, are a set of dull and dyspeptic men, wasting their lives in enervating idleness.

Here we trust to be pardoned for a little digression. With regret it must be observed that the moral and social condition of the Parsees has of late shown signs of a gradual decline. The prediction of Dosabhoy Framjee, Esq., C.S.I., that " the Parsees of twenty years hence will stand far higher in the scale of civilization than even those of our own school," is unfortunately not verified. The Parsees are becoming more Europeanised in their dress, but not in their manners, education, and mental culture. In physical power the Parsees have degenerated, suicide is on the increase, and symptoms of premature decay manifest themselves. The evil of habitual reliance on the purse of relations and friends is on the increase. Marriage has of late become a trade with the lazy and the effeminate, the educated and the uneducated youths. The sooner the Parsees discourage this, the better will it be for their own name and fame, and for the welfare of their co-religionists. Scandal and lying have begun to creep insidiously into the morals of a nation whose ancestors were eminently distinguished by their love of truth. A fondness for medicine among young Parsee gentlemen and ladies may indeed be now considered the rule rather than the exception. Can nothing be done by the leading Parsees to put down the train of evils which threaten to extirpate the remnant of a race once the terror of the surrounding nations? Why do not the Parsee Dustoors* who occasionally

---

* Party spirit and party disputes have led to the recognition of two Dustoors or high priests in Bombay, who being dependent and partial to their own supporters cannot command the respect of all.

give rambling discourses on Farvardagan and Gahambar feasts, preach morality to their people? This first and chief duty ought not to have been ignored or neglected. Morality cannot be maintained without religious education.

It must not however be supposed from the above remarks that we speak thus of the whole Parsee community; they are intended only for those deluded youths who seem to have entirely forsaken the noble virtues of their ancestors. We repeat that the remnant of the ancient Persian race in India is still far above the Hindoos and Mahomedans in point of civilization, learning, enterprise, philanthropy and benevolence, but to bring them to the status of European society, a thorough and sweeping reformation and a sound education are highly needed.

We have no wish to discuss the question of female education. Every right-minded man is convinced of its value. It is defective, but is advancing, and has done a good deal to dispel the darkness, superstition, and ignorance which had prevailed among Parsee women. The fervent hopes expressed by Dosabhoy Framjee, Esq., C.S.I., in his *History of the Parsees*, that "with the increasing sense of the responsibility of educating females, and the great encouragement and support the scheme receives from all quarters, the Parsee female of a quarter of a century hence will rise far superior in intellect to their sisters of preceding generations," are not totally realised. Although no small credit attaches to the originators of the movement which has for its object to diffuse the light and the blessings of education, the success

Plato, Democritus, Hermippos, Pyrrho, and many other Greek philosophers were pupils of the Magi.

The present Magi, or the Dustoors and Mobeds of the Parsees, whose ancestors had previously been in advance of the laity in the exercise of the sciences and arts, and had once a partial control over the most powerful Persian monarchs, have gradually degenerated from their high positions. The Dustoors or high priests have always been respected for their learning and good qualities. Those of Poona are pre-eminent for their public spirit, independence, impartiality and learning. The Mobeds with few exceptions are ignorant and illiterate, and have degraded socially and morally. "Ignorant and unlearned as these priests are, they do not and cannot command the respect of the laity." So writes Dosabhoy Framjee, Esq., C. S. I., author of the History of the Parsees. And why is this? The only answer to be given is, that this disgraceful state of things is caused by the Behdins (laity) their oppressors, who do not even consider them on a footing of equality with themselves. The priests receive the miserable fee of one or two annas for reciting—"parrot-like"—all the chapters of a portion of the sacred writings, and for this wretched remuneration they are expected to become the spiritual guides of the Parsees! Their poverty and loss of power on the one hand, and the unworthy and overbearing conduct of the Behdins on the other, have given rise to discontent among them. Conscious of their own low position in society, they show disregard for their sacred duties, and some of them follow other trades and professions. To the discredit of the Parsees there are to be found among their priesthood, contractors, brokers, confectioners, cooks, liquor-sellers, auction-criers, turband-folders, &c. We would strongly advise the wealthy Parsees, by whom charity was scattered with such lavish profusion during the late share mania time without distinction of caste or creed, to remedy the existing evil by improving their order of priesthood. They should bear in mind that " charity begins at home.'

We find from the sacred literature of the Parsees that Thrita was the first person skilled in medicine. Fargard XX. of the Vendidad gives an account of this physician.*

"Zarathustra asked Ahura-Mazda, Heavenly, Holiest, Creator of the corporeal world, Pure! Who is the first of the men skilled in medicine? Of the acting, of the sovereign, of the able, of the brilliant, of the strong, of the first-established, who kept back sickness to sickness, death to death; who kept back Vazemnô-açti; who kept back the heat of the fire from the body of men?"

"Then answered Ahura-Mazda: Thrita was the first of men, O holy Zarathustra, of the healing, of the active, of the sovereign, of the able, of the brilliant, of the strong, of the first-established, who kept back sickness to sickness, who kept back death to death, who kept back Vazemnô-açti, the heat of the fire from the body of men. He desired a means as a favour from Khshathra-vairya, to withstand sick-

---

* The Fargard contains a few passages which seem to have been interpolated.

ness, to withstand death, to withstand pain, to withstand fever-heat, to withstand the evil rottenness and the dirt which Anramainyus has brought to the bodies of men. Then brought I forth, I who am Ahura-Mazda, the healing trees, many hundreds, many thousands, many tens of thousands, round about the one Gaokerena. All praise we, all laud we, all pray we here to this body of the man. Sickness I curse thee, death I curse thee, pain I curse thee, fever I curse thee, wickedness I curse thee."

" Through whose increase do we smite the Druj?"
" We smite the Druj through increase."
" Whose reign is strengthening for those like us, O Ahura?"

" I combat sickness, I combat death, I combat suffering, I combat fever, I combat evil corruption, the dirt which Anramainyus has created in the bodies of these men; I combat all sickness and all death, all Yatus and Pairikas, all the slaying, wicked (Daevas). Hither may the wished-for Airyêmâ come for joy to the men and women of Zarathustra. For joy for Vôhu-manô; may he grant the reward to be desired after the law. I wish the good purity of the pure. Great be Ahura-Mazda. May Airyêmâ, the desirable, smite every sickness and death, all Yatus and Pairikas, all the slaying, wicked (Daevas)."*

In the seventh Fargard of the Vendidad it is expressly enjoined that a person intending to practise the healing art should first make a trial on the idolators, and if found unsuccessful three times, is incap-

---

* Spiegel's *Avesta, translated by Bleeck*.

able for ever to practise among the Mazdayaçnians (those who invoke the Supreme Being). The fees to be paid to successful physicians are also fixed according to the rank of their patients :—

"Creator! When the Mazdayaçnians wish to make themselves physicians, whom shall they first cure, the Daevayaçnians or the Mazdayaçnians?"

"Then answered Ahura-Mazda: They shall make trial of healing on the Daevayaçnians before the Mazdayaçnians. If he begins to cut a Daevayaçnian for the first time, and he dies; if he begins to cut a Daevayaçnian for the second time, and he dies; if he cuts a Daevayaçnian for a third time, and he dies, then is he incapable for ever. The Mazdayaçnians shall not try (consult) him] afterwards; he shall not cut the Mazdayaçnians; he shall not wound by cutting. If the Mazdayaçnians afterwards try him, if he cuts the Mazdayaçnians, if he wounds them by cutting; then shall he atone for the wound of the wounded (man) with the punishment of the Baôdhovarsta. If he begins to cut a Daevayaçnian for the first time, and he recovers; if he cuts a Daevayaçnian for the second time, and he recovers; if he cuts a Daevayaçnian for the third time, and he recovers; then is he capable for ever. According to (their) wish shall the Mazdayaçnians afterwards make trial of him; he shall cut the Mazdayaçnians as he pleases; he shall heal them by cutting at his will.

"Let him cure a priest for a pious blessing. Let him cure the master of a house for the value of a small beast of burden. Let him cure the ruler of a clan for the value of a middle-sized beast of burden. Let him cure the chief of a tribe for the value of a large beast of burden. Let him cure the ruler of a territory for the value of a chariot with four oxen. If he first cures the mistress of a house, then a female ass is his reward. If he cures the wife of the chief of a clan, then a cow is his reward. If he cures the wife of the chief of a tribe, then a mare is his reward. If he cures the wife of the ruler of a district, then a female camel is his reward. Let him cure a boy from the village for the price of a large beast of burden. Let him cure a large beast of burden for the price of a middle-sized beast of burden. Let him cure a middle-sized beast of burden for the price of a small beast of burden. Let him cure a small beast of burden for the price of small animals, and small animals for the price of food. When many physicians come together, O holy Zarathustra! Physicians with knives, physicians with herbs, physicians with holy sayings, then is it the most healing among physicians who uses the Manthra-Çpenta as a remedy."*

All literary and religious books of the ancient Persians, with few exceptions, were burnt after the conquest of Persia by Alexander, and most of those which escaped destruction were finally destroyed by the Arabs. It is only from the Greek, Roman and Mahomedan writers we derive the greater part of our knowledge of Persian history, but their statements should be received with caution. The Greeks boast that the Persian kings appointed Greek physicians to their courts on account of their superior skill. Allowing this, as we are led to believe, it is not to be supposed that there were no Persian physicians of high professional standing in their own country. Zarathustra, their prophet, ordains: "Let the physician improve and render himself more skilful: his business is to give health." The famous physician and Sanscrit scholar Barzouyeh twice visited India to become acquainted with the literature of the Hindoos, and to collect specimens of Indian medicinal drugs. Among the numerous Sanscrit works he brought with him from India, were the celebrated Fables of Pilpay, which he is said to have translated into Pehlvi at the request of Noshirvan the Just. The other Sanscrit works were translated into Persian either by him or the learned Buzerjmeher. The Persian kings may have followed the fashion of the times, as is now in the countries of

---

* Spiegel's *Avesta*, *translated by Bleeck*.

Europe, to consult foreign practitioners. They seem to have employed not only Greek but Egyptian physicians. Cambyses, the son of Cyrus, requested king Amasis to send him the best eye-doctor from Egypt. An oculist of great repute and skill was chosen out of the kingdom, and ordered to proceed to the court of Persia. The order was obeyed, but the Egyptian doctor, separated from his family, and sent out to a foreign country, meditated vengeance against Amasis. No sooner he had obtained influence with Cambyses than he entered into intrigues, which resulted in the subjugation of Egypt by the Persian king. Darius attached several Egyptian physicians to his court, as we learn from Herodotus himself. Cyrus the Elder had the best physicians in the world (not only for himself, but for those who were in want of them), whom he highly honoured, and favoured with many rich gifts. "I do not consider," said he, "those who possess most and keep guard over most to be the happiest men." We learn from Herodotus that Democedes, the Crotonian, was physician to King Darius. In his early days he had studied medicine, and practised first at Crotona and then at Ægina. He was afterwards the medical adviser of Polycrates, the Greek tyrant of Samos, and was captured among the slaves and detained as a prisoner by the Persians. An amusing story of this physician is thus told by Herodotus :—

"Darius while leaping from his horse while hunting, twisted his foot, and it was twisted with such violence that the ancle-bone was dislocated ; and at first thinking he had about him those of the Egyptians who had the first reputation for skill in the healing art, he made use of their assistance. But they, by twisting the foot, and using force, made the evil worse ; and from the pain which he felt, Darius lay seven days and seven nights without sleep. On the eighth day, as he still continued very bad, some one who had before heard at Sardis of the skill of Democedes the Crotonian, made it known to Darius; and he ordered them to bring him as quickly as possible. They found him among the slaves of Orætes, altogether neglected; and brought him forward, dragging fetters behind him, and clothed in rags. As he stood before him, Darius asked him whether he understood the art. He denied that he did, fearing lest, if he discovered himself, he should be altogether precluded from returning to Greece. But he appeared to Darius to dissemble, although he was skilled in the art; he therefore commanded those who brought him thither to bring out whips and goads. Whereupon he discovered himself, saying that he did not know it perfectly, but having been intimate with a physician, he had some poor knowledge of the art. Upon which, when Darius put himself under his care, by using Grecian medicines, and applying lenitives of the violent remedies, he caused him sleep, and in a little time restored him to his health, though he had before despaired of even recovering the use of his foot. After this cure Darius presented him with two pairs of golden fetters, but Democedes asked him, if he purposely gave him a double evil because he had restored him to health. Darius pleased with the speech, sent him to his own wives; and the eunuchs, introducing him, said to the women that this was the man who had saved the king's life; whereupon each of them, dipping a goblet into a chest of gold, presented Democedes with such a munificent gift, that a servant, whose name was Sciton, following behind, picked up the staters that fell from the goblets, and collected a large quantity of gold."*

' From this time Democedes was much liked and respected, and was admitted to the king's table. But he, not considering it a great honour to become a friend of the king, chose to live in his native country. He preferred freedom and poverty to slavery and riches, and by some stratagem effected his escape. The Persians went in pursuit of him, and when they reached Crotona, they found him in the market and

---

* *History of Herodotus*, by H. Cary, pp. 224, 225.

seized him. Some of the Crotonians, who greatly feared the power of the Persians, were inclined to give him up, but others began beating them with sticks though they expostulated with them in these words—" Men of Crotona, have a care what you do, you are rescuing a man who is a runaway from the king; how will King Darius endure to be thus insulted? How can what you do end well if you force this man from us? What city shall we sooner attack than this? What sooner shall we endeavour to reduce to slavery?" With these menacing words they set sail from Crotona, and after suffering many hardships returned to Persia.

Another Greek named Apollonides of Cos was physician to Artaxerxes Longimanus. He was cruelly put to death for his intrigues.

Artaxerxes Mnemon had two Greek physicians, Polycritus of Mende and Ctesias, as his medical attendants. The latter is said to have healed the wound received by that prince in the battle of Cunaxa. He was the contemporary of Hippocrates, and a descendant of the family of the Asclepiadæ. Ctesias had been first the physician of Cyrus the younger, whom he accompanied in his expedition against Artaxerxes, and was taken prisoner in the battle of Cunaxa. Hearing of his surgical skill Artaxerxes placed himself under his care, and was successfully cured of his wound. He was afterwards appointed as his first physician, in which capacity he resided in Persia for seventeen years, during which he wrote a history of Persia, India, Babylon and Assyria, and also many treatises on medicine.

The Fourth Hippocrates was physician to Roxana,

queen of Alexander the Great, and daughter of King Darius Codomannus.

During the Sassanian dynasty founded by Ardashir, the Magian religion, which had been corrupted and mixed with idolatry by a number of unbelievers, was reformed, arts and sciences were protected, schools were founded, and philosophers and physicians, who from every part of the world resorted to Persia, received every encouragement from the enlightened dynasty. In short, the Sassanian kings liberally patronised the arts and sciences. The Persian king Baharam was not less solicitous for the cultivation of literature and science in his dominions. He himself went to Canoje in disguise to study the laws, religion, &c. of the Hindoos. The number of Greek physicians began to increase in Persia after the capture of the Roman Emperor Valerian by Sapor I. The queen of Sapor, who was the daughter of the Emperor Aurelian, brought with her many Greek physicians. Sapor built the city of Nisapur in honour of her favorite queen, which became celebrated as a great seat of learning. A Greek school of medicine was founded in this city, which sent forth many renowned men, such as Hareth-ibn-Kalda, who first settled at Mecca as a practitioner, but was afterwards appointed by Abu-Beker as his physician, and Bactishua, physician to the Kaliph Almansur, at whose request he translated several Greek and Persian books into Arabic. Noshirvan was a great patron of learning. He invited several men of letters to his capital from other kingdoms, and ordered the best foreign works to be translated into Persian.

CHAPTER VIII.

Zarathustra Spitaman—The age in which he lived—His birth and parentage—His early career—He communicates his Divine mission to king Gustasp—His persecutions—Gustasp becomes a zealous convert to the Zoroastrian faith—Rapid spread of the new religion—Assassination of Zarathustra—His monotheism—His sacred writings—His extant works—Avesta and Hygiene.

We shall now proceed to give the life of an individual of considerable learning in his age, and of extraordinary genius, whose astonishing powers and performances have always been admired by the most profound philosophers and literati in all ages and in every country of the civilized world. We speak with due reverence of Zarathustra Spitaman, the founder of the pure and sublime Magian religion, and the Prophet and Legislator of the Parsees. The Zarathustra Spitaman of the Zend Avesta, deservedly surnamed the Great, is also known as Zoroaster, Zurtosht, Zarades, and Zerdusht. The age in which he lived, and the place of his birth, are not exactly known. He is supposed to have flourished about the year 550 B.C., and to have been contemporary with Darius Hystaspes, whom some authors confound with Gustasp. We are told by some that there were two remarkable persons of this name, the one supposed to be the founder, and the other the reformer, of the Magian religion. Others are of opinion that in ancient times the head of the Magus or high priest was known by the appellation of Zarathustrotemo. Hence the confusion of dates regarding his age. It is not a matter of certainty, but it is most probable that he lived in the reign of Gustasp, about fourteen centuries before the Christian era, in the city of Rai (Zend *Ragha*), situated on the bank of the river Dergic (Zend *Darijaya*).

He was descended from a noble family. His father's name was Poroshaspa, and his mother's name Doghdo. It is said that Poroshaspa received from an angel a cup of wine. He drank it off, and his wife soon after became pregnant. In the sixth month of her pregnancy Doghdo received a warning in a dream, for which an astrologer was consulted, who interpreted it to mean that she would become the mother of a son destined to check the career of Paganism, and to found a religion at once pure and marvellous. After the full period she bore a son to Poroshaspa. The devas (devils) trembled, and the "priest and prophet of the idols" and the wicked and irreligious were thrown into confusion. The impious and evil-doing worshippers of the Devas, getting alarmed, made several attempts to destroy the infant, who miraculously escaped on all occasions. The hand of Providence frustrated their evil designs. "We find it stated," says Pliny, "that Zoroaster was the only human being who ever laughed on the same day on which he was born. We hear, too, that his brain pulsated so strongly that it repelled the hand when laid upon it, as presage of his future wisdom."*

---

* Pliny's *Natural History*, Book VII.

Nothing is known of his early education. We are informed that he visited Chaldea to become a disciple of the Chaldean sages and acquire a knowledge of their writings. But this is a mere conjecture. Having attained the age of thirty, Zoroaster retired to the Alburz mountains. Here he spent ten years of his life in meditation and prayer, living entirely on milk or cheese. In his fortieth year he appeared before King Gustasp with the sacred fire called " Ader Boorzin Meher" in the one hand, and a cypress tree in the other. On being asked the object of his visit, he announced his divine mission in the following terms :—" The Almighty God has sent me to you, and has appointed me a prophet to guide you in the path of truth, virtue, and piety." And added :—" Learn the rites and doctrines of the religion of *excellence*. For without religion there cannot be any worth in a king."* Thus, by a few pathetic words, the Prophet prevailed upon the greatest monarch of his age to receive the religion of God. At first Zarathustra was looked upon with suspicion, and had to encounter opposition from the courtiers of Gustasp. He was even accused of heresy and magic, and thrown into prison. That he was exposed to severe persecution there can be no doubt, for he says in the Gatha Ustavaiti—" To what country shall I go ? where shall I take my refuge ? what country is sheltering the master (Zarathustra) and his companion ? None of the servants pay reverence to me, nor the wicked rulers of the country. How shall I worship Thee further, living Wise ?

---

* *Firdousi.*

"I know that I am helpless. Look at me being amongst few men, for I have few men (I have lost my followers, or they have left me); I implore Thee weeping, thou living God, who grantest happiness as a friend gives *a present* to his friend. The good of the good mind is in thy own possession, Thou True!"*

How the Prophet frustrated the attempts of the devils to destroy him and the worship of one God may be learnt from the nineteenth chapter of the Vendidad.

Zarathustra, by performing several miracles, soon gained the confidence of the king and his councillors, who bowed to him as their Prophet and Legislator, and became zealous converts to the new faith. To his miracles and prophecies it is not necessary to advert in these pages. By the combined efforts of King Gustasp and his loyal subjects, Zoroastrianism rapidly spread through the vast Persian empire. In the first Fargard of the Vendidad are enumerated 16 Aryan countries throughout which the Zoroastrian religion was propagated. Gustasp even refused to pay an annual tribute to Arjasp, king of the proud, idolatrous, and warlike Scythians (Turanians); unless he and his countrymen forsook idolatry and received the Zoroastrian religion. The warlike barbarian, disliking the worship of one Supreme Being, suddenly invaded Bactriana with a strong force, stormed and pillaged Balkh, and Baraturut, one of the Turanian generals, stabbed Zarathustra to death while praying in a fire-temple. The Prophet performed his last miracle by throwing his string of

---

* Haug's *Essays on the Sacred Language, Writings, and Religion of the Parsees.*

beads at the perpetrator of the bloody deed, who instantly fell lifeless on the spot. Gustasp hastily collected an army, attacked the Scythians, defeated them completely, and slaughtered them by thousands to avenge the murder of Zarathustra. The life of the king of Turan was not afterwards spared.

Zarathustra is said to have had more than two hundred disciples, and among them such men as Mediomah his cousin, Isfandiar the son of Gustasp, and the two most learned brothers of the Havogava family, named Furshostar and Jamasp. All took part in converting the Persians and other nations from the worship of idols to the belief of one Supreme Being.

The Zoroastrians have always been the adorers of one God, and haters of idolatry. The enemies of the pure Zoroastrian religion and some ignorant and prejudiced authors accuse the Parsees of adoring fire, sun, moon, &c. The extant works of Zoroaster and the testimony of eminent historians and Zend scholars show that the Parsees and their ancestors have been the worshippers of one God, the Creator and Ruler of the whole universe, under His purest symbols and noble productions. The scripture of the Christians calls Cyrus "anointed of the Lord." Xerxes, during his invasion of Greece, ordered many temples of superstitious idolatry to be destroyed. Cambyses, when he entered Memphis in triumph, stabbed the sacred bull of the Egyptians, and ordered the temples and images to be burnt. The Medes and Elamites under Cyrus destroyed the images of Babylon. "Go up to Elam! besiege O Media! Babylon is fallen, is fallen; and all the graven

images of her gods he hath broken unto the ground."
(Isaiah xxi. 2-9.) The following lines from Firdousi show that the Zoroastrian religion is anti-idolatrous:—

"Nagui ke atash parastan budand
Parastandaye pak yezdan budand."

Sir William Ouseley, speaking of the Parsee religion, says:—"I shall here express my firm belief that the first Persian altars blazed in honour of God alone; as likewise, that the present disciples of Zeratusht or Zerdehest (Zoroaster), both in India and the mother country, Iran or Persia, have no other object when they render to fire a semblance of veneration."*

The same traveller, agreeing with Dr. Hyde in acknowledging the Zoroastrian religion as anti-idolatrous, says:—"I sincerely join in respecting the old Persian worship, and sympathize in lamenting the infamous persecution which has caused its decay."

Sir John Malcolm states it as his opinion:—"God, he (Zoroaster) taught, existed from all eternity, and was like infinity of time and space . . . . . . Light was the type of the good, darkness of the evil spirit; and God had said unto Zoroaster 'My light is concealed under all that shines.' Hence the disciple of that prophet, when he performs his devotions in a temple, turns towards the sacred fire that burns upon its altar, and when in the open air, towards the sun as the noblest of all lights, and that by which God sheds his divine influence over the

---
* Ouseley's *Travels*, Vol. I., p. 108.

whole earth, and perpetuates the works of his creation."*

Forbes in his "Oriental Memoirs" says:—"The vulgar and illiterate worship the sacred flame, as also the sun, moon, and stars, without regard to the Creator; but the learned and judicious adore only the Almighty Fountain of Light, the Author and Disposer of all things, under the symbol of fire. Zoroaster, and the ancient Magi, whose memories they revere, and whose works they are said to preserve, never taught them to consider the sun as anything more than a creature of the Great Creator of the universe; they were to revere it as his best and fairest image, and for the numberless blessings it diffuses on the earth; the sacred flame was intended only as a perpetual monitor to preserve their purity, of which this element is so expressive a symbol."†

Dean Prideaux expresses his sentiments on the Magian religion in the following words:—"They, (the disciples of Zarathustra) abominating all images, worshipped God only by fire. Light was the truest symbol of the good God; and therefore they always worshipped him before fire, as being the cause of light, and especially before the sun, as being in their opinion the perfected fire, and causing the perfectest light. And for this reason in all their temples they had fire continually burning on altars, erected in them for that purpose; and before these sacred fires they offered up all their public devotions, as likewise they did all their private devotions before their private

---

* Malcolm's *History of Persia*, Vol. I., p. 194.
† Forbes's *Oriental Memoirs*, Vol. I., p. 80.

fires in their own houses. Thus did they pay the highest honour to light as being in their opinion the truest representative of the Good God, but always hated darkness as being what they thought the truest representative of the Evil God, whom they ever had in the utmost detestation as we now have the Devil."*

We could recite the opinions of several other eminent authors, but the pages of this volume are not intended for theological discussions. However, we must not omit to state the opinion of the late oriental scholar Dr. Martin Haug, whose writings betray an intimate acquaintance of Zend literature. The following extracts from his " Essays on the Sacred Language, Writings, and Religion of the Parsees," prove that the Zoroastrians are monotheists :—

" Zarathustra Spitama's conception of Ahuramazda as the Supreme Being is perfectly identical with the notion of *Elohim* (God) or *Jehovah*, which we find in the books of the Old Testament. Ahuramazda is called by him ' the Creator of the earthly and spiritual life, the Lord of the whole universe at whose hands are all the creatures.' He is the light and the source of light ; he is the wisdom and intellect. He is in possession of all good things, spiritual and worldly, such as the good mind (*vohu manô*), immortality (*ameretât*), wholesomeness (*haurvatât*), the best truth (*asha vahista*), devotion and piety (*armaiti*), and abundance of every earthly good (*Khshathra vairya*). All these gifts he grants to the righteous pious man, who is pure in thoughts, words, and deeds."

" His real doctrines, untouched by the speculations of later ages, can be learnt only from the old Yasna, chiefly from the Gâthas. The leading idea of his theology was *Monotheism, i. e.*, that there are not many gods, but only one, and the principle of his speculative philosophy *Dualism, i. e.* the supposition of two primeval causes of

---

* Dean Prideaux quoted by Sir W. Ouseley in his "Travels in Persia," Vol. I., p. 123.

the real world and of the intellectual, while his moral philosophy was moving in the *Triad* of thought, word, and deed."

"That his theology was mainly based on monotheism, one may easily ascertain from the Gâthas, chiefly from the second. His predecessors, the Soshyanto, seem to have been worshipping a plurality of good spirits whom they called *Ahuras, i. e.* the living ones who were opposed to the Devas. Spitama, not satisfied with this indistinct expression of the Divine Being, reduced this plurality to an unity. The new name, by which he called the Supreme Being, was *Ahurómazdâo*, which means, that Ahura who is called 'Mazdâo, ... In the Sassanian times the name was changed to *Ahurmazd*, and in modern Persian to *Hormazd* or *Ormazd*, which form is used by the Parsees now-a-days. In the Gâthas we find both words frequently separated and promiscuously employed to express the name 'god,' but no difference of meaning is attached to either. In translating then *Ahura* may best be rendered by 'living' and *mazdâo* by 'wise' or 'Creator of universe.'"

Finally, let us hear what Zarathustra himself says of monotheism in a speech delivered by him before a monstrous meeting. In the third section of the Gâtha Ahunavaiti (Izeshnê XXX.) he thus preaches his doctrine of monotheism to his countrymen:—

"I will now tell you who are assembled here, the wise sayings of the most wise, the praises of the living God, and the songs of the good spirit, the sublime truth which I see arising out of these sacred flames.

"You shall, therefore, hearken to the soul of nature (*i. e.* to plough and cultivate the earth); contemplate the beams of fire with a most pious mind! Every one, both men and women, ought to-day to choose his creed (between the Deva and the Ahura religion). Ye offspring of renowned ancestors, awake to agree with us (*i. e.* to approve of my lore to be delivered to you at this moment)!

"In the beginning there was a pair of twins, two spirits, each of a peculiar activity; these are the good, and the base in thought, word and deed. Choose one of these two spirits! Be good, not base.

"And these two spirits united created the first (the material things); one, the reality, the other, the non-reality. To the liars (the worshippers of the devas, *i. e.* gods) existence will become bad, whilst the believers in the true God enjoy prosperity.

"Of these two spirits you must choose one, either the evil, the originator of the worst actions, or the true holy spirit. Some may wish to have the hardest lot (*i. e.* those who will not leave the polytheistic deva religion), others adore Ahuramazda by means of sincere actions.

"You cannot belong to both of them (*i. e.* you cannot be worshippers of the one true God, and of many gods at the same time). One of the devas, against whom we are fighting, might overtake you when in deliberation (what faith you are to embrace), whispering you to choose the naught mind. Then the devas flock together to assault the two lives, (the life of the body, and that of the soul), praised by the prophets.

"And to succour this life (to increase it), Armaitis came with wealth, the good and true mind; but the soul as to time, the first cause among created beings, was with Thee.

"But when he (the evil spirit) comes with one of these evils (to sow ill weed among the believers), then thou hast the power through the good mind of punishing them who break their promises, O true spirit!

"Thus let us be such as help the life of the future. The wise living spirits are the greatest supporters of it. The prudent man wishes only to be there where wisdom is at home.

"Wisdom is the shelter from lies, the annihilation of the destroyer (the evil spirit). All perfect things are garnered up in the splendid residence of the Good Mind (Vohu-manô), the Wise (Mazda), and the True (Asha) who are known as the best beings.

"Therefore perform ye the commandments which pronounced by the Wise (God) himself, have been given to mankind; for they are a nuisance and perdition to liars, but prosperity to the believers in the truth; they are the fountain of happiness."*

Those who expressed their willingness to forsake

---

* Haug's *Essays*, pp. 141, 142, 143.

idolatry were received into the Zoroastrian community after the following confession:—

"I cease to be a Deva *worshipper*. I profess to be a Zoroastrian Mazdayasna (worshipper of Ahuramazda), and enemy of the devas, and a devotee to Ahura, a praiser of the immortal saints (Amesha spentas), a worshipper of the immortal saints. I ascribe all good things to Ahuramazda, who is good, and has good, who is true, lucid, shining, who is the originator of all the best things, of the spirit in nature (*gâus*), of the growth in nature, of the luminaries and the self-shining brightness which is in the luminaries.

"I choose (follow, profess) the holy Armaiti, the good; she may be mine! I abominate all fraud and injury committed on the spirit of earth, and all damage and destruction of the quarters of the Mazdayasnas.

"I allow the good spirits who reside on this earth in the good animals (as cows, sheep, &c.) to go and roam about free according to their pleasure. I praise, besides, all that is offered with prayer to promote the growth of life. I shall cause neither damage nor destruction to the quarters of the Mazdayasnas, neither with my body nor my soul.

"I forsake the Devas, the wicked, bad, false, untrue, the originators of mischief, who are most baneful, destructive, the basest of all beings. I forsake the Devas and those who are Devas-like, the witches and their like, and any being whatever of such a kind. I forsake them with thoughts, words and deeds; I forsake them hereby publicly and declare that all lie and falsehood is to be done away with.

"In the same way as Zarathustra at the time when Ahuramazda was holding conversations and meetings with him and both were conversing with each other, forsook the Devas: so do I forsake the Devas, as the holy Zarathustra did.

"To what party the waters belong, to what party the trees, and the animating spirit of nature, to what party Ahuramazda belongs, who has created this spirit and the pure man; to what party Zarathustra and Kavâ Vistâspa and Frashostra and Jâmâspa were, of what party all the ancient firepriests (Soshyantô) were, the pious, who were spreading the truth: of the same party and creed *am* I.

"I am a Mazdayasna, a Zoroastrian Mazdayasna. I profess this religion by praising and preferring it to others (the Deva religion), I praise the thought, which is good, I praise the word, which is good, I praise the work, which is good.

"I praise the Mazdayasna religion, and the pure brotherhood, which it establishes, and defends against enemies, the Zoroastrian Ahura religion, which is the greatest, best, and most prosperous of all that are, and that will be. I ascribe all good to Ahuramazda. This shall be the praise (profession) of the Mazdayasna religion."*

From the extracts given above the reader will readily perceive that Zarathustra's theology is based on monotheism, and that he spread his religion not by the sword but by his brilliant oratory.

The following passages in the Behistun inscription, cut on a rock near Kermanshah by order of King Darius, also prove that the worship of the elements did not prevail in Persia after the advance of Zarathustra:

"By the grace of Ormuzd I am king; Ormuzd has granted me the empire."

"By the grace of Ormuzd I crossed the Tigris. I went to Babylon. We fought a battle. Then Ormuzd brought help unto me," &c.

We learn from characters impressed on the coins of King Ardeshir Babikan, a pious and devoted follower of Zarathustra, that he was a believer only in one God:—"The Ormuzd Worshipper, divine Ardeshir, king of kings of Iran, of divine origin from God."

The following legend engraved on the seal of Baharam fully confirms that the ancient Persians adored one God (Ormuzd) and not fire, sun, &c. "Varahran, king of Kerman, son of the Worshipper of Ormuzd, the divine Sháhpúr, king of kings of Iran and non-Iran, of celestial origin from God."

---

* Haug's *Essays*, pp. 163, 164, 165.

The sacred Zend-Avesta, or the Scriptures of the Parsees which Zarathustra had brought with him to the Court of Persia in twenty-one volumes or Nosks, show that he must have been a man of no ordinary genius. The following are the names of all the books in the Zend and Pehlvi languages :—

	Zend.	*Pehlvi.*
1.	Yatha	Setudtar or Setud-Yashts.
2.	A-hoo	Setudgar.
3.	Verio	Vahista-Mathra.
4.	A-tha	Bagha.
5.	Ratoos	Dâın-Dât.
6.	Ussad	Nâdur.
7.	Chid	Pacham.
8.	Hucha	Ratushtâi.
9.	Vungéhoos	Burush.
10.	Dujda	Koshusarub.
11.	Munungho	Vishtasp Nosk.
12.	Sieuthenanam	Chidrusht.
13.	Ungéhoos	Safand.
14.	Muzdaí	Jarasht.
15.	Khusthremchai	Baghan Yesh.
16.	A-hooraí	Nayârum.
17.	Aa	Hûsparûm.
18.	Eem	Domasarûb.
19.	Durregobio	Hûskarûm.
20.	Dadada	Vendidâd.
21.	Vastarem	Hadokht.

The late Dr. Martin Haug observes :—" That such a division into 21 sections really existed, cannot be doubted ; for the names of the several sections, together with the number of chapters they comprise, and the short statement of the chief contents, are still extant." The contents of the 21 Nosks given by Doctor Haug from the two Revâyats now in the possession of Dustoor Noshirvanjee, the learned and worthy High-priest of the Parsees at Poona, are as follows :—

1. *Setudtar* or *setud-yashts* (Zend : çtaota, çtûiti praise, worship) comprised 33 chapters, containing the praise and worship of the *Yazatas* or angels.

2. *Setudgar*, 22 chapters, containing prayers and instructions to men about good actions, chiefly those called *jadûngôi*, *i. e.* to induce another to assist a fellow-man.

3. *Vahista mâthra*, 22 chapters, treating of abstinence, piety, religion, qualities of Zoroaster, etc.

4. *Bagha*, 21 chapters, containing an explanation of the religious duties, the orders and commandments of God and obedience of men, how to guard against hell and to reach heaven.

5. *Dâm dât*, 22 chapters ; contents : knowledge of this and that world (the future life), qualities of their inhabitants ; the revelations of God concerning heaven, earth, water, trees, fire, men and beasts ; the resurrection of the dead and the passing of the bridge *chinvat* (the way to heaven).

6. *Nâdur*, 35 chapters, containing astronomy, geography, astrology, translated into Arabic under the name *Yûntâl*; and known to the Persian by the name *fawâmaz jân*.

7. *Pacham*, 22 chapters, treating of what food is allowed or prohibited, of the reward to be obtained in the other world for keeping the six *Gahambârs* and the *Fravardagan*.

8. *Ratushtâi*, 50 chapters (at the time of Alexander the Great only 13 were extant), treated of the different *ratus* or heads in the creation, such as Kings, High-priests, Ministers, and gave statements as to what fishes are Ormuzd's and what Ahriman's ; there was besides a geographical section in it.

9. *Burush*, 60 chapters (thirteen of which only were extant at the time of Alexander the Great), contents : the code of law for kings, governors, etc.; workmanship of various kinds ; the sin of lying.

10. *Koshusarub*, 60 chapters, (at Alexander's time 15 only were extant), treated of metaphysics, natural philosophy, divinity, etc.

11. *Vishtasp Nosk*, 60 chapters (at Alexander's time only 10), on the reign of King Gustasp and his conversion to the religion and its propagation by him through the world.

12. *Chidrusht*, 22 chapters, was divided into six parts: 1st, on the nature of the divine being, the Zoroastrian faith, the duties enjoined by it; 2nd, on obedience due to the king; 3rd, on the reward for good actions in the other world, and how to be saved from hell; 4th, on the structure of the world, agriculture, botany, etc.; 5th, on the four classes of which a nation consists, viz. rulers, warriors, agriculturists, traders and workmen (the contents of the sixth division are left out).

13. *Safand*, 60 chapters, on the miracles of Zoroaster, the Gahâmbar, etc.

14. *Jarasht*, 22 chapters, on the human life, from the birth to its end and up to the day of resurrection; on the causes of man's birth, why some are born in wealth, others in poverty.

15. *Baghan Yesh*, 17 chapters, containing the praise of high angel-like men.

16. *Nayârum*, 54 chapters, code of law, stating what is allowed, and what prohibited.

17. *Hûsparûm*, 64 chapters, on medicine, astronomy, midwifery, etc.

18. *Domasarûb*, 65 chapters, on the marriages between the nearest relatives (called *qaetvo-datha*); zoology and treatment of animals.

19. *Hûskarûm*, 52 chapters, treating of the civil and criminal law; of the boundaries of the country, of the resurrection.

20. *Vendidâd*, 22 chapters, on removal of uncleanliness of every description from which great defects arise in the world.

21. *Hadokht*, 30 chapters, on the creation, its wonders, structure, etc.

From the contents of the Nosks it will appear that Hûsparûm treated of medicine, astronomy, midwifery, &c., and Domasarûb of zoology. A part of the Chidrusht was devoted to botany. These are lost for ever. The antiquity and authorship of the 21

THE MEDICAL ART. 169

books have not been denied by the ancient Greek and Roman writers. Dr. Haug and other European scholars state that such an extensive literature cannot be the work of a single man; while the Parsees, on the other hand, assert that the sayings of God were revealed to his Prophet Zoroaster. It would exceed the limits of this work to enter into a full discussion of this subject.

All the sacred writings of the Parsees have perished with the exception of Vendidad Sádé, which contains three Zend works, the Vendidad, Yaçna or Izeshnê, and Vispered; the Yashts, and fragments of the Hadokt and Vistasp nosks; and books of prayers called Nyaish, Afrigans, Gahs and Sirozahs. The subjects of these books are so varied that to give an account of them would require separate volumes of no small dimensions; neither have we the talent to discuss the subject fully. We shall therefore only notice a few principal passages relating to hygiene, and containing strict injunctions for the protection of those exposed to contagion, which ought not to be passed over in silence. They are a proof that the great founder of the Parsee religion was acquainted with the best principles of prevention and the best means for the isolation of those exposed to contagion. The religious ceremonies of the Parsees, which are regarded with derision by a few imperfectly educated young men calling themselves Mazdayaçnians, but who are really Devayaçnians, contain some striking truths and lay down sound sanitary regulations for the social interest. The excellencies of the Zoroastrian religion have been acknowledged by the best

Zend scholars of Europe. More than twenty-five centuries after the sanitary teachings of Zoroaster, civilized Europe awoke from its slumber, and framed compulsory laws intended for the enforcement of cleanliness in order to prevent the spread of zymotic diseases. Of the compulsory notification of all cases of an infectious character occurring both in public and private practice in some countries of Europe, our professional readers are not ignorant. From the following account of the ravages performed by the great epidemics, it will be evident that sanitary science was unknown in Europe in the middle ages:—

"The Black Death swept away, within the space of four years, a fourth part of the population of Europe. Some towns in England are stated to have lost two-thirds of their inhabitants, and it is computed that one-half of the entire population of the country perished.

"Of the Sweating Sickness, Bacon says it 'destroyed infinite persons'; Stowe, 'a wonderful number'; and other writers reckon the deaths in the places attacked by thousands.

"Similar representations are given of the ravages of the Plague, of the Petechial Fever, and even occasionally of Intermittent Fever; and the substantial correctness of these statements is confirmed by entries in parish registers still extant, which tell the story of the local outbreaks of those days with graphic and touching simplicity.

"During some of the worst of these visitations, contemporary writers concur in stating, that the living were insufficient to bury the dead; business was suspended; the courts of law were closed; the churches were deserted for want of a sufficient number of clergy to perform the services; and ships were seen driving about on the ocean and drifting on shore, whose crews had perished to the last man.

"We can form no adequate conception of the terror inspired by these events. We have seen alarm in our own day, but then it bordered on maniacal despair. It seemed as if the last judgment had come upon the world, and men abandoned alike their possessions and their friends. The rich gave up their treasures, and laid them at the foot of the altars; neighbours abandoned neighbours; parents their offspring, and brothers their sisters."*

It was not till after the terrible loss of life which resulted from neglecting the principles of health that Europe rose from its lethargy, and saw the importance of a knowledge of hygiene for the improvement of the sanitary condition of the people.

The medical work entitled Husparûm, which is unfortunately lost, might have thrown some light on the contagious diseases prevalent in the vast empire of Persia in the days of Zoroaster. It appears, however, from his extant works that he thought prevention of greater importance than cure; and that he clearly saw and understood that zymotic diseases are communicated to healthy persons—

1. By direct contact with the sick or dead.
2. By poisonous matter applied through the medium of the bed or clothing.
3. Through the medium of the atmosphere.
4. By the reception of morbific matter into the alimentary canal.

We find throughout his writings strict injunctions for the protection of persons exposed to the influence of zymotic diseases. The corpse of a person who had died of a non-infectious disease is treated in the same way as a case of infection, and similarly with regard to their clothing, bedding, &c. The only explanation we can give of this is, that people in his age (as indeed in our own) were not wise in discriminating between infectious and non-infectious diseases; hence

---

* *The Common Nature of Epidemics*, by Southwood Smith, M.D., pp. 38, 39.

to avoid any mistakes we find, in his religious writings, the same rules for the treatment of the dead in general, the purification of their clothes, &c. He understood that a doubt about the contagiousness of a disease in the minds of the people would result in the neglect of proper precautions, and the dissemination of zymotic diseases in various ways. The following passage from Watson's Practice of Physic is so like what Zarathustra might have written, that it reads like a quotation from his works:—" There are a thousand ways in which contagion may be disseminated. It may lurk in a hackney coach; you may catch the complaint from your neighbour in an omnibus, or at the theatre, or at church; your linen may be impregnated with the subtle poison in the house of your laundress, or your coat may convey it from the workshop of your tailor. Even if we doubt about the contagiousness of the disease, we are bound to act as if we had no doubt of the subject."

To preserve purity of body, cleanliness is considered essential for the well-being of a Zoroastrian; and without observing it, all the effect of his religious ceremonies and prayers is lost. Of the importance of cleanliness abundant evidence is afforded in the scripture of the Parsees.*

"I combat the Naçus. I combat direct uncleanness. I combat indirect uncleanness away from the dwelling, the village, the town, the region, away from my own body, away from the unclean man,

---

* The reader will observe that for the passages of the Avesta quoted hereafter in this chapter, we have relied on the authority of Bleeck, who, at the request of Mr. Muncherjee Hormusjee Cama, has translated the Avesta into English from Spiegel's German translation of the original manuscript.

the unclean woman, the lord of the house, the village, the town, the region, away from all pure creatures."—Ven. F. X., v. 12.

"Purity is the best good. Happiness, happiness is to him, namely, to the best pure in purity."—K. A.

"Unwillingly, O holy Zarathustra, shines the sun upon the unclean, unwillingly the moon, unwillingly these stars. For he who purifies makes content, he who removes the Naçus from the unclean. O holy Zarathustra, he makes the fire content,* he makes the water content, he makes the earth content, he makes the cattle content, he makes the trees content, he makes the pure man content, he makes the pure woman content."

"Zarathustra asked: Creator of the corporeal world, Pure! What does that man receive as a reward, when body and soul have separated, who removes the Naçus from an unclean (person)?"

"Then answered Ahura-Mazda. Let them promise this man† as his reward in the next world; the attaining of Paradise."—Ven. F. IX., vv. 161 to 166.

As poisonous matter is sometimes absorbed through the cutaneous surface, daily bathing and frequent ablutions of the exposed parts of the body during the day (such as before meals, prayers and religious ceremonies, and after natural functions,) are religious duties entailed upon every Zoroastrian not only for keeping the body clean, but as a precaution against his receiving contagion into his system, or conveying it to others. A shirt must be worn by the Parsees night and day. The entire body of Parsee corpse-bearers is covered, with the exception of a portion of their face. Even their hands are enveloped in white pouches.

A part of the seventh Fargard of the Vendidad is occupied with some details of the destruction and the disinfection or purification of the bedding and dress

---

* Gratifies.—*Guj. Tr.*   † This man will receive.—*Guj. Tr.*

of a deceased Zoroastrian. The reader will bear in mind that cow's urine was used by the Persians as a purifying or disinfecting agent. The term Naço is employed to any dead matter or decomposed thing. Naçus is that which decomposes or destroys.

"Zarathustra asked Ahura-Mazda : Creator! If several men are together in the same place, or on the same bed and the same mat, if two other persons are there opposite one, or five, or fifty, or a hundred, together with (their) wives.* Then one of these men dies. This one has a bed or a mat with which they cover him. Upon how many of these—the bed and the mat†—does the Drukhs Naçus settle?"

"Then answered Ahura-Mazda : Upon the top of this bed, on the outmost covering thereof, the Drukhs Naçus settles with corruption, rottenness, and impurity."

"Creator! How do these garments become pure again, O pure Ahura-Mazda! which have been placed on the body of a dead dog or a dead man?"

"Then answered Ahura-Mazda! They become pure, O pure Zarathustra! in this way: If they are stained with matter, with dirt, or with vomit, then the Mazdayaçnians shall cut these garments in pieces and bury them. If they are not stained with matter, dirt, or vomit, then shall the Mazdayaçnians wash these garments with cow's urine. If they (the garments) consist of hair, then they shall wash them three times with cow's urine, rub them three times with earth, wash them three times with water, air them three months at the window of the house. If they are woven they shall wash them six times with cow's urine, rub them six times with earth, wash them six times with water, air them six months at the window of the dwelling."

"Creator! how are these garments again suitable after the purification and the washing, for the Zaota, for the Havanan, for the Atarevakhs, the Frabereta, the Aberet, the Açnata, the Raethwiskara, the Çraoshavareza, for the priests, the soldiers, and the husbandmen?"

---

* " With their wives" is not in the *Guj. Tr.*
† The dress and the pillow.—*Guj Tr.*

THE MEDICAL ART. 175

"Then answered Ahura-Mazda : These garments are not serviceable again after the purification and washing not for the Zaota, not for the Havanan, not for the Atarevakhs, not for the Frabereta, not for the Aberet, not for the Açnata, not for the Raethwiskara, not for the Çraoshavareza, not for the priest, not for the warrior, not for the husbandman. If a woman in a Mazdayaçnian dwelling is afflicted with menstruation, or if a limb has been broken, and a wound stains the house, then is this her bed and her mat wherewith they cover her, until she brings out her hands in prayer and praise."

It has been proved that fabrics, which had been exposed to the infection of typhus, cholera, smallpox, scarlet fever, &c. are powerful agents in conveying the diseases at great distances into healthy localities. The following is an instance :—

"An illustration of the dangerous rôle in propagating disease, which the laundry occasionally plays, was given at a recent meeting of St. Olave's Board of Works. The medical officer of health reported that a serious outbreak of typhus fever had occurred at a certain yard, necessitating the removal of five persons to the hospital. On making inquiries, it was found that a young woman who lived with her mother and brother at one of the houses, brought home from the other side of the water some clothes to be washed, which had been worn by a patient suffering from typhus fever. The consequences were immediate and tragic. The two women, the man, and two neighbours were attacked, and four out of the number died in hospital. The house was at once closed, and most of its contents burned, while the Board very rightly directed the medical officer to make further investigation into the circumstances of the fatal importation."*

A contagious disease is sometimes communicated to the healthy by the application of poisonous matter through the bed or clothing, in other words by direct

---

* Vide *Lancet*, Feb. 16, 1878.

contact. Dr. Parkes, speaking of "military ophthalmia," says:—

"In some cases the use of the bedding (pillows and pillow-cases) which has been used by men with grey granulations, has given the disease to others, and this has especially occurred on board transports. In time of war, especially, this should be looked to. If any cases of ophthalmia have occurred on board ship, all the pillows and mattresses should be washed, fumigated, and thoroughly aired and beaten. The transference in this case has been direct, particles of pus, &c. adhering to the pillow and mattresses, and then getting into the eyes of the next comers."

In some countries of Europe measures are taken for the compulsory registration of all cases of infectious diseases; and the bedding, clothing and other articles are either thoroughly disinfected or destroyed. For instance, the family of a poor workman in England, consisting of four boys, were once attacked by scarlet fever and two of them died. As the disease was of an infectious character, he reported the matter to the sanitary inspector. The result was that whatever he possessed was destroyed, and he himself was not permitted to enter the work-shop on account of the infection. The poor man thus describes his misery in a letter to his doctor:—

"Dear Sir,—I cannot rest without letting you know how deeply my poor wife and I feel the terrible position in which we are placed. The workmen under the inspector have torn our house to pieces, our feather beds are destroyed at my expense. I shall be obliged to ask my landlord to let my rent stand over, and through him, he being a guardian, petition for my taxes to be excused."

It must of course be understood that under the provisions of the Sanitary Act the inspector was empowered to destroy the bedding, clothing, &c. of persons ill with infectious diseases. "Sanitary authorities," says Dr. Parkes, " have powers (29 & 30 Vict. c. 90) to remove persons ill with infectious diseases to a proper hospital in special conveyances, to prosecute sick persons frequenting public places or conveyances ; to destroy bedding or clothing, and to disinfect rooms, houses or clothing . . . . . The freest ventilation, supply of water, and means of disinfection are essential. Under the same Act a town is empowered to erect a proper place for disinfecting clothing and bedding, disinfecting chambers (heated by hot air, steam pipes, or gas, and in which a heat of 240 degrees Fahr. can be reached) are now provided in many towns for the immediate disinfection by heat of all soiled clothes taken from patients with any of these diseases."*

The *Lancet* (February 16, 1878) has drawn the attention of the authorities to the " army clothing infection." We cannot do better than reproduce some instructive passages from the same :—

"The uniforms provided by the Army Clothing Depôt were often contaminated by the germs of zymotic diseases."

"Uniforms imported from London fever dens into the British camp may do more to ensure discomfiture than the most gallant onslaught on the part of the enemy."

"The most radical and effective of all measures would involve an entire change in the method of producing uniforms. They should all be made within the walls of Government factories, no clothes should be sent out, none entrusted to contractors; and the whole work ought to be under the constant inspection of medical officers."

Infection is known to cling firmly to woollen and dark-coloured clothes, which are capable of retaining

---

* *Public Health*, by E. A. Parkes, p. 43.

it for a long period. Persons wearing such clothes often convey it from sick rooms into other houses:—

"Woollen clothes are probably the chief media by which animal poisons are carried when they are conveyed in clothes."—Parkes' *Hygiene.*

"Woollen and dark-coloured materials are said to take up the poison (of typhus) most readily."—Robert's *Theory and Practice of Medicine.*

White has always been considered among Zoroastrians as an emblem of purity. "White the similitude of the Mazdayaçnian law."—*K. A.* A white shirt must be worn by the Parsees. All the ceremonies are performed by the Parsee priests in a white dress. The dress of the corpse-bearers is white, and is never worn another time, but soon destroyed.

Typhus fever, scarlatina, and other grave maladies are propagated not only by means of clothes, bedding and furniture, but by letters, books, and even by milk kept in proximity to the sick. The hair and nails have been known to act as carriers of contagious germs. On this account it seems that Zarathustra enjoins the Parsees to bury them. The nails of unclean persons may become the media for the dissemination of the germs of a deadly disease. Though such persons may not contract disease themselves, still they may become its vehicles to others. Very likely Zarathustra perceived the danger attending this form of infection, for in the Avesta we find a repetition of the following verse respecting unclean persons:—" On their nails springs the Drukhs Naçus (devil of destruction)."

The twelfth Fargard of the Vendidad contains

some directions for the purification of the dwelling in which a Zoroastrian dies :—

"When the father dies, or the mother dies, Creator!. How shall I purify the dwellings, how will they become clean?"

"Then answered Ahura-Mazda: Three times let them wash the body, three times let them wash the clothes, three times let them recite the Gâthâs."

Fumigation of the dwelling has also been recommended in Ven. F. viii., v. 7, and other parts of the Zend Avesta.

"They shall fumigate the dwelling with Urvaçna, Vôhu-gaôna, Vôhu-kĕrĕti, Hadhâ-naêpata, and all kinds of sweet-smelling trees."

To check specific diseases prevailing in a building, barrack, or ship, thorough and constant fumigation has been recommended in works on hygiene. Daily experience shows that outbreaks of zymotic diseases occur from specific poisons in the atmosphere, and fumigation is one of the best means for destroying them. Dr. Moore states :—

"In the case of gonorrhœal and other kinds of ophthalmia, it has been frequently remarked that a visit to a ward, where a number of patients are congregated, has been followed by an attack of the malady, even when every care has been taken to avoid coming in contact with the sick, or with any articles near them.

"Thus, latterly in the Orphan Asylum near Prague, an epidemic of ophthalmia broke out, and ninety-two children were attacked. M. Eiselt examined the air with Pouchet's aeroscope, and, in the atmosphere of a ward, where lay a great number of children, a quantity of large pus-cells were found. The cells were noticed on the instrument immediately the air was made to pass through the apparatus.

"In such cases, it may be probable that the pus-globules floating in the air attach themselves to the eyes of healthy individuals, and so excite the disease; but there are other affections which arise from the atmospherical dispersion of the *materies morbi*, and its consequent absorption by the skin, lungs, or alimentary passages. Cholera, yellow fever, malarious fever, influenza, small-pox, plague and the whole of the exanthemata, obviously belong to this class."*

Dr. Moore next discusses the important question of the extension or limits at which the miasm loses the power of exciting disease in a healthy individual :—

" The question naturally arises, at what distance from the bodies of the sick, or from the localities of formation, is the miasm capable of inducing disease ? This can scarcely be reduced to demonstration. Both classes of emanations become fatal, or prove innocuous, according to the extent to which they are diluted by pure air. Miasm may be, roughly speaking, said to diminish as the square of the distance; and, in fresh air, according to Dr. Alison, it does not extend beyond three feet from the patient."

The following passages from the Vendidad will convince our readers that Zarathustra knew the limits at which an individual may approach the localities of the formation of the miasmata, though he is silent respecting the class of diseases which generate them, and the different ways by which they may be communicated to the healthy person :—

The corpse-bearers should sit themselves down three paces away from the pure man, and three paces away from the dead.

The dead body is to be laid in the dwelling thirty paces from the pure man if kept for a longer time than usual.

A woman delivered of a still-born child should keep herself at a distance of thirty steps from the pure man. A woman after having borne a living child

---

* *Health in the Tropics*, by W. J. Moore, p. 25.

should sit three steps remote from the pure man. A person who shall bring her food may approach her to three steps.

It is impossible to avoid the conclusion from the scattered observations by Zarathustra with respect to the treatment of recently delivered women, that some disease of an infectious character must have been prevalent among them. From the foregoing and other passages it will be apparent to the reader that Zarathustra was well acquainted with the risk attending the carriage of the disease by human intercourse, and the means of arresting its progress. If a man wilfully touches a woman recently delivered, or goes and sits down with her, he is considered guilty, and is punished for so doing.

Zarathustra asked Ahura-Mazda : " Creator ! He who with full will pollutes his body with a woman who is affected with marks, signs, and blood, whilst the marks are manifest on her; what is the punishment for this ?"

"Then answered Ahura-Mazda : Let them strike thirty blows with the horse-goad, thirty with Çrāôshô-charana. If he goes (to her) the second time, sits down there the second time, let them strike fifty blows with the horse-goad, fifty with the Çrāôshô-charana. If he goes for the third time, sits down there for the third time, let them strike seventy blows with the horse-goad, seventy with the Çrāôshô-charana. He who lies with a woman who is affected with marks, signs, and blood ; he does no better deed than if he were to burn the unclean body of his own son, and bring the unclean flux to the fire."

The fifth Fargard of the Vendidad contains some rules for the purification of clothes which have come in contact with a woman recently delivered of a still-born child, by whom they may be used, and by whom not, after such purification :—

"Creator! When are these clothes, after cleaning and washing them again, united (with other clothing),* for the Zaota, the Havanan, the Atarevakhsa, the Frabereta, the Aberet, the Açnata, the Raethwiskara, the Çraoshavareza, the priests, the warriors, and the husbandmen?"

"Then answered Ahura-Mazda: These clothes are not again united (*i. e.* to be used) after cleansing and washing, by the Zaota, the Havanan, the Atarevakhsa, the Frabereta, the Aberet, the Açnata, the Raethwiskara, the Çraoshavareza, the priests, the warriors, and the husbandmen. If a woman is suffering menstruation in this Mazdayaçnian dwelling, or if a limb is broken, or the house is stained in consequence of a wound, then this is the bed for it, this is the covering with which they cover, until she brings out her hand with prayer and praise."

What was known twenty-five centuries ago to the Zoroastrians, is beginning to be appreciated at the close of the present century, and yet how many women after child-birth die of puerperal fever annually in Europe from defective sanitation and want of attention to cleanliness? Thousands! From the report issued lately by the Puerperal Fever Committee appointed by the Berlin Obstetrical Society, it appears that 8,872 women die annually of puerperal fever in the Prussian kingdom. Let us hear what Dr. Leishman says of the prevention of puerperal fever to which recently delivered women are liable :—

"It is impossible to exaggerate the importance, in its bearing upon prophylaxis, of the strictest attention to cleanliness on the part

---

* That is, when may they be used again.

of the practitioner, who in an ordinary case should wash his hands not only after but before each examination. Such a precaution would no doubt be scrupulously observed had he just come from a case of scarlatina or erysipelas, or from a *post mortem* examination; but, the more completely the doctrine of septic infection is established, the more clearly does it appear that the great majority of cases of puerperal fever are preventible, and, if so, we may be sure that to act, in every case, as if we had special reasons to fear that we might propagate the disease, is the surest way to reduce the risks to a minimum. For ordinary practice, thorough cleansing with hot water and soap will suffice, and the nail brush should also be used, as below and at the root of the nails are the situations in which septic matters are most likely to be retained. The precaution necessary, where we have any special cause for alarm, consists in a still stricter attention to cleansing the hands, and here, in addition to soap and water, Condy's fluid or carbolic acid should be employed. We must not, however, lose sight of the fact that the finger of the accoucheur is not the only possible conductor of the poison. Unless the nurse directly imports the poison, the fact of her attention being confined to one case at a time renders her less likely to infect a patient than a general practitioner who, in the course of a single day, supposing his obstetric practice to be quite free from fever, may have visited several cases of scarlatina, dressed a wounded limb affected with phlegmonous erysipelas, and performed a *post mortem* examination. But, on the other hand, the nurse in the course of her special duties comes directly in contact with the discharges, so that there is no point of greater importance in the education of these women than the necessity of inculcating strict cleanliness in their own persons as well as in that of their patient. A weak solution of carbolic acid may be habitually employed. Again, the poison may very readily be conveyed by the dress, so that it should be changed where we have previously been in attendance upon a suspicious case. And, in like manner, the linen, napkins, and so forth, are possible vehicles of conveyance; but this, for obvious reasons, is more likely to take place in hospital than in private practice."*

---

* *A System of Midwifery*, by W. Leishman, M.D., pp. 805, 806.

There seems to be but little question that the honour of priority of the discovery belongs to Zarathustra, whose precepts, we regret to say, have been completely misunderstood and disregarded by Parsee youths of trifling attainments.

The seventh Fargard of the Vendidad contains injunctions for the purification of vessels in domestic use, made of gold or silver, which have been polluted by contact with a dead body. It is also enjoined that utensils made of wood and clay are not to be used again, and very rightly so, on account of their porosity.

"Creator! How do the vessels out of which one eats become clean which have been brought to the carcass of a dead dog or man?"

"Then answered Ahura-Mazda: They are clean, O pure Zarathustra! in the following manner: If they are of gold, wash them once with cow's urine, lift them up once from the earth, wash them once with water, then are they clean. If they are of silver, wash them six times with cow's urine, lift them up from the earth six times, wash them six times with water, then are they clean. If they are of earth, wood, or lead, then are they unclean for ever." Ven. F. vii., vv. 183 to 188.

The Parsees have strictly followed the wise rules laid down in their sacred books in laying the bodies of the dead on a flat polished stone in their dwellings, and in carrying them on an iron bier. Porous materials are never used for the purpose, as they become saturated with impurities. Zarathustra asked: "Creator! Where shall we carry the bodies of the dead, O Ahura-Mazda! Where shall we lay them down?"

"Then answered Ahura-Mazda: On the highest place, O holy Zarathustra! On iron, stone, or lead" (inferior metal—*Guj. Tr.*) Ven. F. vi., vv. 92, 93 and 96.

Again, it is declared in the Avesta that the Mazdayaçnians should bring food to a lying-in woman on inferior metals.

"Wherewith shall he bring her food, wherewith shall he bring her fruit?"

"On iron, lead, or the meanest metal." Ven. F. xvi. To keep the water pure and free from pollution is a religious duty entailed upon the Zoroastrians by God, as an action beneficial to mankind.

"The waters praise we, the dropping, flowing, forward-running, the arising from Ahura, the well-working, having good fords, the well-flowing, well-washing, desirable for both worlds." Yaçna xxxviii., vv. 7 to 9.

"I praise the water: Ardvî-çûra, the pure, the full-flowing, healthful; averse to the Daevas, devoted to the faith in Ahura, the praiseworthy for the corporeal world, the worthy of adoration for the corporeal world, the pure for those which further life, the pure for those which further the cattle, the pure for the furtherers of the world, the pure for the furtherers of the kingdom, the pure for the furtherers of the region." Yaçna lxiv., vv. 1 to 6.

If a man who has come in contact with a dead body in a jungle, pollutes water without purification by getting into it, he is, according to the Zoroastrian law, punished with four hundred blows with the horse-goad, four hundred with Çrâôshô-charana. Ven. F.

viii. Men who defile water by bringing a dead body to it, are considered unclean for ever.

"Creator! How do those men become clean, O pure Ahura-Mazda! who bring a corpse with dirt to the water or the fire with uncleanness!"

"Then answered Ahura-Mazda. They are unclean, O pure Zarathustra! The wicked who have defiled themselves with corpses are the most helpful to the dog Madhakha; they are most helpful to the drought which destroys the pasture, those who have defiled themselves with corpses; they are most helpful to the winter which the Daevas have created, which kills the dogs, is full of snow, the slowly passing, wounding, evil, wicked-knowing, those who have defiled themselves with corpses; the Drukhs Naçus springs on their nails, then are they unclean for ever." Ven. F. vii., vv. 65 to 71.

The following is the punishment appointed for those through whose negligence water is polluted by any of the bones of a dead person:—

"Creator! If they do not fasten them, and the carnivorous dogs and birds take some of the bones to the water and the trees; what is the punishment for this?"

"Then answered Ahura-Mazda: Strike their sinful bodies two hundred strokes with the horse-goad, two hundred with the Çrãôshô-charana." Ven. F. vi., vv. 98 to 100.

No one will deny the truth of Zarathustra's precepts regarding the sin of polluting water. There are facts which prove the dissemination of certain specific diseases by drinking water. Instances have occurred of typhoid, cholera, &c., which were distinctly traced to the use of water contaminated by the poison of those diseases. Dr. Parkes, in his excellent "Manual of Practical Hygiene," observes:—

1. "An endemic of diarrhœa, *in a community*, is almost always owing either to impure air, impure water, or bad food. If it affects a number of persons suddenly, it is probably owing to one of the two last causes, and, if it extends over many families, almost certainly to water.

2. "Diarrhœa or dysentery, constantly affecting a community, or returning periodically at certain times of the year, is far more likely to be produced by bad water than any other cause.

3. "A very sudden and localised outbreak of either typhoid fever or cholera is almost certainly owing to introduction of the poison by water.

4. "The same fact holds good in cases of malarious fever, and especially if the cases are very grave, a possible introduction by water should be carefully inquired into."

Dr. Moore, in his work entitled "Health in the Tropics," writes:—

"That the germs of cholera may be conveyed through the medium of water there exists, unfortunately, little doubt."

"That impure water has a powerful influence over the intensity of cholera outbreaks is unquestionable. . . . Dr. Sutherland in 'A Report to the Board of Health' states:—'A number of the most severe and fatal outbreaks were referable to no other cause except the state of the water supply,' and this especially where the water was obtained from wells into which the contents of sewers, privies or the drainage of grave-yards had escaped."

"Camp latrines should not be placed on running streams, as the communication of zymotic disease through the medium of water has been so thoroughly proved, that no doubt remains that such a course may be fraught with the greatest danger."

In order not to defile water or eatable things by saliva, the Parsee priest puts a *padan* on the face whilst praying. The Parsees cannot eat or drink out of the same vessel with another who touches it with his lips and tongue, or thrusts his fingers, spoon, or knife into his mouth and back again into the same vessel. The importance of this time-honoured custom is borne out by the testimony of several recent observers. Instances have occurred where some diseases were communicated to the healthy by means of saliva. Drs. Maury and Dulles of Philadelphia have described fourteen cases in which syphilis was communicated by indiscriminate tattooing. The tattooer had suffered from syphilis, and had extensive mucous patches in the mouth. "Whilst tattooing he frequently wetted the needles in his mouth, and, in some cases, he also moistened the pigments (vermillion and Indian ink) with saliva. The details of twenty-two cases, which were thoroughly examined and their histories taken, are minutely recorded by the authors. Special care was taken to exclude the possibility of the syphilis having been acquired in any other way than by the tattooing. In fourteen cases the evidence makes it absolutely certain that this was the mode by which the virus was introduced into the system."*

The *Lancet*, April 6, 1878, under the heading "The Dangers of Bread and Cheese," observes :—

"Some Swiss medical papers have expatiated on the risks attending the sale of bread and cheese. The cheese is generally tasted by means of a knife, which is allowed to touch both the tongue and lips of the purchaser, but is rarely if ever cleaned. The Swiss do not remove the sample from the knife with their fingers, as is the custom in England, but thrust this implement into their mouths and then back again into other cheeses, thus conveying to them a slight

---

* The *Lancet*, March 23, 1878.

THE MEDICAL ART.   189

but possibly dangerous moisture from the mouth. In the bakers' shops the small loaves or rolls are handled over and over again by the customers. The one seeks a soft, the other a hard crust, a new or a stale loaf. A multitude of individuals, who are not generally distinguished for their cleanliness, particularly in respect to their nails where zymotic germs are scarcely exposed to the purifying influence of the air, pressing their thumbs down into a dozen or more rolls before they make a single purchase. Disease could thus be rapidly conveyed from one family to another."

The Avesta abounds in passages directed against the nails of unclean persons. "On their nails springs the Drukhs Naçus."

The different methods of disposal of the dead were not overlooked by Zarathustra. He was well acquainted with the danger to the public health arising from the burning and burial of the dead. The decomposition of the body buried is very slow, and dangerous to the health of the people. If the body is burned the same process   and less detrimental to the public health i   ed. Zarathustra saw that both wer   v principles; hence he cons   t that admit of no

" Creator! If the Mazdayaçnians going afoot, running, riding, or driving, come to a fire in which dead bodies are burning, where they are burning or cooking dead bodies, how shall the Mazdayaçnians conduct themselves ?"

"Then answered Ahura-Mazda: He shall beat on this (fire)* which is roasting the bodies. They shall beat it.† They shall drag away the dead.". . . . . Ven. F. viii., vv. 229 to 236.

Zarathustra even ordains punishment for those who defile the earth by throwing about one of the smallest bones of a dead man:—

" Creator! He who throws away the bone of a dead dog or a dead man, were it only so large as the top joint of the little finger, and there melts out upon it (the earth) grease and marrow ; what is the punishment for this ?"

"Then answered Ahura-M   rike thirty strokes with the horse   Çraôshô-charana."

The pur   ut the largest

                                  lead
                                  size
                                  t is

                                  'e
                                  '.

tisement enjoined for throwing about a corpse is most rigid :—

"Creator! He who throws away the whole body of a dead dog or a dead man, and grease or marrow runs out there; what is the punishment for this?"

"Then answered Ahura-Mazda: Strike a thousand blows with the horse-goad, a thousand with the Çraôshô-charana."

Latest researches establish beyond doubt that the great truths advanced by Zarathustra with regard to the burying and burning of the dead are based on sound principles of health. The late Dr. Parkes, Professor of Military Hygiene in the Army Medical School, Netley, says :—

"Burying in the ground appears certainly the most insanitary plan of the three methods. The air over cemeteries is constantly contaminated, and water (which may be used for drinking) is often highly impure. Hence, in the vicinity of graveyards two dangers to the population arise, and in addition, from time to time, the disturbance of an old graveyard has given rise to disease. It is a matter of notoriety that the vicinity of graveyards is unhealthy."

"It is true that the impurities in burning can be well diffused into the atmosphere at large, and would not add to it any perceptible impurity. But if the burning is not complete, fœtid organic matters are given off, which hang cloud-like in the air, and may be perceptible, and even hurtful."*

The same author in another little work on Public Health writes :—

"The law of England now allows no burial grounds in large cities, nor burial under churches, and consequently cemeteries are provided at convenient distances from towns. These cemeteries ought to have a dry soil, so that the ground water shall never rise high enough

---

* *Manual of Practical Hygiene*, by E. A. Parkes, M.D., F.R.S. Second edition, pp. 475, 476.

to meet the corpse, or to float it up in the vault, as sometimes happens; there should be good drainage, and the water should not run into any watercourse from which drinking-water is taken . . .

"Bodies decay in very various times according to soil, access of air, amount of pressure, &c. In some cases a corpse may be destroyed in three years, but as a rule, when ground has to be used over again, a period of from five to thirty years is allowed in different countries before re-interments."*

In our age of sanitary improvement, experience has shown that the air over cemeteries is always more or less contaminated by effluvia arising from the slow decomposition of bodies. The breaking out of a zymotic disease from the opening of a burial ground or cemetery, and the danger to the health of the people caused thereby, cannot be doubted. Dr. Moore observes:—

"It may seem superfluous to state that a barrack or hospital should not be built over an old grave-yard, or on or near ground charged with organic matter."

"Dr. Gibb informs us that an epidemic of small-pox was the result of the opening of a cemetery at Quebec, where, years since, a large number of patients, the victims of variola, had been buried."

"Some few years ago a party of prisoners were employed making a road in the Guntoor district, and in cutting away the soil came upon a number of remains of persons who had died of cholera in the famine year of 1838. The disease broke out with great violence amongst these workmen."

"A number of coolies, employed on railway works in the neighbourhood of Salem, in cutting through an old burial ground, came upon a spring of apparently pure water. Many who drank of this water were seized a few hours after with cholera of a very severe type."

"Care should be taken that camps are not pitched on old graveyards, or over ground charged with organic matter . . . . . . When the first division of the army arrived at Varna, 13th June, 1854, they were healthy, till they encamped at Aladyn. There they

---

* *Public Health*, by E. A. Parkes, pp. 46, 47.

unfortunately took the same site which the light division had formerly occupied, and then cholera, preceded by diarrhœa, broke out.

" On the 20th October, 1854, the battle of the Alma was fought, and afterwards the 4th Division encamped on ground recently occupied by the Russians ; cholera also raged in this camp."*

The question of the best way in which dead bodies are to be disposed of has been much discussed of late. Burial in the earth gives rise to nuisance, and is considered injurious to health. Cremation is less hurtful when properly managed, and as a matter of health is preferable to burial. What then is the best method of disposing of the dead, which ought to be wholly innocuous to the public health? Let us examine the practice of exposure of the dead on elevated sites to the vultures and other carrion birds. The Zoroastrian religion is perhaps the only one which enjoins that their dead bodies should be exposed on the tops of rocks in a tower, there to be consumed by vultures. The practice, though revolting to those unaccustomed to it, is the best and most sensible when looked at in a sanitary point of view. The Dakhmas or "Towers of Silence" are built on the tops of hills remote from a populous locality. The cost of building one of the largest in Bombay was more than two lakhs of rupees. The construction of the Dakhma or Parsee "Tower of Silence" is thus described by Prof. Monier Williams in a letter that appeared in the London *Times* of the 28th January 1876:—

" Imagine a round column or massive cylinder 12 or 14 feet high, and at least 90 feet in diameter, built throughout of solid stone, except in the centre, where a well, 10 feet deep and 45 in diameter,

---

* Moore's *Health in the Tropics*, pp. 124, 188, 193, 262.

leads down to an excavation under the masonry, containing four drains at right angles to each other, terminated by holes filled with charcoal. Round the upper surface of this solid circular cylinder, and completely hiding the interior from view, is a stone parapet 14 feet in height. This it is which, when viewed from the outside, appears to form one piece with the solid stone work, and being, like it, covered with chunam, gives the whole the appearance of a low tower. The upper surface of the solid stone column is divided into 72 compartments, or open receptacles, radiating like the spokes of a wheel from the central wall, and arranged in three concentric rings, separated from each other by narrow ridges of stone, which are grooved to act as channels for conveying all moisture from the receptacles into the well and into the lower drains. It should be noted by-the-bye, that the number ' 3 ' is emblematical of Zoroaster's three precepts, and the number ' 72 ' of the chapters of Yasna— a portion of the Zend-Avesta.

"Each circle of open stone coffins is divided from the next by a pathway, so that there are three circular pathways, the last encircling the central well, and these three pathways are crossed by another pathway conducting from the solitary door which admits the corpse-bearers from the exterior. In the outermost circle of the stone coffins are placed the bodies of males, in the middle those of females, and in the inner and smallest circle, nearest the well, those of children."

The body after having been laid in one of the open stone receptacles is consumed by vultures within fifteen minutes, leaving nothing behind but a skeleton exposed to the elements. Any one acquainted with the two systems, viz., that of burial and of exposure, cannot fail to see the superiority of the latter. The method of interment is decent in appearance but unscientific; that of exposure, though almost revolting to the sensibilities of nations who bury their dead in the ground, is scientific. Suppose we are dealing with two corpses exposed to our view in a state of decomposition, the question is—will the one surrounded with innumerable worms, or the other which is rapidly devoured by vultures, be a nuisance prejudicial to health? We may also reasonably ask which of the two is preferable? Prof. Monier Williams justly observes:—" I could not help thinking that, however much such a system may shock our European feelings and ideas, yet our own method of interment, if regarded from a Parsee point of view, may possibly be equally revolting to Parsee sensibilities. The exposure of the decaying body to the assaults of innumerable worms may have no terrors for us, because our survivors do not see the assailant; but let it be borne in mind that neither are the Parsee survivors permitted to look at the swoop of the Heaven-sent birds. Why, then, should we be surprised if they prefer the more rapid to the more lingering operation? and which of the two systems, they may reasonably ask, is more defensible on sanitary grounds?" In Dr. Parkes' Practical Hygiene we find the remarkable statement that the best way in which dead bodies are to be disposed of is by burying them in the sea. "Accustomed as we are," he says, "to land burial, there is something almost revolting, at first sight, at the idea of making the sea the sepulchre, or of burning the dead, yet the eventual dispersion of our frames is the same in all cases; and it is probably a matter merely of custom which makes us think that there is a want of affection, or of care, if the bodies of the dead are not suffered to repose in the earth that bore them. . . . . . In reality neither affection nor religion can be outraged by any manner of disposal of the dead, which is done with proper solemnity and respect to the earthly dwelling-place of our friends. The question should be placed entirely on sanitary grounds, and we shall then judge it rightly." Again, this enthusiastic partisan of sea burial writes :—" In the burial at sea, some of the body would go at once to support other forms of life more rapidly than in the case of land burial, and without the danger of evolution of hurtful products, and in the vast abyss of the ocean the remains would rest until the trumpet shall sound which shall order the sea to give up its dead !"

Had Dr. Parkes been acquainted with the Parsee plan of disposal of the dead, he would have very likely preferred it to sea burial, and written in favour of it. However, the agitation and discussion of the question of sea burial is an important step towards deciding the best plan of disposing of the dead; for we are already informed of "a new method of inhumation of bodies" by Dr. Panizza of Barcelona, in which the bodies are placed in open cemeteries exposed to the air, and covered with animal charcoal. In the lapse of time, with the progress of sanitary knowledge, the day will come when exposure of the dead bodies on the tops of hills in properly constructed towers will supersede burning and burial in all the civilized countries of the world, and sickness and mortality from zymotic diseases will then be mitigable to a very great extent.

In conclusion, we may hope that the contents of this chapter will be acceptable to a large circle of Parsee readers, and will help others better qualified to devote their leisure hours to this important subject, which demands the most attentive consideration.

The shameless indifference of a few imperfectly trained Parsees and their wilful blindness in not following the minute observances in their sacred writings are to be deplored, especially at a time when the nature of contagia, and their mode of action upon the system, are questions which have of late engaged the attention of many eminent men of the profession. There is no doubt that many contagious diseases are of foreign climates, some are frequently met with in Europe and America, and others in Asia. But this should not deter the most sceptical Parsee from observing the rules laid down in his religion for preventing the spread of contagious diseases, which are certainly not intended for any particular climate.

CHAPTER IX.

Rome without Physicians throughout the Republic—Opposition to Greek Philosophy and Physic—Archagathus—Medicine practised by Slaves—Asclepiades—His simplicity of Treatment—His Inventions—His Theory of Disease—His Death—Themison—State of Medicine during the Empire—Celsus—Survey of his treatise *De Medicina*—Pliny—Thessalus—Clinical instruction—Andromachus—Aretæus—Character of his writings—Dioscorides—Cælius Aurelianus—Galen—His wanderings—His knowledge of Anatomy—Of Physiology—Of Pathology—Active Treatment —Influence of his writings—Oribasius—Ætius—Alexander Trallianus—Paulus Ægineta.

Alexandria flourished for nearly three centuries under the Ptolemies, when the Romans, who were for a long time extending their conquests in every direction, besieged it B. C. 48. Ptolemy made a brave resistance, but his army was defeated by the Romans under Julius Cæsar, and he himself was slain in the engagement. It was at this time that the library of Bruchion, which contained 400,000 volumes, was accidentally burnt to ashes. The library of Serapion escaped destruction, but after some centuries was burnt by order of Khalif Omar. After the conquest of Alexandria by Cæsar its schools of medicine still maintained a high degree of reputation, and for many centuries sent forth a succession of physicians to almost every country of the civilized world.

In the early ages of the Republic the Romans,

being continually engaged in wars with foreign nations, had neither opportunity nor taste for literature, science or arts. About a hundred and fifty years before the Christian era philosophy first attracted their share of attention. A few Greek philosophers who were banished from their native country, and had emigrated to different parts of Italy, diffused a taste for learning among the Roman youth. But foreign philosophy soon met with opposition from the older citizens, and the Greek philosophers were banished from Rome by a decree passed by the senators. Cato says of the Greek philosophers and physicians—"Whenever that nation shall bestow its literature upon Rome, it will mar everything, and that, all the sooner, if it sends its physicians among us."* Philosophy did not gain a firm footing till the arrival of an Athænian embassy at Rome. It also received a fresh impulse from a Roman citizen named Lucullus. He was the first Roman who during his stay in Greece had the opportunity of becoming acquainted with the learning and philosophy of the Greeks, and upon his return to Rome inspired his countrymen with a love of learning, and instituted a library which soon became a resort of learned men.

In medicine the Romans were first instructed by the Etruscans, and afterwards by the Greeks. We are told that throughout the Republic, Rome was without physicians, and that medicine was practised by the priests and slaves, or by anybody at his own risk and peril. A person of high rank, who ignorantly administered a remedy that caused the death of a

---

* Pliny's *Natural History*, book XXIX., chap. 7.

patient, was punished with exile, while one of low rank was punished with death.

Epidemic diseases were attributed by the Romans to the anger of the gods. When a pestilence raged in Rome the Sibiline books were consulted, and by their counsel the worship of Æsculapius was introduced at Rome B. C. 293:—

> "A wasting plague infected Latium's skies;
> Pale, bloodless looks were seen, with ghastly eyes;
> The dire disease's marks each visage wore,
> And the pure blood was changed to putrid gore:
> In vain were human remedies applied;
> In vain the power of healing herbs was tried."

The Romans, tired of the havoc performed by the pestilence, first implored the aid of Apollo, who advised them to consult his son Æsculapius:—

> "The assistance, Roman, which you here implore,
> Seek from another and a nearer shore;
> Relief must be implored, and succour won,
> Not from Apollo, but Apollo's son;
> My son to Latium borne, shall bring redress,
> Go with good omens, and expect success."

Ambassadors from Rome immediately sailed to Epidaurus, where Æsculapius had a temple dedicated to him. The god of health, moved with the afflictions of the Romans, accompanied the ambassadors in the form of a serpent. The ship at length arrived in the Tiber with her "serpentine god," who was received with joyful acclamations by the people:

> "The world's great mistress, Rome, receives him now;
> On the mast's top reclined he waves his brow,
> And from that height surveys the great abodes
> And mansions, worthy of residing gods,

> The land, a narrow neck, itself extends,
> Round which his course the stream divided bends;
> The stream's two arms, on either side, are seen,
> Stretch'd out in equal length; the land between,
> The isle, so call'd from hence derives its name:
> 'Twas here the salutary serpent came;
> Nor sooner has he left the Latian pine,
> But he assumes again his form divine,
> And now no more the drooping city mourns,
> Joy is again restored, and health returns."*

From the time of Julius Cæsar the profession was held in better repute. He honoured those who practised in Rome with the right of citizenship. During the Empire worthy practitioners received the title of Archiater or Physician-in-Chief. Military medical service was first organised by Augustus. Even in the reign of that monarch slaves were not prohibited to practise medicine, but were in great demand.

In the latter period of the Republic, Rome was visited by a physician named Archagathus. He was a Peloponnesian by birth, and is said to have been the first foreign surgeon who settled at Rome in the time of the Consuls Æmilius and Livius to practise medicine and surgery, B.C. 219. He was first received by the Romans with high esteem, and a public subscription was raised to buy a shop for him. Shortly after he received from them the title of Vulnerarius or wound-curer. But he soon incurred the displeasure of the people, for his practice consisted in the frequent use of the knife, cautery and caustics. He was afterwards so much disliked that he received from them the nickname of *Carnifex*, or public executioner.

---

* *Ovid*, translated by Dryden, Pope, and others, vol II., p. 189.

After Archagathus the knowledge and practice of medicine continued to be much in the same state for a century. In Rome at this period no one remained who deserved to be called a physician. The knowledge of medicine was confined to the priests and slaves, and was disgraced by the intermixture of superstition. Among the slaves who practised medicine, Antonius Musa and Scribonius Largus are celebrated names. The former was physician to the Emperor Augustus, whom he rescued from a dangerous malady by means of cold baths and the eating of lettuces, which were prohibited by the emperor's own physician C. Æmilius. Musa was handsomely rewarded for his services, permitted to wear a gold ring, and exempted from taxes. A statue was erected in his honour by the Roman people, and placed near that of Æsculapius. He was a zealous methodic, and is supposed to be the author of "De Herba Botanica" and "Detuenda Valetudine." Scribonius Largus, who lived in the reign of Claudius, deserves notice chiefly for a few improvements which he made in pharmacy.

We should not omit to mention that after Archagathus most of those who obtained some reputation among the Romans were either Greeks or Asiatics. Rome, during neither the Republic nor Empire, produced hardly a medical man of genius. In fact, with the exception of Celsus hardly an individual can be named who acquired any eminence in the art of medicine.

Next after Archagathus should be mentioned Asclepiades, a native of Bythinia, who, about a century before Christ, and in the time of Pompey the Great, visited Rome, where he taught rhetoric, but with little or no success. He next applied himself to the study of medicine, and after practising for a short time in Alexandria returned to Rome as a legitimate practitioner of medicine, and settled there for the remainder of his life. He was a man of some learning and talents. As a zealous, attentive and successful practitioner he was much esteemed and honoured by the Romans. It is told of him that he once "breaking in upon the funeral ceremony saved the life of a man who was actually placed on the funeral pile." Asclepiades belonged to the sect of the Empirics, and chiefly distinguished himself by his opposition to the principles and practices of his predecessors, and in particular attacked and strenuously declaimed against the writings of Hippocrates. He condemned the use of blood-letting, purgatives, and other powerful drugs in the treatment of diseases. He says that the chief duty of a physician is to cure safely, speedily and pleasantly. *"Tuto cito et jucunde."* His practice was very simple, and we are informed that he paid more attention to diet, friction, bathing, exercise, and the liberal allowance of wine, than to the administration of active remedies. He said that exercise was "the common aid of physic." The first attempt at treating some disorders by the shower-bath was made by him. He was the inventor of Lacti Pensiles, or swinging beds for the sick, and made use of the trumpet for relieving nervous pains. We are told that he was the first to divide diseases into the two important classes of acute and chronic, and to propose the operation of bronchotomy. " In his physiological principles," says Dr. Bostock, " Asclepiades is said to have been a follower of Epicurus, and to have adopted his doctrine of atoms and pores, on which he attempted to build a new theory of disease, by supposing that all morbid action might be reduced into obstruction of the pores and irregular distribution of the atoms. This theory he accommodated to his division of diseases, the acute being supposed to depend essentially upon a constriction of the pores, or an obstruction of them by a superfluity of atoms; the chronic upon a relaxation of the pores or a deficiency of the atoms."[*] Mithridates having heard of his fame, invited him at his court to appoint him as his household physician, but Asclepiades, unwilling to leave Rome, refused his request, and dedicated his works to that monarch as a mark of respect. The death of this celebrated practitioner of Rome was peculiar. It is said that "he, fearing lest he should fall sick, and so lose his credit, threw himself downstairs, and died." Asclepiades is accused of having vilified the principles and practices of the ancients in order to obtain popularity. We are inclined to believe that he is unduly blamed by some writers because he rejected blood-letting and the use of virulent drugs; in short, he did not servilely follow his predecessors in practising antiquated theories, but mainly relied on diet and regimen, and the employment of simple remedies. It is a well known fact that in medicine, as in other sciences and arts, as soon as one changes from one doctrine to another, or points out old esta-

---

[*] *History of Medicine,* prefixed to the Encyclopædia of Practical Medicine, vol. I.

blished errors, some pretended advocates of liberality of thought immediately rise up in arms and charge the reformer with heresy.

Themison was another of the ancient celebrated Greek physicians. He was a native of Laodicea, and lived in the first century of the Christian era. He was a pupil of Asclepiades, whose practice he followed most particularly in his early age, but afterwards zealously upheld the principles of the methodics. He is said to have been the first person to bring into public notice the use of leeches. He was the author of several works, none of which is extant.

Aurelius Cornelius Celsus was one of the most eminent of the ancient authors, and the first native of Rome who acquired a considerable degree of celebrity as a writer on medicine over any of his countrymen. Very little is known of his history. It seems probable that he lived at Rome in the time of Augustus and Tiberius. As Pliny has not mentioned the name of Celsus in his sketch of the history of medicine, it is probable that both were contemporaries. Doubts have been entertained whether he practised medicine, or studied it as a part of philosophy. If we peruse his writings we shall perceive that he very probably practised physic. But his fame rests chiefly on his medical writings, which we believe are at this day studied by the students of medicine in London who prepare themselves for examination at Apothecaries' Hall. The treatise on medicine "De Medicina" in eight books is a work of great research, and is still read with admiration for its intrinsic excellence.

Book i.—The author begins with a short sketch of the history of medicine from the time of Æsculapius to his own, and condemns in strong terms the practice of Herophilus and Erasistratus of dissecting criminals alive as both cruel and useless. "Nothing is more foolish," says he, "than to think that a man has been so in his life-time as he is found when he is dying or already dead."* He next ably discusses the tenets of the rival sects of the Dogmatists or Rationalists, the Empirics, and the Methodics, and admits the uncertainty of the medical art, as will appear from the following passages :—

"Physic is a conjectural art, but such as neither conjecture nor experience itself can make always successful."†

"He that has been cured with the usually successful medicines, has by the contrary ones been effectually restored."‡

In selecting a physician, he says, "you ought to prefer a physician that is your friend, to a stranger, if their knowledge is equal."‡ The subjects of exercise and diet are next taken up :—

"A sound, healthy and active man (if he is at his own liberty) ought not to confine himself to any rules, neither has he any need of the physician or the quack. He ought to lead a various course of life, be sometimes in the country, sometimes in town, but yet oftener in the country; he ought to sail, hunt, sometimes rest, but oftener be in exercise; since laziness slackens and dulls the body, but labour strengthens and makes it firm; the former hastens old age, the latter prolongs youth."§

"Too lazy a life should be avoided, for there may happen a necessity to work."‖

---

* *Sentences of Celsus*, translated by Sir Conrad Sprengell, Kt., p. 290.
† Ibid., p. 292.   ‡ Ibid., p. 296.
§ Ibid., p. 297.   ‖ Ibid., p. 308.

"Sweat ought for the most part to be the end of exercise, or certainly a lassitude, which may be on this side (not amounting to) fatigue."*

"We ought to know that a draught of cold drink is very pernicious to him that has worked himself into a sweat ; and likewise hurtful to those whose sweat has ceased after being fatigued with a journey."†

He then lays down some general rules of diet :—

"Too great fulness is never profitable. Too much abstinence is often prejudicial. But intemperance is always better in drink than in meat."‡

"We must take care that in the time of health we do not lavishly consume and destroy those things which should be our defence against diseases."§

"Neither is it good to eat too much after long fasting, nor to fast too long after much eating."||

Book ii.—A portion of this book is devoted to the consideration of the different seasons of the year and their influence upon the health and age of the people, together with the diseases most prevalent in them :—

"The spring time is most wholesome ; next to that is the winter ; the summer is most dangerous ; but the autumn worst of all. And as for seasons, those are the best that are the most constant, whether hot or cold ; and the worst are those that are most changeable ; and hence it is that the autumn is pernicious to so many."¶

"Clear days are the most wholesome ; rainy weather is better than that which is only cloudy and foggy. In the winter such days are best as are without wind ; in summer such as are accompanied with a westerly wind."**

"The winter is the greatest enemy to old, the summer to young people."††

---

* *The Eight Books of Celsus*, literally translated by J. W. Underwood, vol. I., p. 42.
† Sprengell's *Celsus*, p. 309. ‡ Ibid., p. 303.
§ Ibid., p. 300. || Ibid., p. 306.
¶ Ibid., p. 318. ** Ibid., p. 319. †† Ibid., p. 322.

The diseases peculiar to all ages are next enumerated:—

"The middle age is most safe, which is infested neither by the heat of youth, nor by the cold of old age. Old age lies opened (exposed) more to long (chronic) diseases, youth to acute."*

Old people, he says, are subject to urinary difficulties, dyspnœa, pains of the joints and of the kidneys, paralysis, nightly watchings, and chronic diseases of the eyes. "The fat generally are suffocated by acute diseases and by difficulty of breathing, and often die suddenly." Youth is subject to acute diseases, epilepsy, consumption, cholera, insanity, and spitting of blood. Children are most exposed to diarrhœa, convulsions, aphthæ, vomiting, purulent discharge from the ear, and scrofula. After thus enumerating the diseases to which children are most liable, he goes on to say:—

"If any kinds of diseases have fallen upon an infant, and have been ended neither by puberty nor by the first connexions, nor in a woman by the first monthly (courses), for the most part they are long; yet more often childish diseases which have remained very long are terminated (at that period).†

The author next carefully lays down some general rules of prognosis in fevers. He has treated the subject so admirably that it is our opinion no physician of the present day can excel him in this respect. He carefully drew his rules of prognosis in fevers by observing the position and movements of the sick while asleep and awake, the countenance, the respiration, the temperature, the various secretions and excretions of the body, &c. Sudden emaciation,

---
* Underwood's *Celsus*, p. 75.   † Ibid., p. 82.

hurried breathing, delirium in the very beginning of the fever, cold feet and hands (the abdomen being hot), shiverings after a sweat, sordes, black vomitings, and dark-coloured and offensive urine, are considered the worst signs. But if along with these we observe the following appearances, death is almost certain:—" Acute nostrils, the temples having sunk, hollow eyes, the ears cold and languid, and gently turned in the lowest parts ; the skin of the forehead hard and stretched, the colour (complexion) either black or very pale."* If besides these the following symptoms show themselves, death is near at hand. Intolerance of light, eyes half closed, pale or distorted lips and nostrils, loss of sight and hearing, sinking towards the foot of the bed, picking up of the bed-clothes, cold extremities, frequent gapings, chatterings of the teeth, a constant sleep, unconsciousness, pale nails and fingers, a sudden dryness, paleness, or lividity of a long standing ulcer, inability to swallow, convulsions, &c. We will not weary our readers with all the favourable symptoms mentioned by Celsus.

In the following sentences the author expresses his belief in the healing power of nature and the pernicious effects of physic when administered to the healthy :—

"We ought to know that it is nature that performs the cure, the art administers the instruments of it."†

"Physic is not always good for the sick, but is always hurtful to the healthy."‡

The above passages are worthy the consideration of those dishonest practitioners who for the sake of

---

* Underwood's *Celsus*, vol. I., pp. 93, 94.
† Sprengell's *Celsus*, p. 332.   ‡ Ibid., p 342.

a trifling gain undermine the health of persons who seek their advice for complaints which do not exist in their bodies. But the doctors are not alone to be blamed; the patients themselves have a share in the destruction of their own health. There are persons who have been known to consume medicine almost daily; some through ignorance and vanity, others to excite the sympathy of their friends and relations.

Book iii.—The author commences with a few remarks on the nature and dietetic treatment of acute and chronic diseases. A person suffering from acute disease is to be fed sparingly, and from chronic plentifully. "Rest and abstinence," he says, "are the best of all remedies, and abstinence alone cures without any danger."

A portion of the treatise contains observations on fevers and their nature and treatment. The time when food and drink ought to be given most conveniently to a person suffering from fever, together with their quantity, quality, and frequency, is discussed at some length :—

" The morning time is for the most part more remiss (easier) to the sick, some think (food) ought to be given then. But if it answers (succeeds) it ought to be given not because it is morning but because there is a remission to the sick."*

In selecting the proper time for food and drink he cautions physicians not to be deceived by the pulse, for he says:—

" We give the most credit to the pulse, although deceitful, and not to be relied on; because it beats faster or slower according to the sex, age, and nature of bodies."†

---

* Underwood's *Celsus*, vol. 1., p. 216.
† Sprengell's *Aphorisms of Celsus*, p. 359.

Celsus also knew perfectly well that exercise, fear, anger and other passions of the mind excite the pulse, and thus advises physicians :—

"An experienced physician should not as soon as he enters go instantly to feel the patient's pulse; but let him first sit down with a cheerful countenance, and ask him how he finds himself; and if he finds that he is under any fear or uneasy apprehensions, let him endeavour to hearten him by some plausible discourse, and then he may proceed to feel the patient's pulse."*

Before prescribing nourishment, Celsus attached great importance to the strength, age and habit of persons laid up with fever, for he says :—

"One thing to be always observed is that the physician should consider the strength of the patient, which when it abounds he ought to weaken by abstinence; if any weakness is to be feared he must allow meat, for it is his duty that he neither load his patient with superfluous matter, nor weaken him too much by hunger."†

"Nor, by Hercules, is it sufficient (for) the physician to look to only the fevers themselves, but also the habit (condition) of the whole body, and to direct the treatment to it, whether strength abounds, or is wanting, or some other affections intervene."‡

Children, he says, ought not to be treated as adults, neither are they to be incautiously bled, purged, nor tormented with hunger or thirst.

Delirium coming on in fever is next brought into notice and its treatment laid down. He says that delirium, although a serious symptom in fever, is not always dangerous, and that sleep is particularly necessary to those suffering from it :—

"Phrenetics can hardly be brought to sleep tho' it is very necessary for them; for it is by that they are mostly restored."§

---

* Sprengell's *Aphorisms of Celsus*, p. 360. † Ibid., p. 355.
‡ Underwood's *Celsus*, vol. I., p. 220.
§ Sprengell's *Aphorisms of Celsus*, p. 374.

The remaining portion of the book is devoted to the subjects of insanity, dropsy, consumption, epilepsy, jaundice, elephantiasis, apoplexy, paralysis, &c. Speaking of consumption, he says that it is a very dangerous disease, most common between the ages of eighteen and thirty-five. He recommends long sailing, change of climate, carriage exercise, milk diet, meal mixed with suet and afterwards boiled, &c. If these means fail, and the body becomes more wasted, then he says "there is need for stronger aids." The "stronger aids" consisted in searing with red-hot iron the parts under the chin, on the throat, on both sides of the chest and below the shoulder blades. Celsus is scarcely to be blamed on this account when we know that such a rude and cruel operation is practised even by a few enlightened practitioners in our *age of progress*. As for epilepsy, he says that it is more common in males than in females. As precautionary measures he advises those affected with it to guard against a precipice, bath, fire, and all calefacient things; also to avoid the sun, cold, wine, venery, anxiety, &c. It is his belief that the disease often disappears on the appearance of menses in females, and at the age of puberty or first connections in young men. His method of treating the disease is unnecessarily severe. Blood-letting, scarifications, cupping, purgatives, and red-hot iron, to evacuate the pernicious humours, are the weapons he recommends in this distressing malady; and to complete the cure, to drink the warm blood of a recently slain gladiator! He next comes to the subject of jaundice, called the "royal disease." Fever supervening on jaundice is considered dangerous, especially when there is hardness of the right side of the præcordia, but jaundice coming on after the seventh day of fever is safe " provided the præcordia being soft." A jaundiced patient, he says, should have "a more ornamented bed and chamber, with sport, with jest, with games, with frolic, by which (things) the mind might be exhilarated." On this account, he observes, jaundice was called by the ancients the " royal disease."

Book iv.—This book is devoted to the consideration of a few internal diseases. It opens with an enumeration of the internal viscera of the human body, together with their respective positions. His description of the symptoms of diseases, though brief, is accurate, and shows an acute power of observation. The treatment laid down in some diseases is judicious, and reflects credit upon the author. In the treatment of others he servilely follows Hippocrates in his doctrine of humours by tormenting the sound neighbour of a diseased part, in the same way as Diocles recommends, in his epistle to King Antigonus, to gargle the mouth with marjoram tea for headaches in order to evacuate the unhealthy humours from the head!

Book v.—This book, devoted to pharmaceutical preparations and their uses, to wounds, and to antidotes against poisonous substances, is fairly written. Celsus, although admitting the utility of medicines in a great number of diseases, prefers Asclepiades' method of curing in some by regulating the diet as most beneficial. " It is the business of a quack," he says, " to magnify the smallest matter, that he may be thought to have performed miraculous cures."

Celsus hints that injuries of the cranium at the base and the spinal marrow, wounds of the heart, small intestines, kidney, and large blood-vessels around the fauces, are fatal. Persons wounded in the lungs, liver, membrane of the brain, spleen, large intestines, womb, and bladder, seldom recover. Wounds inflicted in the arm-pit, in the popliteal space, in the joints, and in the course of large blood-vessels, are dangerous. "The safest wound of all is that which is in the flesh." An incised or straight wound, he says, is better than a contused or curved wound, and adds:—

"A boy or young man is sooner cured than an old man; one that is healthy, than one that is weak; one that is moderately slender or full, than one that is immoderately so; a sound habit of body, than a corrupt one; one that is used to exercise, than an inactive lazy person; a sober temperate man, than one that is addicted to drinking and venery."*

The danger from loss of blood and inflammation after the infliction of a wound is distinctly stated. The treatment of hæmorrhage by plugging, cold water, vinegar, pressure, "ligature of the veins in two places about that which has been struck," and cautery, is described, together with the after-treatment. Any foreign body or clots of blood are to be removed from a wound before sewing it. If the wound is gaping, *clasps* are to be put on to bring the edges together. If both are inadmissible, either a sponge dipped in vinegar, wine, or cold water, or plaster is to be applied and afterwards bandaged. The danger of gangrene

---

* Sprengell's *Aphorisms of Celsus*, p. 394.

following tight bandages is noticed. For the treatment of hæmorrhage he advocates the use of wine internally :—

"And many also dying during (fainting) out of a flow forth of blood are to be refreshed with wine before any treatment; which wine is otherwise most hostile to a wound."*

The author next lays down some general rules of prognosis. Much swelling of a wound is a token of severe inflammation and is dangerous, but when there is no swelling at all, it is a token of the death of the part, and is most dangerous. Further on he writes :—

"That fever is dangerous and pernicious, which either happens even upon a slight wound, or continues after the inflammation is over, or causes a delirium."†

"A bilious vomit, which proceeds not voluntarily or immediately after a wound, or while the inflammation continues, is an ill sign only in those whose nerves or nervous parts are wounded."‡

"If a wound is either livid, black, or of a various colour, we must know it is an ill sign."§

"A white or red wound is the best."

The danger of erysipelas and gangrene supervening upon wounds is pointed out. Erysipelas of the head and neck is considered most dangerous. The causes of gangrene are violent inflammation, extreme heat or cold, and tight bandaging. It also occurs in old age and to persons of bad constitution. The disease is not considered very difficult of cure if it begins in a youth, if the muscles and nerves are healthy or but slightly affected, and if it is circumscribed. If the disease extends notwithstanding the

---

* Underwood's *Celsus*, vol. II., p. 87.
† Sprengell's *Aphorisms of Celsus*, p. 396.
‡ Ibid., p. 397. § Ibid., p. 398.

excision or burning of the part, then there is no chance of saving the limb. "There is," he says, "the wretched but only remedy of cutting off the limb, which dies by little and little, that the other part of the body may be safe." Fever, delirium, and an irritable stomach in gangrene are fatal signs, and "most die under a cold sweat."

Book vi.—Nearly the whole of this book is occupied with diseases of the scalp, eyes, ear, nose, mouth, &c. and does not merit notice.

Book vii.—This treats of surgery. Here, Celsus again speaks of the uncertainty of the medical art, and contends that as the same medicines often prove salutary, and often fail in a given disease, it is doubtful whether the restoration to health be attributed to them or to the favourable constitution of the patient. He does not stop here, but adds that health is often restored without medicines; that the sick who are in vain drugged for a long time sometimes recover their health when all the medicines are discontinued; that the diseased eyes being "harassed a long time by physicians, sometimes become healthy without these (medicines)." These words of an ancient eminent author, given out with such frankness, should put to shame some of those disreputable practitioners who, to earn their maintenance, entail a great amount of misery and suffering upon their credulous patients.

A surgeon, says Celsus, should possess the following qualifications:—

"A surgeon ought to be a young or middle-aged man, of a strong, steady and never-trembling hand; as ready with the left hand as with the right; of a piercing clear eye; he must be of an undaunted courage, and unmerciful; fully resolved to go through with the cure he has undertaken; unmoved at the cries of his patient, lest he either make greater haste than is convenient, or cut less than is necessary. He must in short do everything without the least appearing motion or concern at the complaint of his patient."

Sprains, abscesses and fistulæ, and the modes of extracting different kinds of weapons from the body, are first brought into notice. Diseases of the eye are next considered, and their surgical treatment accurately explained. The operations for the removal of pterygium and staphyloma are minutely described. The operation for the depression of cataract is described with precision. The patient, he says, should be seated opposite the light, his head and eye steadied by an assistant, a bandage being applied to the other eye. The surgeon should sit a little higher in front of him. If it is the right eye the operation should be performed by the left hand, and if left by the right hand. A sharp needle is then to be introduced into the sclerotic midway between the cornea and outer corner of the eye. When it enters into an empty space, nothing, he says, resists the operator. It should be inclined and pushed against the cataract, which should be gently pressed below the region of the pupil. For relaxation of the eyelid Celsus describes an operation not unlike that practised at the present day by removing a horizontal flap of skin from the lid, and closing the wound by means of sutures. The practice of tapping the abdomen in dropsy was known to Celsus. It consisted in first introducing an instrument carefully into the abdominal cavity, and then inserting a leaden or brazen canula through which the water escaped. The canula was then closed, and either left in the wound or removed to be introduced the next day. Penetrating wounds of the abdomen with perforation of the small intestines are considered fatal. Wounds of the large intestines, he says, can be sewed up, and they sometimes unite. These though dangerous are not necessarily fatal. If the protruded intestines are gangrenous, there is not the least chance of recovery. If they are of natural colour they should be speedily replaced. The man should be laid on his back with his hips elevated, and gentle efforts made by the surgeon to reduce them. If the aperture is small, and the protrusion cannot be pushed back, the wound is to be enlarged, and its sides kept apart by an assistant with his fingers or two hooks. The protruded gut having been cleansed with water, to which a little of oil may have been added, should be carefully replaced by the surgeon. The portion that has protruded last should be reduced first, and *vice versâ*. If a portion of the omentum is mortified, it must be cut off, and the sound one gently reduced in its appropriate place. The edges of the abdominal wound are next to be brought together by means of sutures and plasters covered up with wool or sponge expressed out of vinegar, and supported by a light bandage. Celsus passes from wounds of the abdomen to the consideration of hydrocele and hernia. If reduction of the hernia cannot be effected by the taxis, if there be vomiting with pain in the scrotum extending up to the groins and abdomen, then the means recommended to be resorted to are blood-letting and abstinence if the strength permit; poultices to the tumour, hot bath, enema, and lastly the operation for cutting open the sac. It is quite clear that long before the time of Celsus, the operation of lithotomy or cutting for the stone in the bladder was known to the Greeks, but Celsus is the first writer whose directions for performing the operation are still extant. His method of performing it, known as the " Celsus's method," though now abandoned, was adopted by some European surgeons as late as the sixteenth century. We also learn through his writings that Ammonius, the celebrated lithotomist of Alexandria, was the first to show the importance of breaking the stone, when too large for extraction, by introducing an instrument through the wound in the perineum. " A hook," says Celsus, " is to be so insinuated behind the stone as to resist and prevent its recoiling into the bladder even when struck, then an iron instrument is used of moderate thickness, flattened towards the end, thin but blunt, which being placed against the stone, and struck on the further end cleaves it, great care being taken at the same time that neither the bladder itself be injured by the instrument nor the fragment of the stone falls back into it." Leaving aside the minor operations of surgery so well described by Celsus, let us now pass on to the examination of his last book.

Book viii.—It treats of fractures and dislocations; injuries of the head are first considered. If a person has received a blow on the head, the surgeon, he says, should in the first instance observe whether there is loss of speech, insensibility to light, bleeding from the ears or nose, coma, vomiting, torpor, inconsistency of mind and "relaxation or distension of the nerves." If these symptoms are met with, they indicate fracture of the skull, with injury to the membrane of the brain. In these cases there is little chance of recovery, and the operation of trepanning is necessary. To ascertain whether the bone is broken or not, Celsus advises us to carefully introduce a probe through the wound, and if the bone felt be smooth and slippery, there is no evidence of fracture; if rough, it is almost certain that fracture exists. He cautions us not to be deceived by sutures because they are equally rough. The fracture by *contrecoup* was known to him, for he distinctly writes that sometimes the head is struck on one side and fracture occurs on the other. If a person who has been struck heavily on the head presents bad symptoms, and if no fissure is detected in the wounded part, it is good practice, he says, to open the opposite side in a soft or swollen place (if there be any), when a fracture may be detected; for a broken bone, if not speedily treated, is followed by inflammation of the brain. In extravasation of blood within the cranium without fracture it appears that his line of practice consisted in incising the skin over the seat of extravasation and excising the bone. Celsus remarks that the ancients unnecessarily applied the instruments in every split or broken bone, but it is much better in some cases to try other means. In the mean time the patient should be carefully watched, and if bad symptoms occur, the surgeon should not hesitate to operate. The operation of trepanning in the different varieties of fracture of the skull is carefully described. The remaining portion of the book, which is devoted to simple and compound fracture of other bones, is fairly written, and gives a clear account of the modes of reducing fractures and dislocations, together with proper bandaging and the application of splints.

Another author of great celebrity who deserves to be mentioned on this occasion, although not belonging to the medical profession, is Pliny the Naturalist. He was born in the year A.D. 23. The place of his birth is not certain. In his youth he heard the lectures of Apion, the grammarian at Rome. At the age of twenty-two he travelled over Egypt, Greece, and Africa. After serving a few years in Germany he was made commander of a troop of Roman cavalry. His reputation procured him the friendship of Vespasian, Emperor of Rome, who promoted him to the rank of Prefect of the Roman fleet at Misernum. But Pliny has acquired immortal fame, not by his valour in the battle-field, but by his zeal in the pursuit of knowledge in the natural sciences and arts known in his time. His work on natural history in thirty-seven books, which he published in the year A.D. 77, has survived to our time. It contains a great deal of information not only upon animals, plants, and minerals, but upon geography, medicine, astronomy, the fine arts, and a variety of other subjects. "His work," says Buffon, "as varied as nature herself, always paints her in her most attractive colours." Pliny died in the year A.D. 79, at the age of fifty-six. To form a true opinion of his merits we refer the reader to his work on Natural History.

After Celsus and Pliny came Thessalus, who from a low and obscure condition rose to distinction. He was born at Tralles in Lydia in the first century of the Christian era. He was the son of a weaver, and himself followed the same trade in his youth. He afterwards applied himself to the study of medicine, and practised in Rome in the time of Nero, to whom he dedicated one of his works. He was a follower of Themison, and is supposed to be one of the founders of the dogmatic sect. He spoke in very low and insulting terms of the ancients and their system. It is no wonder that a man of mean birth and imperfect education, as he was, should show contempt for his predecessors and contemporaries. He was never sparing in his own praises, and presumptuously styled himself the " Conqueror of Physicians." He valued himself highly as the discoverer of a new theory in medicine. By these and other cunning acts he made a large fortune in practice. From the time of Thessalus it was the custom in Rome for physicians to visit their patients followed by all their disciples. Martial exclaims:—

> " I'm ill, I send for Symmachus ; he's here,
> An hundred pupils following in his rear,
> All feel my pulse with hands as cold as snow ;
> I had no fever then,—I have it now !"

Another physician, Andromachus, was born at Crete in the time of Nero, Emperor of Rome. He is celebrated for his invention of Theraica, an absurd combination of medicines known by the name of *Theraica Andromachi*. This once famous compound was rejected from the British Pharmacopœias about the beginning of the present century. The active ingredient of this preparation was the flesh of vipers, and it was for many ages esteemed the best antidote for wounds inflicted by bites of venomous animals. Andromachus was physician to Nero, and was the first to receive from him the honourable title of *Archiater* or Physician-in-Chief. An archiater was not necessarily a physician to an emperor. There were two classes of Archiatri in the Roman Empire, the *Archiatri sancti palatii*, or physicians of the Palace, and the *Archiatri populares*, or physicians of the people. The office of the former was more honourable. They were men of distinction who enjoyed many privileges, such as the exemption from all taxes, &c., the latter were paid by the State, but were chosen by the people. There was a certain number of them in each city who attended the sick poor *gratis* as paid medical officers, but who were allowed to take fees for professionally attending the families of the rich.

Aretæus, commonly called the "Cappadocian," was one of the most eminent of the ancient physicians. He was a Greek by birth, and it is conjectured that he practised in Rome either in the reign of Nero or Vespasian. Belonging originally to the Pneumatic sect, whose principles he adopted and maintained, he is said to have afterwards joined the Eclectics. He was an accurate observer of the symptoms of disease, and in many respects followed the opinions of Hippocrates. Dr. Bostock, who appears to be a champion of heroic treatment, bestows high praises upon this ancient writer, because " he freely administered active purgatives; he did not object to narcotics; he was much less averse to bleeding," and above all he made use of a variety of drugs. This system of treatment Dr. Bostock is pleased to call "simple and sagacious!" Aretæus was the first practitioner that made use of blisters. Before his time the Greeks and Romans employed sinapisms. He wrote eight books "on the Causes, Symptoms, and Cure of Acute and Chronic Affections," which are extant, and reflect credit upon the author. The particular symptoms of diseases and the means of forming a correct diagnosis are, with few exceptions, clearly stated. Take for example his description of tetanus :—" Pain and tension of the tendons and spine, and of the muscles connected with the jaws and cheek; for they fasten the lower jaw to the upper, so that it could not easily be separated even with levers or a wedge. But if one, by forcibly separating the teeth, pour in some liquid, the patients do not drink it but squirt it out, or retain it in the mouth, or it regurgitates by the nostrils ; for the isthmus faucium is strongly compressed, and the tonsils being hard and tense, do not coalesce so as to propel that which is swallowed. The face is ruddy, and of mixed colours, the eyes almost immoveable, or are rolled about with difficulty; strong feeling of suffocation, respiration bad,"* . . . . . The causes of this formidable disease are sufficiently clearly stated as follows:—" The causes of these complaints are many ; for some are apt to supervene on the wound of a membrane, or of muscles, or of punctured nerves, when, for the most part, the patients die, for 'spasm from a wound is fatal.' And women also suffer from this spasm after abortion; and, in this

---

* *The Extant Works of Aretæus,* edited and translated by Francis Adams, LL.D., p. 247.

case, they seldom recover. Others are attacked with the spasm owing to a severe blow in the neck. Severe cold also sometimes proves a cause; for this reason, winter of all the seasons most especially engenders these affections; next to it, spring and autumn, but least of all summer, unless when preceded by a wound, or when any strange disease prevails epidemically."*

The pathology of Aretæus in a majority of diseases is erroneous, and his system of treatment unnecessarily severe. We certainly are somewhat surprised that a learned man like Dr. Adams should admire his rules of treatment. In almost all the acute and in the majority of chronic diseases he recommends general blood-letting, scarification, purgatives and cautery. The cause of " cephalæa" or chronic headache is " coldness with dryness," and " vertigo is formed from a humid and cold cause." The latter " when connected with yellow bile, mania is formed; when with black, melancholy; when with phlegm, epilepsy; for it is liable to conversion into all these diseases."† Aretæus seems to have based his system of treatment on the Hippocratic doctrine of humours. Besides evacuating the diseased humours " upwards and downwards," he employed sialogogues and sternutatories to evacuate them by the mouth and nose. The following is a specimen of his treatment of chronic headache. After a repetition of blood-letting and free purging " we are to open the

---

* *The Extant Works of Aretæus*, translated by F. Adams, pp. 246, 247.

† Ibid., p. 296.

straight vein (*temporal?*) on the forehead, for abstraction by it is most efficacious, the amount, about a hemina (*half-pint?*) or a little more. But we must not evacuate further, for we must avoid emptying the vessels. Then, having removed the hair with a razor, we are first to apply one cupping instrument to the vertex, and another between the scapulæ, without drawing blood; but along with the instrument applied to the vertex, we are to scarify unsparingly, for the purpose of attracting the redundant fluid and of making an incision in the deep-seated parts. For remedial means applied even to the bones are beneficial in cephalæa. When the wounds are cicatrised we are to excise a portion of the arteries. . . . . In all cases we are to bring off phlegm, first evacuating the bowels, either by a purgative draught or by a clyster; and sometimes from the nostrils by sternutatories; and sometimes from the mouth by sialogogues." And again : " we are to abstract blood from the inside of the nostrils, and for this purpose push into them the long instrument named *Katiádion*, or the one named *Toryne,* or in want of these, we must take the thick quill of a goose, and having scooped the nervous part of it into teeth like a saw, we are to push it down the nostrils as far as the ethmoid cells, then shake it with both hands so that the part may be scarified by its teeth. Thus we shall have a ready and copious flow of blood; for slender veins terminate there, and the parts are soft and easily cut." But the Cappadocian hero of physic does not stop here. Even when the pains cease, after these things "we must go on." he adds, "to the conclusion of the system of treatment; for the mischief is apt to return, and frequently lurks in the seat of the disease. Wherefore, having removed the hair with a razor (and this also is beneficial to the head), we are to burn with heated cauteries, superficially, down to the muscles; or if you wish to carry the burning to the bone, you must avoid the muscles, for the muscles when burnt occasion convulsions."*

To do justice however to Aretæus we should observe that his accessory treatment and general hints and instructions adapted to the peculiarities of each case are rational. For example, a patient suffering from inflammation of the brain "ought to be laid in a house of moderate size, and mild temperature—in a warm situation if winter, and in one that is cool and humid, if summer; in spring and autumn, to be regulated according to the season. Then the patient himself, and all those in the house, are to be ordered to preserve quiet; for persons in phrenzy are sharp of hearing, are sensitive to noise, and easily become delirious. The walls should be smooth, level, without projections, not adorned with frieze or paintings; for painting on a wall is excitant. And, moreover, they catch at certain false appearances before their eyes, and grope about things which are not projecting, as if they were so; and any unreal occasion may be a cause sufficient to make them raise their hands. Length and breadth of the couch moderate, so that the patient may neither toss about in a broad one, nor fall out of a narrow bed. In plain bed-clothes, so

---

* *The Extant Works of Aretæus*, by F. Adams, pp. 458, 459, 460, 461.

that there may be no inducement to pick at their nap. But on a soft bed, for a hard one is offensive to the nerves; as in phrenetics, above all others, the nerves especially suffer, for they are subject to convulsions. Access of their dearest friends is to be permitted; stories and conversation not of an exciting character; for they ought to be gratified in everything, especially in cases where the delirium tends to anger. Whether they are to be laid in darkness or in light must be determined by the nature of the attack; for if they are exasperated by the light, and see things which exist not, and represent to themselves things not present, or confound one thing with another, or if strange images obtrude themselves upon them; and in a word, if they are frightened at the light, and the things in the light, darkness must be chosen; but if not, the opposite state."* At the commencement of the disease he advises liquid farinacious diet, but "if the disease be prolonged, the customary food must not be abstracted, but we must give nourishing articles from the cereals, in order to support the patient; and when there is need, of the flesh of the extremities of beasts and fowls, mostly dissolved in the soups; these ought to be completely dissolved during the process of boiling."†

One of the most renowned physicians who belonged to the sect of the Eclectics was Archigenes of Apamea. He settled in Rome as a practitioner of medicine in the reign of Trajan, and was highly respected for his

---

* *The Extant Works of Aretæus*, by F. Adams, pp. 378, 379.
† Ibid., p. 381.

professional attainments. Among his several works was a treatise on the pulse.

Dioscorides, one of the most celebrated physicians of his time, and the first authority on materia medica, was a native of Anazarba in Cilicia. He is supposed to have flourished in the second century of the Christian era, in the reign of Hadrian. It was to materia medica that he did the most real service. He travelled in distant countries for investigating this branch of the medical art. His valuable treatise on materia medica, in five books, was considered as a standard work for more than fifteen centuries. It contains the names, description and medicinal virtues of more than six hundred plants. "For more than fifteen hundred years," says Dr. Russell, "his was the only work upon the subject held as an authority; and Dioscorides was no less slavishly copied in his department, than was Galen servilely obeyed in the other branches of the art of medicine. It was the fashion to find everything in Dioscorides. It was a firm belief as late as the sixteenth century, that not a plant grew in Germany, France or England which had not been described by Dioscorides. Even when potatoes were introduced into Europe, the learned found no difficulty in discovering them in Dioscorides."*

Cælius Aurelianus, a contemporary of Galen, was another celebrated physician who flourished in the second century A.D. Whether he was a native of Greece or Italy is uncertain. He was a zealous Methodic, and maintained the principles and practice of that sect. He was an accurate observer of the

---
* Russell's *History of Medicine*, p. 121.

phenomena of disease, and treated the Hippocratic doctrine of humours with contempt. He also differed from him and his followers with respect to the confidence which they placed in the healing powers of nature for the cure of disease. He was averse to bleeding, purgatives, and other active remedies, and trusted much to diet, bathing, exercise, friction and abstinence. He wrote several books on acute and chronic diseases, and is said to have inserted in them matter relating to surgery.

Among the more celebrated writers of his age the most renowned for the celebrity of his name and for the extent of his writings was Galenus Claudius, generally styled Galen. He was born at Pergamus about A.D. 131. His father Nicon, who had attained reputation as a man of learning, gave him an excellent education in his childhood. At the age of fifteen he was placed under the best philosophers for useful learning. Galen was destined to the life of a physician. His father having dreamt that Galen should follow the profession of medicine, placed him at the age of seventeen under a physician to begin his medical studies. For nearly three years he studied under the best masters in his own country. After his father's death, which took place in the year A.D. 150, he left his native city Pergamus to prosecute his studies under the most eminent professors. He first travelled to Smyrna to study under Pelops the physician. After this he went to Corinth to hear the lectures of Nemesianus. He also proceeded to Alexandria, where he was instructed by Heraclianus, the anatomist. In A.D. 158 he returned to Pergamus, where he accepted the office of surgeon to the school of gladiators, and obtained great reputation in his profession. In A.D. 161 he quitted his home on account of some popular disturbance, and visited Rome. He remained in that famous capital for four years, during which time he wrote many books on philosophy and medicine, gave public lectures, and greatly distinguished himself by his successful practice. His fame excited the intolerable envy of his professional brethren. Galen knew that it was a common practice in the corrupt city to get rid of a successful rival by poison, and for fear of losing his life, he withdrew privately from Rome to Pergamus. "It is clear," says Dr. Russell, "there could have been no satisfaction in practising among a vulgar, brutal, greedy, licentious, pauper populace; and as for the slaves, they had no life to be saved; their bodies were their masters; and physicians were even required to perform the most horrible mutilations upon them, since we are sometimes compelled, against our will, by persons of high rank to perform this operation—writes Paulus Ægineta. Among the upper ten thousand alone and the strangers who congregated to the capitol could anything like a satisfactory practice be sought."*

Galen had hardly reached home when he was summoned by the Emperors M. Aurelius and L. Verus to appear before them at Aquileia. In obedience to their mandates he left Pergamus, and hastened towards the camp at Aquileia, and joined the Emperors A.D. 169. Shortly before his arrival a fearful pes-

---
* Russell's *History and Heroes of Medicine*, p. 76.

tilence had been raging in the camp. The two Emperors with Galen and a few followers made a hasty retreat towards Rome. Verus died on the way, and Aurelius and Galen reached safely. When the Emperor left Rome a second time for his German campaign, he chose Galen as the fit person to take medical charge of his son Commodus, a boy nine years of age. Having been recommended in a dream to leave Rome, Galen, after an absence of several years, set off towards Pergamus, touching at the island of Lemnos on his way to know the composition of a celebrated nostrum called "Terra Lemnia." After this nothing whatever is known of him. It is conjectured that he died in Sicily at the age of eighty. Galen was the author of a considerable number of medical and philosophical works, some of which were consumed in his lifetime, others have come down to us. He shows the importance of studying philosophy as a part of medicine, and remarks that "the best physician is also a philosopher." We have already said in another part of the work that in former times there were three medical sects, which had their separate schools and professors. The adherents of these divergent schools of medicine were for centuries at variance with each other. About the time of Themison two other sects had arisen, the Pneumatic and the Eclectic; so that at the time of Galen there prevailed in all five sects in Rome. Galen did not adopt the tenets of any particular sect, but chose from each what was most important, and adhered and followed in most particulars the principles and practice of Hippocrates, whose writings he highly admired. Those who attached themselves to any particular sect were called slaves. His conduct towards the distinguished followers of Erasistratus, who then practised at Rome, and who did not coincide with his views, was undignified.

Galen paid much attention to the study of anatomy, and the knowledge he acquired in this department was greater than that of any of his predecessors. He became acquainted with the structure of the body not by dissecting the human subject, but from experimenting upon apes, monkeys, goats, and other animals. "In one passage, however," says Dr. Greenhill, "he mentions that those physicians who attended the Emperor M. Aurelius in his wars against the Germans had an opportunity of dissecting the bodies of the barbarians."

In physiology and morbid anatomy he excelled the ancients. He was the first to observe by experiments made on the lower animals that after the application of a ligature to the main artery, the indirect supply of blood carried into the limb preserves its vitality, in other words, collateral circulation goes on, and mortification does not necessarily follow. Even the carotids, he says, may be tied without serious injury to life, and adds that those who attributed the loss of voice to the tying of the carotids were mistaken; that this occurrence happened only when the contiguous nerves were included in the ligature. The ancients believed that the arteries contained air. Galen was the first to show that these vessels contain blood in the living subject; and recommends twisting the artery in hæmorrhage. When this method fails, he directs us to apply a ligature. He was also the first to divide the causes of diseases into the *predisposing* and *exciting*.

The pathology of Galen was inaccurate, and his hypothesis respecting the properties of medicines absurd and incorrect. His practice was founded upon the principle *contraria contrariis curantur*. For instance a disease which was hot in the first and cold in the second degree, must be combated by a remedy possessed of opposite qualities, that is by one which was cold in the first and hot in the second degree. "He could only see everywhere hot and cold, dry and moist." He fancied that medicines possessed the four inherent qualities of cold, moisture, heat and dryness. Each of these four qualities was again divided into four degrees, that is, a plant was cold in the first, hot in the second, dry in the third, and moist in the fourth degree; or hot in the first, moist in the second, &c. Opium, he says, is cold in the fourth degree. Even " in the London Dispensatory of 1721," remarks Dr. Paris in his Pharmacologia, "we find the *hot* and *cold* compound powders of pearl." "It is quite clear," says Dr. Russell, " that his practice of medicine had all the fatal faults of his idol Hippocrates, besides a large contingent due to himself." To be brief, he, like Hippocrates, whose doctrines he professed to revive, was never sparing in the use of bleeding, cauteries, purgatives, &c. It was he who propagated the use of blisters, and gave birth to polypharmacy. Such a rude system of treatment, followed and recommended by the heads of our profession, gave rise to homœopathy.

Galen, with all his imperfect notions of pathology, was very successful in his diagnosis and prognosis of disease, indeed he boasts of "never having found himself wrong, with the help of God, in his prediction." In his prognosis he attached great importance to the critical days and to the strength and frequency of the pulse. In materia medica he is considered next to Dioscorides. He was the founder of the new prevailing fashion of combining a number of simples in one prescription. At the request of the Emperors M. Aurelius and Septimius Severus he prepared for them the famous compound medicine known by the name of *Theriaca*, which when taken daily was long known as an antidote against poisonous drugs and the stings of venomous animals. He had a superstitious belief in the efficacy of charms and amulets against certain bodily ailments.

Galen's reputation as a surgical writer is not so great as several other writers of antiquity, nor is he famous for any invention in this department. He was a voluminous writer, and is celebrated for having been the author of more than two hundred treatises, of which 137 are still extant. They contain a vast deal of information not only upon medical science, but upon philosophy. Properly speaking, he has written an encyclopædia of the knowledge of medicine in his age. His works have exercised a powerful influence upon the state of medicine in all its branches, and were held in high estimation for fifteen centuries. The followers of Erasistratus protested against his heroic treatment, but in vain. Galen's eloquence and opinion prevailed, and his immense influence swayed the medical world for centuries. Making every allowance for the spirit of the age, he has always been justly ranked among the greatest writers on medicine. In the words of Dr. Aikin, " his own mass and modern improvements have now in great measure consigned his writings to neglect, but his fame can only perish with the science itself."

Oribasius, a native of Sardis, and a disciple of Zeno the philosopher, flourished in the fourth century. He was a contemporary and an intimate friend of the Roman Emperor Julian, who appointed him to the office of Quæstor of Constantinople. He accompanied the Emperor in his expeditions against the Franks and Persians. Both were unfriendly to the doctrines of Christianity. On the death of Julian, which took place in the year A.D. 363, Oribasius was banished, and his property confiscated by the succeeding emperor, but was afterwards liberated. He wrote a considerable number of works, of which three are considered to be genuine, viz., the *Collecta Medicina* in seventy books, more than half of which has now disappeared; the *Synopsis* consisting of nine books; and the *Defacile Parabilibus* in four books.

Ætius, an eminent Greek physician, was born at Amida in Mesopotamia. He lived towards the end of the fifth or beginning of the sixth century. He studied medicine at Alexandria, and practised for some time in Constantinople. In his writings there is very little that can be called original. It must however be admitted that he is more full on some subjects relating to surgery than any of his predecessors. The virtue of the magnet in curing certain diseases was known to him, as appears from the following passage:—" We are assured that those who are troubled with the gout in their hands or their feet, or with convulsions, find relief when they hold a magnet in their hand."

The next author of importance, Alexander Trallianus, who is supposed to have lived in the middle of the sixth century, was born at Tralles in Lydia. He was the son of a physician, and his reputation as a practitioner was brilliant. Although a mere compiler, yet his writings contain much more original matter than those of Ætius. He was a firm believer in the efficacy of charms and amulets.

The next medical writer after Alexander is Paulus Ægineta, who lived in the seventh century, and laid the foundation of obstetrical science. He was more celebrated for his skill in treating diseases of women than his predecessors. His work *De Re Medica*,* in seven books, contains much useful matter. The fifth and sixth books devoted to surgery are most original. With the death of Paulus we may date the decline of the Greek and Latin schools of medicine.

---

* Translated into English by Francis Adams.

CHAPTER X.

Decline and fall of the Roman Empire in the West—Rise of the splendid Empire of the Saracens—Destruction of the Alexandrian Library—Accession of the house of Abbas—The Caliphs Almansur, Harun-al-Rashid, and Almamun—Their love of learning and patronage to Arts and Sciences—Empire of the Saracens in the West and of the Fatimites in Egypt—Library of Cordova—Foundation of a College at Bagdad—Magnificence of the Saracen Courts—Medical schools—Addition of new drugs to the *Materia Medica*—Discoveries in Chemistry—Celebrated Arab Physicians.

With the death of Constantine the Great in A.D. 337, the Roman Empire began to decline. More than half a century was spent in a series of civil dissensions, yet Rome retained its former grandeur. With the death of Theodosius the Great may be dated the misfortunes and degeneracy of the Roman Empire. Theodosius with a fatal policy divided the Empire between his sons Arcadius and Honorius. To the former he left the dominion of the Eastern and to the latter that of the Western Empire, A.D. 395. About this time hordes of barbarians overran the Roman provinces from all directions. The Goths, the Huns, the Vandals, the Heruli, and other barbarous nations ravaged and desolated the Empire on all sides. The Persians, under their kings Sapor Cobad and Khosroo, made frequent encroachments on the eastern provinces, and Justinian was forced by the latter to purchase a humiliating peace by the cession of a portion of his territory and the payment of an enormous sum of money to defray the expenses of the war. The Goths, under their leader Alaric, made an entry into Rome, and plundered the city, A.D. 410. It was taken and plundered a second time by the Vandals under Genseric, A.D. 455. To complete the wreck, Italy was finally conquered by the Heruli under Odoacer, their prince, who forced the weak monarch Augustulus to abdicate his throne. Thus the once mighty and magnificent Empire of the West fell to pieces by the destructive policy of its rulers and the shameful corruption and vices of its inhabitants, A.D. 476. The Eastern Empire escaped destruction at this period. Although in a declining state, its fall was retarded for many ages.

Another power gradually arose on the fall of the Roman Empire in the West. The beginning of the seventh century was distinguished by the rise of the splendid empire of the Saracens. The Arabians, before the time of Mahomed, were a lawless and barbarous people, claiming their descent from Abraham and Ishmael, and professing a religion full of superstition and idolatry. They had no taste for literary pursuits. The healing art and indeed all the other arts and sciences were in a state of utter degradation. The inhabitants of Arabia were divided into several independent tribes. Some of these carried the produce of their land across their wide deserts, and sold it in distant countries; others obtained their livelihood by plunder. The principal articles of export were balm, incense, myrrh, cassia, cinnamon, ginger, storax, aloes, pepper, benzoin, stibium, honey and sugar. Some of these were used by the ancients in their religious ceremonies. The sugar exported by the Arabs was not considerable, and was used only for medicinal and religious purposes. "To what purpose," says Jeremiah, addressing his superstitious countrymen, "cometh there to me incense from Sheba, and the sweet cane from a far country? Your burnt offerings are not acceptable, nor your sacrifices sweet unto me" (chap. vi. 20). Inoculation was known and practised by the Arabs as a preventive of small-pox, from the earliest period, nor are the modern Arabs ignorant of it. "Mothers perform this operation on their children by opening the skin of the arm with the prickle of a thorn or the point of a needle charged with infected matter." The priests, an influential class who guarded their temples and idols, were ignorant of letters. Their principal duties consisted in interpreting oracles and dreams and studying astrology. With such a rude and wandering nation the healing art must have been in a degraded state. Towards the end of the sixth and beginning of the seventh century Mahomed and his successors converted them from idolatory to the belief of one God. From this period the Arabs began to emerge from obscurity into splendour. For more than a century and a half they devoted their whole attention to the extension of their dominions in every quarter, and to propagating Mahomedanism by the sword. It was when they were masters of Alexandria that the celebrated Alexandrian library, consisting of several hundred thousands of volumes, was burnt by order of

Caliph Omar, A.D. 640. Amron, the lieutenant of the Caliph, was, by the solicitations of his friend John the Grammarian, disposed to preserve the library. The consent of the Caliph was asked, who replied as follows :—" If these writings of the Greeks agree with the book of God, they are useless, and need not be preserved; if they disagree, they are pernicious, and ought to be destroyed." The order was obeyed, and the immense number of volumes were consumed in the four thousand baths of this extensive city for six months. Nearly two centuries were spent in bloodshed and the interpretation of the Koran. This happened in the time of the nineteen Caliphs of the house of Omar called Ommiades, who ruled the Saracenic empire. After them the Abbasides of the line of Abbas ascended the throne in succession, and reigned as Caliphs of the Saracens. This dynasty of Abbas introduced a taste for literature among the Arabs. About this time the fanaticism of the Mahomedan conquerors had abated with their extensive conquest, and the Caliphs of the family of Abbas, finding that most of the conquered nations had received the Mahomedan religion, turned their attention to learning and the sciences, and became rather the protectors than destroyers of literature.

The medical profession was held in better esteem about the time of Mahomed. An Arab physician of some professional reputation, named Hareth-ibn-Kalda, who had received his medical education in the Greek school, founded by Sapor in Persia, settled to practise in Mecca. The prophet occasionally favoured him with his conversation, and Abubeker appointed him his physician. A celebrated Christian physician named George Bactishua, also educated at the school of Nisapur in Persia, was physician to the Caliph Almansur. He translated at his request several Greek and Persian works on medicine into the Arabic language. Almansur on his succession to the Caliphate removed the seat of the empire from Cufa to Bagdad, where literature, sciences and arts began to be cultivated. He had so much taste for literary acquirements that whenever he travelled at a distance he selected for his companions a hundred learned men.

The Caliph Harun-al-Rashid, who is made to play so large part in the *Arabian Nights*,* invited into his capital learned men from distant countries; and liberally rewarded those who collected and translated Greek and other works into Arabic. In his reign Bagdad for the first time became renowned as one of the celebrated seats of learning. By virtue of a law issued by him a school was annexed to every mosque. John-ibn-Mesue, a Nestorian Christian physician of Damascus, who had settled in Bagdad, was appointed by him to superintend the schools in his empire. In the beginning of his reign he was not inclined to encourage Christians of high literary and scientific attainments. But two fortunate circumstances occurred owing to which the Caliphs afterwards patronised and esteemed them. These were

---

* The authorship of the *Arabian Nights* seems legendary, and was originally derived from a Persian or perhaps Indian source. Harun-al-Raschid was not the author, as the work was translated into Arabic in the time of Caliph Mansour, who came to the throne A.D. 754, or thirty years before Harun-al-Raschid (786-809).

the cures performed upon himself and an Egyptian female who was his favourite, by the superior skill of Christian physicians.

His son Almamun was the Augustus of Arabian literature. He eclipsed the fame of his predecessors, and surpassed them in learning. He collected crowds of literati around him. Bagdad became the great centre of literature and science, where the learned of every country, without any distinction of caste or creed, lived under his liberal patronage. To encourage literature he bestowed high offices in the State only upon the distinguished scholars. From the literary men who flocked to his capital, he chose for his companions the most celebrated Greek, Persian and Chaldean scholars; and founded a society of learned men, electing John-ibn-Mesue, the celebrated physician and highly accomplished Greek scholar, as their president. The governors of his provinces and the ambassadors in foreign courts were ordered to collect the most valuable books and manuscripts. In a treaty of peace with the Greek Emperor Michael III., one of the conditions required was, that he should give up the whole collection of his books. Trains of camels laden with Greek, Egyptian, Persian and Hebrew books and manuscripts were seen entering Bagdad from every direction. By the command of the Caliph the principal books were translated into Arabic by learned men, and the copies circulated among the people. After translating the manuscripts, the originals, instead of being deposited in a safe place, were unfortunately burnt by his order. The general superintendence of these translations was conferred upon John-ibn-Mesue, who was also made a professor of the celebrated school of Bagdad. He and his disciple Honain, another distinguished Christian physician, translated the works of Hippocrates, Galen, and other renowned physicians into Arabic. After the death of Almamun learning was propagated with equal zeal and to a considerable extent by his successors. The last of the dynasty of the Abbasides was the Caliph Mostanser, who founded a grand college at Bagdad. In his reign this city was besieged and taken by the Tartars, under the grandson of Zengiskhan, and Mostanser was slain. The prosperity and glory of the Arabian empire in the East ceased with the life of this prince. The division of the Saracenic empire into the Caliphates hastened its downfall.

After the conflict betwen the Ommiades and the Abbasides, and the fall of the former in the East, one of their family, Abdalrahman, who had fled to Spain, founded the splendid kingdom of Cordova in the West. The Fatimites ruled over Africa and Egypt, and their capital was Cairo. The Caliphs rivalled each other, not only in pomp and luxury, but in the splendour and magnificence of their numerous colleges, libraries, &c. The most distinguished seats of Arabian learning were at Bagdad, Bussora, Bokhara, Damascus, Balkh, Ispahan, and Samarcand in Asia; at Cairo, Alexandria, and Kairwan in Egypt; at Morocco and Fez in Barbary; and at Cordova, Seville, Granada, and Toledo in Spain. Alexandria for a second time became the depository of literature and science. It had twenty schools of philosophy. The royal library of the Fatimites in Cairo comprised

1,00,000 manuscripts, which were lent to the students of that city as well as those of Alexandria. Al-hakem, a zealous promoter of learning, founded at Cordova a library of 400,000 volumes. The other cities of Spain had seventy libraries. Besides public libraries every learned man had a library of his own. "A private doctor refused the invitation of the Sultan of Bokhara because the carriage of his books would require four hundred camels." "The Vizier of a Sultan devoted a sum of two hundred thousand pieces of gold to the foundation of a college at Bagdad, which he endowed with an annual revenue of fifteen thousand dinars. The fruits of instruction were communicated, perhaps, at different times, to six thousand disciples of every degree, from the son of the noble to that of the mechanic ; a sufficient allowance was provided for the *indigent* scholars, and their merit and industry was repaid with adequate stipend."* The Caliphs not only vied with each other in establishing schools, colleges and libraries, but in the pomp and magnificence of their courts. The historian Abulfeda thus describes the magnificence of the Caliph Moctader, at the time when he gave audience to a Greek ambassador :—

" The Caliph's whole army, both horse and foot, was under arms, which together made a body of one hundred and sixty thousand men. His State officers, the favourite slaves, stood near him in splendid apparel, their belts glittering with gold and gems. Near them were seven thousand eunuchs, four thousand of them white, the remainder black. The porters, or door-keepers, were in number seven hundred. Barges and boats, with the most superb decorations, were seen floating upon the Tigris. Nor was the palace itself less

---

* Gibbon's *Roman Empire*, vol X., p. 43.

splendid, in which were hung up thirty-eight thousand pieces of tapestry, twelve thousand five hundred of which were of silk embroidered with gold. The carpets on the floor were twenty-two thousand. A hundred lions were brought out with a keeper to each lion. Among the other spectacles of rare and stupendous luxury, was a tree of gold and silver spreading into eighteen large branches, on which as well as on the lesser boughs sat a variety of birds made of the same precious metals as the leaves of the tree. While the machinery affected spontaneous motions, the several birds warbled their natural harmony. Through these scenes of magnificence, the Greek ambassador was led by the vizier to the foot of the Caliph's throne."*

Nor was the palace of the Caliph of Cordova less magnificent and costly than of Bagdad :—

"Three miles from Cordova, in honour of his favourite sultana, the third and greatest of the Abdalrahmans constructed the city, palace, and gardens of Zehra. Twenty-five years, and above three millions sterling were employed by the founder: his liberal taste invited the artists of Constantinople, the most skilful sculptors and architects of the age, and the buildings were sustained and adorned by twelve hundred columns of Spanish and African, of Greek and Italian marble. The hall of audience was encrusted with gold and pearls, and a great basin in the centre was surrounded with the curious and costly figures of birds and quadrupeds."† . . .

Of all the sciences and arts the Arabs have done the greatest service to the medical art. The principal cities of the extensive Saracenic empire possessed eminent medical schools. After a regular course of study the students were subjected to a searching examination by the *Hakimbashi*, or chief physician, and those found qualified received certificates to practise. In the city of Bagdad alone were eight hundred and sixty licensed practitioners of medicine.

---

* *Abulfeda*, quoted by Gibbon, vol. X., pp. 37, 38.
† Ibid., vol. X., pp. 38, 39.

We are greatly indebted to the Arabs for the introduction of mild aperients, such as rhubarb, manna, cassia, senna and tamarinds, into the materia medica. They also deserve the credit of having added to their Pharmacopœias many plants unknown to the Greeks, as camphor, musk, saffron, nux vomica, myrobalans, nutmegs, mace, cloves, and many other simple medicines. With these they also inserted several absurd remedies, such as gold, silver, pearls, bezoar, and precious stones. They were the first to publish authorized Pharmacopœias, and to introduce into practice juleps, conserves, syrups, and electuaries. The statements of modern writers that the Arabs were the first to make use of blisters is without foundation. Aretæus, who practised in Rome in the beginning of the second century of the Christian era, while speaking of the treatment of epilepsy, says:—
" In all cases we are to use rubefacient applications to the head ; namely, the common ones, as described by me formerly ; and a still more powerful one is that from cantharides, but for three days before using it the patient must drink milk as a protection of the bladder, for cantharides are very injurious to the bladder."* The origin of the terms camphor, naphtha, syrup, jalap, alcohol, alkali, alembic, aludel, and alchemy is derived from the Arabic. The shops of the apothecaries were superintended by the magistrate of the city to prevent the adulteration of drugs by unprincipled dealers. It was also the duty of the magistrate to see that all the drugs were genuine and sold at reasonable prices.

---

* *The Extant Works of Aretæus,* by F. Adams, pp. 469, 470.

To the Arabs we are also indebted for our knowledge of chemistry. They surpassed all the ancient nations in this branch of medicine, and may be regarded as its inventors. By their zealous and persevering search after the philosopher's stone capable of transmuting the baser metals into gold, and after the elixir of life for prolonging human existence, they discovered and became acquainted with many chemical substances. The operation of distillation is described by them, and the distinction of vegetable and mineral alkalies proved. The three mineral acids, namely, the nitric, sulphuric, and the muriatic, were discovered by the Arabs, who also knew the method of preparing alcohol. They were also aware of the existence of phosphorus, and were acquainted with the preparations of many chemical compounds, as we shall presently see.

The Arabians excelled the Greeks and Romans in their knowledge of botany. Their works on this subject contained two thousand more plants than the materia medica of Dioscorides. Anatomy and surgery were not cultivated with the same zeal as pharmacy, chemistry, and botany. Religious prejudices and respect for the dead prevented the Arabs from dissecting human bodies. But they obtained their knowledge of anatomy by dissecting lower animals and by examining skeletons in the cemeteries. In their works on surgery the Arabs borrowed almost everything from Paulus, Archigenes, Antyllus, and other Greek writers.

We now come to the celebrated names which impart considerable lustre to the medical literature of the Arabs. The names of Hareth-ibn-Kalda, George Bactishua, John-ibn-Mesue, and his pupil Honain, have been already mentioned.

Ibn Phara and Albiruni distinguished themselves as botanists. The former held the office of curator of the botanical garden of the Sultan Alnasar; the latter is said to have travelled all over India for forty years to acquire a knowledge of the nature and virtues of Indian plants and minerals.

Serapion and Alkhendi were two other physicians of some celebrity. The former wrote several treatises on medicine; the latter is particularly celebrated for his skill in philosophy and medicine.

The first and most distinguished of the Arabian chemists was Geber (supposed to be a Zoroastrian, converted to Mahomedanism), who lived in the eighth century. He was acquainted with the preparations of muriatic and sulphuric acids, nitrate of silver, caustic potash, and corrosive sublimate. He was familiar with the process of distillation, sublimation, and many other chemical phenomena. He is said to have written a considerable number of works on chemistry, out of which only four small treatises have come down to us. Modern writers assert that he derived his knowledge of chemistry from the works of the ancient Hindoos.

The other names of greater importance are Rhazes, Ally Abbas, Avicenna, Albucasis, Avenzoar, Averroes, and Ibn Beithar. Al-Rasi, or Rhazes as he is commonly called, flourished in the tenth century. He was a native of Rai in Persia. At the age of thirty he applied himself to the study of medicine, and working steadily and hard passed through a brilliant career as a student. He soon obtained such a degree of reputation that he was appointed director of the hospital in his native city. Here he acquired much experience in the practice of medicine, and became so famous that he was called the Arabian Galen. He became not long afterwards professor in the college of Bagdad, where he distinguished himself as an able and enthusiastic lecturer. His fame and influence spread through distant countries, and he was invited to Cordova by Caliph Almansur of Spain, where he spent the remainder of his days in pomp and dignity. He died about the year 986. Rhazes wrote several treatises on medicine and chemistry; but he is more celebrated for the many improvements which he made in pharmacy, and also as an author of a treatise on small-pox and measles. He was the first to give a full description of these diseases. He dedicated his *Liber ad Almansorem* to his patron the Caliph Almansur, and also wrote a small treatise on quacks. He was a firm believer in alchemy and the elixir of life. In his work entitled *Continens*, Rhazes is said to have borrowed almost everything connected with surgery from Paulus, Antylhus and Archigenes.

The next author of importance who lived in the tenth century is Ally Abbas, surnamed the Magian. He is supposed to be the descendant of a Zoroastrian priest.. His reputation as a physician was great, and he did much to promote the study of medicine. In surgery, although he professes to have copied almost everything from Paulus, yet he has introduced many original observations and improvements of his own.

His principal work, called *Al-maleki*, or Royal Work, was read and highly esteemed until the appearance of the *Canoon* of Avicenna.

The reputation of Al-Rasi and Aly Abbas was eclipsed by Abdulla-ibn-Sina, designated by the hakeems of India Bu-ali-Sina, and by the Christians Avicenna, a man of considerable learning in the age in which he lived, and the author who has acquired the greatest celebrity by his labours in enriching the medical literature of the Arabs. He was born at Bokhara in the year 980. At an early period he studied under Abu-Abdulla, a philosopher. He soon afterwards left Bokhara to study philosophy and medicine in the famous school of Bagdad, where he evinced much ability, diligence and attention. At a later period he was highly respected by the people for his professional reputation, and deservedly obtained from them the appellation of Sheikh Reyes, or the prince of physicians. He attained to such a considerable degree of popularity that the Sultan consulted him on the occasion of his son's illness, which did not yield to the treatment of the court physicians. He succeeded in curing the prince, whereupon he was chosen by the Sultan as his physician, and afterwards as his vizier. Shortly after, his good fortune forsook him, and he was dishonoured and thrown into prison. After a time he was liberated, and again reinstated to the dignity of a vizier. But Avicenna, apprehensive of a future danger, was obliged at length to escape in disguise for the safety of his life. He became dissipated, and indulged freely in wine, which undermined his constitution, and he died at Hamadan, in Persia, of intestinal inflammation, in the fifty-sixth year of his age. Among the Arabian authors none stands so high in point of literary reputation as Avicenna. The numerous writings of this distinguished physician were held in high estimation and read with admiration until a late period. His principal work, entitled the *Canoon*, consisting of five books, contains a vast deal of information on all subjects connected with medicine. It is an encyclopœdia of the medical literature of his time. The merit of this work was so great that for many ages it was the only text book in the principal medical schools of Europe. In the practice of medicine he was a follower of Galen. He translated the works of Aristotle into Arabic.

After Avicenna came Albucasis, the most eminent Arab surgeon. It is not a matter of certainty, but it is probable that he was a native of Cordova in Spain. He had a better knowledge of anatomy and surgery than any of his predecessors, and gained considerable fame as a bold and skilful operator. He was the inventor of a few surgical instruments, and wrote three books on surgery, which contain more original matter than is to be found in any of the works of his predecessors. They were received as text books in many schools.

Among the Saracens of Spain Avenzoar and Averroes had the reputation of being skilled in medicine. Abdelmalek-ibn-Zohr, commonly designated by the Christians Avenzoar, was a native of Seville. He obtained considerable fame by his successful practice, and is chiefly celebrated for the few improvements which he made in medicine and pharmacy. He was the first to introduce bezoar into the materia medica. His favourite study was the discovery of antidotes for poisonous substances. He is also celebrated as having been the author of a work entitled *Tassyr*. He died in the year 1168 at a very advanced age.

Averroes was a pupil of Avenzoar. He was born at Cordova in the twelfth century. He was a man of high birth and perfect education; a more accomplished scholar than a practitioner of medicine. On account of his superior talents he was appointed the chief magistrate of Cordova. His fame soon excited the envy of his rivals, who wrongfully accused him of want of faith in the Mahomedan religion. He was tried for heresy before the Sultan, by whom he was excommunicated, his goods confiscated, and he himself forced to reside among the Jews in Cordova. Tired of persecution, he was obliged at length to escape from Cordova to Fez, where he was soon detected and arrested by the magistrate of that city. The King and council of Fez met, and it was agreed and decided that Averroes, who was a disbeliever of the divine origin of Mahomedanism, should be brought out of the prison to the gate of the mosque on occasions of public prayers, and the worshippers who entered it should be allowed to spit upon his face. After suffering this degrading punishment patiently for some time, he showed repentance, and procured an acquittal from the king, who permitted him to return to Cordova, where he was once more restored to his former honours. Averroes with all his varied acquirements did not neglect medicine, but studied it with assiduity, and wrote works, the principal of which, entitled *The Universal*, was for some time held in high estimation.

Averroes was succeeded by Al-Beithar, or Ibn-Beithar, who deserves to be mentioned on this occasion as being the most eminent of all the Arabian botanists. He was a native of Malaga, and flourished in the thirteenth century. In his zeal for obtaining a knowledge of botany he is said to have travelled over the greater part of Europe, Africa, Arabia, and India. He wrote three books; the first on medicinal plants and their virtues; the second on metals and minerals; and the third on animals. The materia medica of Ibn-Beithar contains a greater number of medicinal articles than that of any Greek, Roman or Arabian physician, or even the British Pharmacopœia of our present day. It also contains much original matter. In his latter days Ibn-Beithar had the honour to become the vizier to the king of Damascus. He died in the year 1248. From the death of Ibn-Beithar we may date the decline of the Saracenic school of medicine.

CHAPTER XI.

Christianity and Medicine—Medical Practice engrossed by Monks and Clergy—Their superstitious practices—Decrees of Popes and Councils—Praiseworthy efforts of Charlemagne—Relics of Saints—Astrology blended with Medicine—Charms and Amulets—Strange Prescriptions—Royal Touch for the cure of King's Evil—Proclamation—School of Salerno—Dissection of dead bodies—Mondini—Roger Bacon—His learning—Curious receipt—Arnoldus de Villa Nova—Linacre—Foundation of the Royal College of Physicians of London.

We have already said that to the Arabs is due the merit of saving literature and science from universal decay after the downfall of the Roman Empire. The introduction of Christianity did not at all contribute to the improvement of the healing art. Christianity rather checked than promoted its progress. Europe for many centuries produced hardly a Christian physician of literary and professional reputation. Christ, we are told, cured by miracles, but of his miraculous cures it is not necessary to allude in these pages. One of the apostles of Christ is designated "Luke, the beloved physician." In the succeeding ages some men, calling themselves Christians, but who worshipped images, saints, and relics, pretended to cure the sick by the aid of supernatural means. Europe became enveloped in the greatest ignorance and darkness. Learning and the sciences were in a state thus described by a historian:—" Law neglected, philosophy perverted till it became contemptible, history nearly silent, poetry rarely and feebly attempted, art more and more vitiated." The healing art shared the same fate. It took refuge in churches and monasteries. To the latter institutions, hospitals were afterwards attached. In short the monks and clergy chiefly engrossed the practice of physic, who had also recourse to prayers, holy water, and other superstitious practices. To put a stop to their *mala praxis*, the Council of Montpelier, held in 1162, issued a decree forbidding the priests to practise medicine. By proclamations made by the Lateran Council, held in 1123 and 1139, it was ordered that no monk or priest should practise the healing art. Pope Innocent II., in a Council at Rheims, forbade the monks to study and practise medicine, A. D. 1131. In the year 1215 Pope Innocent III. effectually prohibited the priests from practising surgery.

Praiseworthy efforts were made by Charlemagne to rouse Europe from the state of literary lethargy into which it had fallen. He invited from distant countries men of distinguished acquirements, employed learned men to translate Arabic works into Latin, and founded Universities in Paris, Bologna, Pavia and Osnaburg. But all his good attempts failed, and he could not overcome the ignorance and barbarity of the time. Learning and the sciences were regarded with indifference and contempt, and were replaced by ecclesiastical study. The priests and monks, who were sunk in vice, were rather the enemies than the promoters of literature. They practised enchantment, astrology, &c. as belonging to their sacred function. It was the general belief at that period that all diseases were of celestial origin, and could only be cured through the intercession of the priests and monks. The belief in charms, amulets, astrology, incantations, and other vulgar superstitions, were not relinquished till the sixteenth century. Sanctified wells dedicated to patron saints were visited by the sick on religious days, and many foolish ceremonies were performed on the occasion. "The relics belonging to saints," says Pettigrew, "have been esteemed of equal efficacy in removing diseases: the belt of St. Guthlac and the felt of St. Thomas of Lancaster were sovereign remedies for the headache, while the penknife and boots of Thomas-à-Becket, and a piece of his shirt, were found most admirably to aid parturition."* According to Brand the following saints were invoked against various diseases :—

St. Anthony against inflammations.
St. Apollonia and St. Lucy agaist the toothache.
St. Benedict against the stone and poison.
St. Blaise against bones sticking in the throat, fire, and inflammations.
St. Christopher and St. Mark against sudden death.
St. Clara against sore eyes.
St. Genow against the gout.
St. Job and St. Fiage against the venereal disease
St. John against epilepsy and poison.
St. Liberius against the stone and fistula.
St. Maine against the scab.

---
* Pettigrew *On Medical Superstitions*, p. 42.

St. Margaret against danger in child-bearing, also St. Edine.
St. Martin for the itch.
St. Marus against palsies and convulsions.
St. Maure for the gout.
St. Otilia against sore eyes and headache, also St. Juliana.
St. Petronilla and St. Genevieve against fevers.
St. Quintan against coughs.
St. Romanus against devils possessing people.
St. Ruffin against madness.
St. Sebastian and St. Roch against the plague.
St. Sigismund against fevers and ague.
St. Valentine against the epilepsy.
St. Venisa against green-sickness.
St. Wallia or St. Wallery against the stone.
St. Wolfgang against lameness.*

In Brand's *Popular Antiquities* the following ridiculous passage, quoted from *The Husbandman's Practice, or Prognostication for ever*, occurs:—"Good to purge with electuaries, the moon in Cancer; with pills, the moon in Pisces; with potions, the moon in Virgo; good to take vomits, the moon being in Taurus, Virgo, or the latter part of Sagittarius; to purge the head by sneezing, the moon being in Cancer, Leo, or Virgo; to stop fluxes and rheumes, the moon being in Taurus, Virgo or Capricorn."†

When an epidemic of sweating sickness raged in Europe, the members of the College of Physicians of Paris, instead of helping the poor despairing victims

---
* Brand's *Popular Antiquities*, vol I., pp. 356, 357.
† Ibid., vol. III., p. 143.

of this frightful disease, gave the following worthy judgment:—" We, the members of the College of Physicians at Paris, having after mature consideration and consultation in the present mortality, collected the advice of the old masters, are of opinion that the constellations, with the aid of nature, strive, by virtue of their divine might, to protect and heal the human race."*

One Mr. W. Kemp, M.A., speaking of plague, writes in a pamphlet dedicated to Charles II.:—" One cause of breeding the pestilence is that corruption of the air, which is occasioned by the influence of the stars, by the aspects, conjunction and opposition of the planets, by the eclipse of the sun and moon, and by the consequences of comets."

Even as late as the beginning of the eighteenth century, astrology seems to have been blended with medicine. In Mortlake churchyard, says Mr. Davis, is a monument dated 1715, upon which is inscribed —" John Partridge, astrologer, and Doctor of Medicine, who made physic for two kings, and one queen, to wit, Charles II., William III., and Queen Mary."

Mr. Davis also quotes from a work dedicated to a member of Parliament, dated 1647, and entitled " A modest Treatise of Astrologie by William Lilly, " the following astrological aphorisms which, the author says, " are beneficiall for Physicians":—

" He that first enters upon a cure in the hour of Mars, shall find his patient disaffected to him, and partly disdain and reject his medicines, his pains ill-rewarded, and his person slighted."

" He will be infinitely oppressed who in the hour of Mars shall first get an *hot* disease, and in the hour of Saturne a *cold* one."

---

* *Sprengel*, quoted by Russell.

"When Jupiter is the author of the sicknesse he demonstrates affection of the liver."

"Mars being the cause of faver, and in Leo shows ebolition or a boyling of the humours, continual burning favers whose originall cause springs from the great veines near the heart."

"Saturne is cold and dry, melancholic, *earthly*."

"Jupiter governeth all infirmities in the *liver*; of colours, sea green or blew a mixt yellow *or green*."

"Mars in nature hot and dry, he delighteth in red colour, and in those savours which are *bitter*, sharp and burn the tongue."

"Venus, in colours she signifieth white."

"Mercury, in the elements he is the water."*

"I knew," writes a learned man, "some honest and religious nuns, confined in the strictest manner, who unfortunately contracted the venereal disease from the peculiar state of the air, together with that of the putrid humours and the weakness of their habits of body."

As a charm for the ague the following lines were uttered up the chimney on St. Agnus's eve by the eldest female in the family :—

> "Tremble and go!
> First day shiver and burn
> Tremble and quake!
> Second day shiver and learn
> Tremble and die!
> Third day never return."†

The following is a charm for the cramp :—

> "Cramp be thou painless!
> As Our Lady was sinless
> When she bare Jesus."‡

For the cure of ague, Elias Ashmole in his diary of 11th April 1681, gives the following vulgar opinion:

---

* *The Chinese*, by J. F. Davis, vol. III., pp. 48, 49.
† Brand's *Popular Antiquities*, vol. I., p. 38.
‡ Ibid., vol. III., p. 311.

" I took early in the morning a good dose of elixir, and hung three spiders about my neck, and they drove my ague away. Deo Gratias!"

The following curious amulet to avert the plague is from the pen of an apothecary to the French King in the eighteenth century:—" Preservation against the plague:—Take three or four great toads, seven or eight spiders, and as many scorpions; put them into a pot well stopp'd, and let them lye some time, then add virgin-wax, make a good fire till all become a liquor, then mingle them all with a spatula, and make an ointment, and put it into a silver box well stopp'd, the which carry about you being well assured that while you carry it about you, you will never be infected with the plague."*

A quack, named John of Audelay, addressed the following letter to Lord Burleigh, Secretary of State to Queen Elizabeth:—

" Be of goode comfort and plucke up a lustie, merrie hearte, and then shall you overcome all diseases, and because it pleased my goode Lord Admiral lately to praise my physicke I have written to you such medicines as I wrote unto him which I have in my boke of my wiffe's hand *proved upon herself and mee both*, and if I can get anything that may do you goode you may be well assured it shall be a joye unto me to get it for you. A good medicine for weakness or consumption:—Take a pig of nine days olde, and slaye him, and put him in a skillat with a handfull of spearmint, and a handfull of red fennell, a handfull of livewort, half a handfull of red neap, a handfull of clarge, and nine dates cleaned, picked, pared, and a handfull of great raisins, and picke out the stones, and quarter of an ounce of mace and two stickes of goode cinnamon bruised in a mortar, and distil it with a soft fire and put it in a glass and set it in the sun nine days, and drinke nine spoonfulls of it at

---

* *Ten Thousand Wonderful Things*, by E. F. King, pp. 42, 43.

once when you list! A compost:—item—take a porpin otherwise called an English hedge-hog, and quarter him in pieces, and put the said beast in a still with these ingredients: item—a quart of redde wyne, a pinte of rose-water, a quarter of a pound of sugar—cinnamon and two great raisins. If there be any manner of disease that you be aggreaved withal, I pray you send me some knowledge thereof, and I doubt not but to send you an approved remedie. Written in haste at Greenwiche Ye 9 of May 1553 by your trewe heartie friend JOHN of AUDELAY."*

The belief in the efficacy of the royal touch in curing scrofula or King's Evil is another specimen of the folly and credulity of mankind. The practice is said to have originated with Edward the Confessor, and ended with Queen Anne. With the accession of George I. of the House of Hanover the practice was discontinued. The French claim that the practice arose with one of their kings. Whether it took its origin with the French or English, there can be no doubt that for centuries it extensively prevailed upon the Continent. Thousands of persons at different times flocked from all parts of the country to be cured of the disease by the royal touch. Louis XIV. is said to have touched sixteen hundred persons affected with the King's Evil on Easter Sunday, 1686. The Turkish ambassador in the court of King James I., having heard of his gift of healing, requested his Majesty to exercise the sacred touch upon his son, who was afflicted with the disease. Pettigrew gives the following extract of a letter upon the subject written by one Pory to Sir Dudley Carleton, ambassador at the Hague, dated 7th November 1618:—"On Sunday the new Venetian ambassador Signor Donati had his

---

* *Ten Thousand Wonderful Things*, by E. F. King, pp. 671, 672.

first audience, and on Tuesday the Turkish Chiaus who means to have a bout also with Holland. His speech to the King (as my Lord Chancellor told me) was:—Sultan Osman, my great master, hath sent your Majesty a thousand commendations and a thousand good wishes both to your Majesty, and to the prince your sonne, and hath commanded me to present unto you these his Imperial letters. In fine, after his Majesty had asked him many questions the Turke said his son was troubled with a disease in his throat, whereof he understood his Majesty had the guifte of healing; whereas his Majesty laughed heartily, and as the young fellove came neare him, he stroked him with his hande, first on the one side and then on the other: marry without Pistle or Gospell."*

The nobility and gentry, as well as the priests and physicians were never sparing in their praise of the royal gift of healing. Peter of Blois, chaplain to his Majesty Henry II., the Rev. Dr. William Tooker, chaplain to Queen Elizabeth, and canon of Exeter, and others, have admitted in their writings the efficacy of the royal touch. Jeremy Collier, author of an ecclesiastical history of Great Britain, speaking on the subject remarks:—" To dispute the matter of fact, is to go to the excesses of scepticism, to deny our senses, and be incredulous even to ridiculousness."

Among the remedies for scrofula one Boorde, in his *Breviary of Health*, recommends the royal touch, with a few words of advice to the king as follows:—" For this matter, let every man make frendes

---

* Pettigrew *On Medical Superstitions*, p. 134.

to the kynges majestie, for it doth perteyne to a kynge to helpe this infirmitie by the grace of God, the which is geven to a kynge anointed. But forasmuch as some men doth judge divers tymes a fystle or a French pocke to be the Kynge's Evyll, in such matters it behoveth not a Kynge to meddle with all."* We are not informed whether this Boorde was a quack or a legally qualified practitioner of medicine ; neither is it of any importance to compare and contrast the one with the other, when we see the writings of the latter in that age always more or less tinged with quackery. Take for example John of Gaddesden of Merton College, Oxford, physician to Edward II., and an "illustrious writer" on medicine, recommending as a last resource the royal touch in scrofula after the failure of known remedies. This is the same Gaddesden who treated cases of small-pox on Avicenna's plan, viz., by wrapping and surrounding them with everything red. "When the son of the renowned King of England," says he, "lay sick of the small-pox, I took care that everything around the bed should be of a red colour ; which succeeded so completely that the Prince was restored to perfect health without the vestige of a pustule remaining."

William Clowes, Surgeon to Queen Elizabeth, and the author of a work on scrofula, wrote as follows on the efficacy of the royal touch :—"The *King's* or the *Queene's* Evil ; a disease repugnant to nature : which grievous malady is known to be miraculously cured and healed by the sacred hands of the queene's

---

* Brand's *Popular Antiquities*, vol. III., p. 302.

most royall majesty even by divine inspiration and wonderfull worke and power of God, above man's skill, arte, and expectation, through whose princely clemency a mighty number of her majestye's most royall subjects, and also many strangers borne, are dayly cured and healed which otherwise would most miserably have perished."*

Proclamations were issued calling upon those troubled with the malady to appear at an appointed time for cure. The following public proclamation was published in the " Newes " of the 18th of May 1664:—" His Sacred Majesty (Charles II.) having declared it to be his royal will and purpose to continue the healing of his people for the Evil during the month of May, and then to give over until Michaelmas next, I am commanded to give notice thereof, that the people may not come up to town in the interim, and lose their labour."† Ceremonies were performed and prayers read on the occasion of touching. Every one who applied to be touched was presented with a piece of gold, the love of which, it is said, attracted many not suffering from the complaint. So great was the number that applied for relief, that in later times no person was presented to the king unless he obtained a certificate from the surgeon.

It remains for us now to give an outline of the lives and labours of those who more or less contributed to, and the great events which materially influenced, the advancement of the medical art. We have already stated that Christianity did nothing for a period of

---
* Pettigrew On Medical Superstitions, p. 132.
† Ten Thousand Wonderful Things, p. 42.

some centuries either to promote it, or save it from falling into neglect. Now we pass on to those followers of the Christian faith who played a creditable part (making every allowance for the age in which they lived) on the stage of medicine; and who took much pains, directly or indirectly, to foster the healing art by bringing it from a low and neglected state into maturity and perfection.

The first school of medicine was founded at Salerno, where students resorted from different countries of Europe to study medicine. Here they were taught the works of Hippocrates and Galen which the Arabs had carefully preserved. No candidate was admitted into the college who had not acquired a fair amount of knowledge and education, for we learn from one of the statutes of the school:—" Since it is impossible for any one to make progress in medicine without a knowledge of logic, we will and command that no one be admitted to the study of medicine until he has been for at least three years engaged in the study of logic." No student was allowed the right to practise without passing academical examinations, and obtaining a diploma signed by the professors.

Other schools, in the course of time, sprang up at Montpellier, Bologna, Vienna, Paris, Padua, Pavia, Milan and Rome. Frederick granted permission to dissect a dead body in Bologna every five years. Mondini, a professor in the university of that city, is said to have been the first person who, taking advantage of this license, dissected a human subject, A.D. 1315, and who afterwards published anatomical plates of the human body. In 1374 the faculty of

Montpellier succeeded in obtaining from the Vatican the right of public dissection. In the next century Pope Sixtus IV. authorised the dissection of human subjects in all the universities. This circumstance diffused a general taste for the study of anatomy, and conduced greatly to the improvement of this branch of medicine.

Albertus Magnus, Roger Bacon, Arnoldus de Villa Nova, and his pupil Raymond Lully, are a few names of celebrity in the thirteenth century. All of them were celebrated alchemists. The most celebrated among them, Roger Bacon, a man of remarkable genius, was an English Franciscan monk. He first studied at Oxford, then at Paris, and after having obtained the degree of Doctor he returned to England. He was learned in all the ancient languages, and was the first inductive philosopher of his age. He cultivated chemistry, medicine, mechanics, optics, and astronomy, with some success, and was acquainted with the preparation of gunpowder. Roger Bacon perfectly knew the opposition which great reformers and learned men always meet with, and remarks at the beginning of one of his works:—" There are four impediments to knowledge; first, too great dependence upon authority; second, allowing too great weight to custom; third, the fear of offending the vulgar; fourth, the affectation of concealing ignorance by the display of a specious appearance of knowledge." The extraordinary genius of Bacon excited the envy of the Franciscan monks, who accused him of magic, and, still worse, of dealing with the devil, for which he was excommunicated by the

Pope, and imprisoned for ten years. During his imprisonment he wrote a treatise entitled " On the means of preventing the Corruption of any Constitution and the Infirmities of Old Age," which he dedicated to the Pope. The elixir invented by Petro de Maharancourt is recommended by Bacon to his Holiness. "For the preparation of this elixir," says the inventor, " you must take that which is temperate in the fourth degree, that which swims in the sea, that which vegetates in the air, that which is cast out by the sea, that which is found in the bowels of a long-lived animal, a plant of India, and two creeping things which are the food of the Tyrians and Egyptians, and let them all be properly prepared." The ingredients of this curious and mysterious prescription were interpreted by Roger Bacon to be " gold, pearl, rosemary, spermaceti, the bone found in a stag's heart, lignum aloes, and serpents."

Arnoldus de Villa Nova, a professor in the university of Barcelona, while engaged in the pursuit of alchemy, accidentally discovered many chemical processes and compounds. He was the first to find out spirits of wine to be a solvent for active vegetable principles. This discovery led to the introduction of tinctures in general use.

Thomas Linacre, a celebrated English physician, and one of the most learned Greek scholars of his day, was a native of Canterbury. He began his studies at the university of Oxford, and afterwards travelled into Italy, where, under the patronage of the celebrated Lorenzo de Medici he acquired a taste for learning. Returning to England he became physician to

Henry VII., and afterwards to Henry VIII. He taught the Greek language at Oxford, where he had such famous men as Sir Thomas Moore and Erasmus for pupils. He translated many of Galen's works, and took a conspicuous part in the establishment of medical professorships in the universities of Oxford and Cambridge, and in founding the Royal College of Physicians of London, which had the effect of partially putting a stop to irregular practice; for it is certain that after the institution of the College of Physicians, quacks guilty of *mala praxis* or fraud were occasionally punished in a summary manner. "A counterfeit doctor," says Stow in his *Chronicles*, "was set on horseback, his face to the horse's tail, the same tail in his hand as a bridle, a collar of jordans about his neck, a whetstone on his breast, and so led through the city of London, with ringing of basins, and banished. Such deceivers no doubt are many, who, being never trained up in reading or practice of physic and chirurgery, do boast to do great cures, especially upon women, as to make them straight that before were crooked, corbed, or crumped in any part of their bodies, &c. But the contrary is true; for some have received gold, when they have better deserved the whetstone."

CHAPTER XII.

Paracelsus—His Travels—Azoth and Arcanum—Professor at Basle—He burns the writings of Galen and Avicenna before his class—Rejects the doctrine of humours and the law of contraries—His eccentric behaviour and dissipated habits—His favourite sword—His death—Jerome Cardan—His early education—Magic and Astrology—Is consulted by Edward VI.—He dies by starvation—Vesalius—Servetus—Is burnt to death for improving anatomy—Galenists and Chemists—Opposition to the use of chemical remedies.

At the end of the fifteenth and beginning of the sixteenth century Europe emerged from the darkness and ignorance of the middle ages. This period may be considered as the era, in the history of Europe, of the revival of polite literature, sciences and arts. The first great event which materially influenced the literature of the period was the invention of the art of printing by John Guttenberg at Strasburg, 1440. The other great events which awakened a spirit of enterprise, discovery, and inventions, and which conduced to the diffusion of learning, were the discovery of America by Christopher Columbus, the discovery of the passage of the Cape of Good Hope to the East Indies by Vasco de Gama, and the spread of the Reformation begun by Luther.

The end of the fifteenth and the whole of the sixteenth century produced bold innovators in the prac-

sumptuously styled himself the " monarch of physicians." The only person of whom he spoke with some respect was Basil Valentine, his reputed tutor. [Basil Valentine was a German Benedictine monk, who first used antimonial preparations, and discovered liquor ammonia.]

The fame of Paracelsus obtained for him a professorship in the University of Basle, A.D. 1526. Such was his arrogance, that, not content with condemning the practice of preceding physicians by reproachful words, he, at the commencement of his introductory lecture, burnt the works of Galen and Avicenna before his class; "declared to his audience that if God would not impart the secrets of physic, it was not only allowable but even justifiable to consult the devil," and added that his beard had more experience than all the schools of Basle; that the buckles of his shoes possessed more knowledge than Galen or Avicenna, and that the hair on the back of his head knew much more than all the authors taken together. Thus the eccentric professor struck with boldness a severe blow to the time-honoured Galenic system of medicine, which, up to his time, prevailed in all the medical schools.

Paracelsus spoke in strong terms of the doctrine of humours and the method of treating diseases by their contraries. "What you call humours," he says, "are not diseases—that is, the disease which makes these humours. How can a physician think to discover the disease in the humours, when the humours spring out of the disease? It is not the snow which makes the winter, but the winter the snow; for although the snow is gone, the winter remains. You mistake the product of disease for disease itself." Again he says :—" *Contraria contrariis curantur ;* that is, hot remedies cure cold diseases. That is false; the whole design is false. There is no proof of a disease being hot, or a remedy being cold."* Instead of giving hot remedies in cold diseases, and cold remedies in hot diseases, we must discover, he says, a proper specific or arcanum for every disease. According to him arcanum is the invisible and indwelling spirit upon which depends the virtue and power of a thing in subduing the disease.

Paracelsus soon after his appointment became dissipated, openly vicious, and fell into habits of excessive drinking. It is said of him that he was ignorant of Latin, and as he could not write correctly in his own vernacular tongue, he dictated most of his treatises in the night when drunk. So says Oporinus, his secretary or chemical assistant. An unfortunate circumstance compelled Paracelsus to leave Basle. A wealthy church functionary at Basle, named Cornelius von Lichtenfels, who was suffering from the agony of gout, offered to give Paracelsus a hundred florins if he freed him of his sufferings. Paracelsus consented, and succeeded in giving him great relief only by the administration of three pills of his *laudanum.* The churchman finding himself so rapidly restored to health, refused to pay the stipulated money, but offered him his usual fee. The disrespect shown by this shabby patient towards him and his profession was enough to rouse the indignation of a fanatic like

---

* *Schultz*, quoted by Russell, p. 165.

Paracelsus. He claimed in the court of Basle from his patient one hundred florins for a visit and three pills. The magistrate decided in favour of the defendant, and allowed only the usual fee, whereupon Paracelsus, in a fit of rage, abused the magistrate, the churchman, and the whole city of Basle! The matter was brought before the notice of the town-council, and the result was the expulsion of Paracelsus from Basle.

Armed with his *elixir vitæ* and specifics, he again began to ramble through different parts of Europe, at this time not for the acquisition of knowledge, but for attracting patients by his wonderful cures, to the disgrace of physicians of the school of Galen. Wherever he travelled he attacked and assailed with fury the doctors and their system. His drunkenness, with its attendant vices, however, kept pace with his fame, nay, it increased to the height of abomination. "During two years Paracelsus was drunk every day, never undressed himself, and went to bed with his famous sword by his side, which he used occasionally to draw and flourish about the room to the infinite alarm of the much-enduring Oporinus," his secretary, who lived with him. One day at Salzburg, Paracelsus in his usual manner gave offence to a doctor by the severity of his attacks, and the consequence of the provocation was that "he was pitched out of a window at an inn by the doctor's servants, and had his neck broken by a fall." At last he died in the hospital of St. Sebastian of that city, at the early age of forty-eight, A. D. 1541.

Such is the career of this extraordinary man. We have called him a quack because he had all the manners, etiquette, impudence and pretensions of a quack. He pretended to be possessed of an elixir of life, and yet he died at the age of forty-eight. But Paracelsus with all his faults was gifted with the power of making discoveries and improvements in chemical science. He introduced mercury and many other new remedies into practice which up to this time figure in our medical books, and was the first to practise external metallo-therapy on the bodies of sick persons. His name is also famous in the history of medicine as the founder of a new sect, and as a reformer of the antiquated system of medicine.

Another "wonderful compound of wisdom and folly" was Jerome Cardan, an Italian, who was born in Pavia, A. D. 1501. He first applied himself to the study of Latin and mathematics. With the reputation of a great mathematician, Cardan, at the age of nineteen, began to give public lectures in Euclid, and for a short time obtained the appointment of Rector of the university of Padua. In his twenty-fourth year he obtained the degree of doctor of medicine, and acquired celebrity by his successful practice. In treating diseases he called to his aid magic and astrology, and was better known to many by the appellation of the "magician" than as a physician. His fame spread through distant countries, and he was invited to Scotland by the Archbishop of St. Andrews to be consulted for a serious disorder from which this prelate had been suffering. The Archbishop was cured, and Cardan received a handsome reward. On his way back to Italy he passed through London, where he was consulted by Edward VI., who desired to know from him, by calculating his nativity, the length of time he would live. Cardan gave his judgment that the king was destined to live a long life, but contrary to his predictions his majesty died within a year. After his return from London he spent some time in Bologna and Rome. In the latter city he walked about like a maniac in the Scottish costume. "For a few steps he walked with a slow measured tread as if at a funeral; then broke into a run as if flying from the police."

Cardan was a man of peevish and melancholy temper. He lived in penury, and was once thrown into jail by his creditors, yet nothing could induce him to accept the honourable and lucrative post of physician to the king of Denmark or of England. Cardan had predicted his own death in 1576, and it is said that in order to verify his statement he starved himself to death. Cardan was a man of genius. He made many important contributions to philosophy, mathematics, and medicine, and boldly rejected long-existing errors in practice.

In the sixteenth century great attention was bestowed on improvements in anatomical science. As an anatomist Vesalius was unequalled in his time. To him belongs the honour of being the first who published an anatomical work without paying regard to the authority of Galen, whose errors he ventured to expose. He was wrongfully accused of having dissected a *living* subject, and was condemned to make a pilgrimage to the Holy Land. On his way back he was shipwrecked and lost.

Servetus, who flourished in the same century, had

some idea of the pulmonary circulation. He pointed out that the septum of the heart is solid, and not porous as Galen supposed, and demonstrated that the passage of blood from the right to the left side of the heart was not through porosities in the septum but through the lungs. The old school became intolerant of this increase of knowledge. The Genevese burned the book in which it was described, and the unfortunate author was burnt to death as a heretic in 1553 by the instigation of Calvin.

The whole of the sixteenth century was a period of revolutions in medicine: a period of innovations and theories, controversies and discussions. The medical profession was divided between the rival sects of the Galenists and chemists. The chemists complained of the imperfection of the Galenic system of medicine and the inertness of the remedies employed by its professors. On the other hand, the introduction of chemical remedies and their merited success met with opposition from the Galenists. The chemical physicians were called in derision *Chemikers*, and were persecuted as charlatans. To bring antimony into disrepute, the French doctors (Galenists) even solicited government interference, and the result was the passing of an edict by the Supreme Council of Paris in 1566 prohibiting the use of antimonial preparations. Guy Patin, a physician of Paris, wrote in strong terms against their use, and gave a long list of persons killed by them. What is more remarkable, the same Government in the year 1666 not only revoked the sentence passed upon antimony, but purchased in the year 1720 from a French surgeon a secret medicine called Panacea Glauberiana, which was afterwards discovered to be nothing than a preparation of antimony known as Kermes mineral. We must not omit to mention that by a decree passed in the year 1615 by the Royal College of Physicians of Paris, "chemical medicines were condemned, and intèrdicted from all Pharmacopœias, and all judges were implored to inflict severe chastisement on all who prescribed, administered, and exhibited those poisonous remedies."*

---

* *Guy Patin*, quoted by Russell, p. 224.

CHAPTER XIII.

Van Helmont—He studies Medicine—Rejects the writings of the ancients—His humility—His Archæus—Lord Bacon—His early career—His employment of the word *Idolæ*—Healing Art uncertain and unprogressive—Remedies pointed out—Descartes—His early education—Studies Medicine—His notions about the production of Motion and Animal Heat—Boyle—Imperfection of the curative branch of Medicine—Simple medication—Rationale of specifics.

After Cardan, another philosopher and physician of superior talents was John Baptista van Helmont, born at Brussels, A. D. 1577. He was early sent to Louvaine, where he diligently devoted himself to the regular course of studies. Nor were philosophy, medicine and the other sciences neglected. With his usual zeal and assiduity Van Helmont examined and mastered the writings of Hippocrates, Galen, Dioscorides, Avicenna, and other authors; and came to the conclusion that they were not fruitful of any good. The faculty of medicine of Louvaine, perhaps fearing a struggle with their would-be antagonist, appointed him at the age of seventeen a Lecturer on Surgery in the Academy of that city.

"Gifts can move gods, and gifts our god-like kings."

But no gift in the world could ever move this bold and restless spirit. Day after day thinking of the imperfection of the ancient systems of medicine, he grew impatient to throw off the yoke of authority. The revolution, however, came at last. His hostility towards the Galenists and their practice assumed a great variety of forms. Van Helmont had a large fortune left him by his parents, which he made over at the first opportunity to his sister, so that if he chanced to discover something new in the field of medicine he might not be accused of avarice by those jealous of him. He then modestly resigned the honourable post of lecturer, complaining of his own incompetency and the deceit of the pretentious professors in appointing inexperienced youths like him as lecturers. He also declined to receive the degree of master of arts, saying that he had not mastered a single art. Rejecting in strong terms the former systems, Van Helmont became desirous of penetrating into the mysteries of chemical philosophy, hoping to discover in it the only effectual system which he could not from the writings of the ancients. After many years of unwearied and tedious labour he came to the conclusion that there is inherent in the living system an immaterial specific agent which he named *Archæus*, and explained all the physiological actions in the living body to its presence. He also said that *Archæus* not only determined the phenomena of health but of disease.

Van Helmont died in the sixty-seventh year of his age, of pleurisy. His opponents assert that his aversion and obstinate refusal to be bled, gave occasion to his death. Van Helmont distinguished himself as a physician of great talents and enthusiasm. The knowledge which he acquired in the field of investigation and experiment was not employed like Paracelsus in bargaining with the sick for florins, but in a manner suitable to his dignity. For several years he gave medical advice *gratis* to the poor, and provided them with medicines at his own expense.

In the seventeenth century Francis Bacon, Descartes, and Robert Boyle gave to the world their works on philosophy, mathematics, and mechanics, which contributed to the rapid progress of science and art.

Francis Bacon was born in London in the year 1561. He was the son of Sir Nicholas Bacon by his second wife Ann. His early education was obtained at Cambridge, where he studied and rejected the writings of the old philosophers. At seventeen he was sent to Paris with Sir Amias Pawlet, ambassador to that court, and at nineteen he wrote a book "On the State of Europe." On his return to England he engaged in the study of law in Gray's Inn, and made surprising progress. At the age of twenty-two he became one of Elizabeth's counsellors, and in the year 1593 a member of Parliament for Middlesex. He was created a knight by James I. In 1605 appeared his great work "On the Advancement of Learning." He was first appointed solicitor-general, and after having obtained many places of honour, received the appointments of attorney-general, privy councillor, keeper of the great seal, and high chancellor of Great Britain. He was invested with the title of Baron Verulam, and was afterwards made Viscount of St. Albans. In 1620 he published his work the "Novum Organum." From this time the fortunes of this great philosopher commenced to decline. An accusation of bribery and corruption was brought against him, for which he was tried, and sentenced to be imprisoned and fined forty thousand pounds. He was soon, however, liberated, after which he lived in retirement, and devoted the remainder of his days to study. He died in the year 1626.

Bacon was a profound philosopher and unquestionably one of the greatest men of his time. He rejected the false method of observing systems, theories, and speculations to attain the knowledge of nature, and impressed the necessity of observation and experiment before arriving at general truths. He exposed the errors of false reasoning, and also pointed out the various circumstances which retarded the advancement of useful knowledge. According to him there was a tacit submission to received opinions, prejudices, and false notions (called by him *Idolæ*), which were so many fetters on the progress of knowledge, and only required to be broken in order to make discoveries and improvements. Four species of *Idolæ* are described by him: 1, *Idola Tribus;* 2, *Idola Specus;* 3, *Idola Fori;* 4, *Idola Theatri*. "We observe," says he, "that idols are the deepest fallacies of the human mind; for they do not deceive in particulars, as the rest, by clouding and ensnaring the judgment, but from a corrupt disposition, or bad complexion of the mind which distorts and infects all the anticipations of the understanding. For the mind, darkened by its covering the body, is far from being a flat, equal, and clear mirror that receives and reflects the rays without mixture, but rather a magical glass, full of superstitions and apparitions.

Idols are imposed upon the understanding, either (1) by the general nature of mankind; (2) the nature of each particular man; (3) by words or communicative nature. The first kind we call idols of the tribe, the second kind idols of the den; and the third kind idols of the market. There is also a fourth kind, which we call idols of the theatre, being superinduced by false theories, or philosophies, and the perverted laws of demonstration."*

" The idols of the tribe are inherent in human nature, and the very tribe or race of man; for man's sense is falsely asserted to be the standard of things; on the contrary, all the perceptions, both of the senses and the mind, bear reference to man and not to the universe, and the human mind resembles those uneven mirrors which impart their own properties to different objects, from which rays are emitted and distort and disfigure them.

" The idols of the den are those of each individual; for everybody (in addition to the errors common to the race of man) has his own individual den or cavern which intercepts and corrupts the light of nature, either from his own peculiar and singular disposition, or from his education and intercourse with others, or from his reading, and the authority acquired by those whom he reverences and admires, or from the different impressions produced on the mind, as it happens to be preoccupied and predisposed, or equable and tranquil, and the like; so that the spirit of man (according to its several dispositions), is variable, confused, and as it were actuated by chance; and Heraclitus said well that men search for knowledge in lesser worlds, and not in the greater or common world.

" There are also idols formed by the reciprocal intercourse and society of man with man which we call idols of the market, from the commerce and association of men with each other; for men converse by means of language, but words are formed at the will of the generality, and there arises from a bad and unapt formation of words a wonderful obstruction to the mind. Nor can the definitions and explanations with which learned men are wont to guard and protect

---

* *Advancement of Learning.*

themselves in some instances, afford a complete remedy—words still manifestly force the understanding, throw everything into confusion, and lead mankind into vain and innumerable controversies and fallacies.

"Lastly, there are idols which have crept into men's minds from the various dogmas of peculiar systems of philosophy, and also from the perverted rules of demonstration, and these we denominate idols of the theatre: for we regard all the systems of philosophy hitherto received or imagined as so many plays brought out and performed, creating fictitious and theatrical worlds. Nor do we speak only of the present systems, or of the philosophy and sects of the ancients, since numerous other plays of a similar nature can be still composed and made to agree with each other, the causes of the most opposite errors being generally the same. Nor, again, do we allude merely to general systems but also to many elements and axioms of sciences which have become inveterate by tradition, implicit credence and neglect."*

Let us now glean a few passages from his writings to show how much he contributed towards the advancement of the art of healing. Medicine, says Bacon, is an uncertain and conjectural art which "has been rather professed than laboured, and yet more laboured than advanced, as the pains bestowed thereon were rather circular than progressive, for I find great repetition and but little new matter in the writers of physic." He admonishes physicians to leave off generalities and bestow their earnest attention to particulars, and to examine diligently and accurately things in order to make new discoveries. He then reproaches physicians who, in their ignorance, give up cases as hopeless and incurable when beyond their power to cure, instead of diligently setting to work for the discovery of appropriate remedies. "Since to pronounce diseases incurable," he says, "is to establish negligence and carelessness,

---

* *Novum Organum.*

as it were, by a law, and screen ignorance from reproach." Even when there are not the slightest hopes of recovery he advises doctors to attend their patients to improve their own skill as well as to mitigate the most painful and distressing symptoms. "We esteem it," he says, "the office of a physician to mitigate the pains and tortures of diseases as well as to restore health; and this not only when such a mitigation, as of a dangerous symptom, may conduce to recovery; but also, when there being no farther hopes of recovery, it can only save to make the passage out of life more calm and easy . . . . . But the physicians of our times make a scruple of attending their patients after the disease is thought past cure, though, in my judgment, if they were not wanting to their own profession and to humanity itself, they should here give their attendance to improve their skill, and make the dying person depart with greater ease and tranquillity."*

He next justly complains in the following terms of the want of specific medicines:—"Though the present physicians tolerably pursue the general intentions of cures, yet they have no particular medicines which by a specific property regard particular diseases; for they lose the benefit of traditions and approved experience by their authoritative procedure in adding, taking away, and changing the ingredients of their receipts at pleasure, after the manner of apothecaries substituting one thing for another, and thus haughtily commanding medicine, so that medicine can no longer command the disease;" and he adds, "the

---

* *Advancement of Learning.*

methods of cure in use are too short to effect anything that is difficult or very considerable . . . . To see the daily labours of physicians in their visits, consultations, and prescriptions, one would think that they diligently pursued the cure, and went directly in a certain beaten track about it; but whoever looks attentively into their prescriptions and directions, will find that the most of what they do is full of uncertainty, wavering, and irresolution, without any certain view or foreknowledge of the course of the cure."*

Rêné Descartes, a celebrated French philosopher, was born in 1596. He was early sent by his father to the Jesuits' college of La Flèche, where he made rapid progress in the study of the Greek and Latin languages, and then applied himself to the study of logic, mathematics, and morals. After spending eight years in the college he returned to his parents, dissatisfied with the ancient systems of philosophy, which, he said, were obscure and defective, at the same time hoping to discover a better method of philosophy. At the age of seventeen he was sent to Paris, where he was induced to study mathematics. This pursuit he soon relinquished, and at first entered the Dutch, and subsequently the Bavarian army, and greatly distinguished himself at the battle of Prague. Changing his mind he quitted the army, and once more resolved to devote himself to the study of mathematics. The labours of this able and penetrating man were also for many years employed profitably upon philosophy. " Besides this he paid no slight attention to medicine, anatomy, and chemistry; he spent a whole winter in

* *Advancement of Learning.*

dissecting and examining animal bodies, and in chemical operations." Regarding medicine, many of his opinions and assertions are extravagant. Dismissing his doctrine of atoms and pores, let us hear how he explained the production of motion and animal heat: " Heat and the motion of the limbs proceed from the body, and thoughts from the mind; but the mind cannot give motion and heat to the body. The more vivid and subtle parts of the blood, which heat rarifies in the heart, are incessantly entering into the cavities of the brain, and form animal spirits, which are in the brain separated from other less subtle parts of the blood. These animal spirits, which are corporeal, excited as by the soul itself, so also the action of external objects upon the senses, are the immediate cause of all the original motions of the body. Whence all the limbs may be moved by means of the objects of sense and the animal spirits without any action of the soul."*

Descartes after many years of wandering arrived at a state of perfection, and published his philosophical works, which were favourably received by a majority of learned men of his age. Four months before his death this illustrious philosopher was invited by Queen Christina to Stockholm, where he became her instructor in philosophy. He died in that city in 1650. Sixteen years after, his remains were brought to Paris.

Another distinguished philosopher who understood medicine was the Honourable Robert Boyle. He was the youngest son of the Earl of Cork, and was born at Lismore in Ireland in 1627. During the greater part of his life Boyle occupied himself with

---

* Enfield's *History of Philosophy.*

philosophical pursuits. It is foreign to our present object to give even a brief outline of the life and labours of this distinguished man. His reputation as a philosopher is amply acknowledged by learned men. Boyle was not only a profound philosopher but a tolerable physician. We cannot pass over in silence his few sensible observations in regard to the art of healing, as they deserve attention. His estimation of the profession is expressed in the following words :—

"Though I ignore not that it is a much more fashionable and celebrated practice in young gentlemen to kill men than to cure them; and that mistaken mortals think that it is the noblest exercise of virtue to destroy the noblest workmanship of nature, yet, when I consider the character given of our great Master and Exemplar in that Scripture that sayeth 'that he went about doing good, and healing all manner of sickness and all manner of diseases among the people,' I cannot but think such an employment worthy of the very noblest of his disciples; and I confess that if it were allowed to me to envy creatures so much above us as are the celestial spirits, I would much more envy that welcome angel's charitable employment, who at set time diffused a healing virtue through the troubled waters of Bethesda, than that dreadful angel's fatal employment, who in one night destroyed a hundred and fourscore thousand fighting men."

Boyle reproaches physicians for paying too little attention to the curative part of their profession. We cannot do better than reproduce an instructive passage from his work :—

"I cannot forbear to wish that divers learned physicians were more concerned than they seem to be to advance the *curative* part of their profession, without which three, at least, of four others may prove, indeed, delightful and beneficial to the physician; but will be of very little use to the patient *whose relief is yet the principal end of physic*. . . . I had much rather that the physician of any friend of mine should keep his patient by powerful medicines from dying, than tell me punctually when he shall die, or show me, in the opened carcass, why it may be supposed he lived no longer."

The uncertainties and evils of compound medicines we shall let him tell in his own words:—

"It seems a great impediment to the further discoveries of the virtues of simples, to confound so many of them in compositions, for in a mixture of great number of ingredients it is hard to know what is the operation of each or any of them, that I fear there will scarce, in a long time, be any progress made in the discovery of the virtues of simple drugs, till they either be oftener employed single, or be but few of them employed in one remedy."

"I fear that when a multitude of simples are heaped together into one compound medicine, though there may result a new crisis, yet it is very hard for the physicians to know beforehand what that will be; and it may sometimes prove rather hurtful than good, or at least by the coalition the virtues of the chief ingredients may be rather impaired than improved."

His remarks on the rationale of specifics are also worth quoting:—

"Finding at every turn that the main thing which does prevail with learned physicians to reject specifics is, that *they cannot clearly conceive the distinct manner of the specifics working*, and think it utterly improbable that such a medicine, which must pass through digestions in the body, and be whirled about by the mass of the blood to all the parts, should, neglecting the rest, show itself friendly to the brain, for instance, or the kidneys, or fall upon this or that juice or humour, rather than any other. But to this objection, which I have proposed as plausible as I can make it, I shall at present but briefly offer these two things:—

"First, I would demand of these objectors a clear and satisfactory, or, at least, an intelligible application of the manner of working of divers other medicaments that do not pass for specifics. Why the glass of antimony, though it acquire no pungent, or so much as manifest taste, whereby to vilicate the palate, is both vomitive and cathartic? For I confess, that to me even many of the vulgar operations of common drugs seem not to have been hitherto intelligibly explained by physicians, who have yet, for aught I have observed, to seek for on account of the manner of how diuretics, sudorifics, &c., perform their operations."

CHAPTER XIV.

Harvey—His medical career—Physician to Charles I.—Discovers the circulation of the Blood—Is persecuted by his colleagues—Claim of Cesalpinus to the discovery—Sylvius de la Boe—Disease and Chemical Actions—His system of cure—Willis—Rise of the Mathematical School—Borelli—Bellini—Mechanical Theory—Sydenham—His early career—Specifics wanted—Fermentation and Depuration—Nature cures diseases—Rheumatism cured by Whey—Simplicity of Prescriptions—History of the Peruvian Bark—Prejudice against its use—Oliver Cromwell dies of an ague—Sydenham's testimony in favour of Bark and his mode of using it—Richard Talbot—His success in curing agues.

The reputation of Van Helmont was somewhat eclipsed by his contemporary Harvey, a name celebrated in the annals of medicine for the discovery of the circulation of the blood. Harvey was born at Folkestone in 1578. After a course of instruction at Cambridge he obtained the degree of B.A. at the age of nineteen. Italy was at this period the great seat of learning which attracted scholars from distant countries. Harvey entered the university of Padua to study medicine under the famous Fabricius de Aquapendante. After an absence of four years he returned to England, and took his degree of M.D. at Cambridge, became a Fellow of the College of Physicians, occupied the post of Physician to St. Bartholomew's Hospital, and lectured upon the circulation of the blood. In the year 1628 he published his great work on the motion of the heart and blood, which he dedicated to Charles I., who five years after appointed him to the post of court physician. Harvey was with the king when the great battle of Edgehill was fought between the Royalists and Parliamentary forces in 1642. The battle was won by the king, who three years after lost the battle of Naseby, and fled to the Isle of Wight, where he was imprisoned. In 1646, that is three years before the king was beheaded, Harvey left his service. Harvey's second work was on Generation, which he published in 1651. He died at an advanced age in 1657. Alas! even Harvey did not escape the persecutions of his colleagues, and was called the "circulator" or quack for his magnificent discovery, and the Paris faculty decreed that no lectures should be delivered in the university on the circulation of the blood as taught by Harvey.

The Italians claim that Harvey derived his knowledge of the circulation of the blood from one of their countrymen. A bust has lately been placed in the university of Rome in honour of Professor Andrea Cesalpino, of the university of Pisa, with an inscription claiming for him that he knew and taught the circulation of the blood previous to Harvey. Professor Scalzi, in a speech delivered by him on the occasion of the ceremony in the university of Rome, speaks thus:—" The great discovery which was to cause a general commotion in the fields of all biological science, was announced firstly by Cesalpinus in the five books of the Peripatetics in the year 1571, with such simplicity of words, with such candid modesty, that it is not to be wondered at that it became known to very few of the learned of Italy, and only to solitary foreigners. It was great good fortune for William Harvey that, finding himself from 1598 to 1602 in Padua, studying medicine, he was able to learn the new doctrine from Fabrizio d'Aquapendante, whose renown as an eminent anatomist attracted students from beyond the Alps; then returning in 1602 to London, he studied to profit by the teaching received in the Padua school, with all the industry of ingenious research in most diligent experiments, and after seventeen long years announced it in private circles; and twenty-six years having elapsed— namely in 1628—printed and published it. He would have done much more to enhance his fame, which was really very great, if he had guarded himself from giving forth as the fruit of his own studies a discovery which was all Italian. Overcome by the desire to render his name famous with such a marvellous discovery, he did not hesitate to say, with as much pomp of words as Cesalpinus—of the whole the true discoverer—had said with simplicity and modesty, that he had made known to the astonished, learned things which were new and not previously heard of in the scientific world."* It is generally admitted that Realdus Columbus, the teacher and predecessor of Cesalpinus, taught the pulmonary circulation in the university of Pisa. It is an undisputed fact that Cesalpinus makes use of the term "circulation," but on perusing a few passages from his writings on the subject, it will appear that his description of circulation is confused and incoherent, and not given in a clear and lucid manner. To

---

* Vide *Lancet*, Feb. 3, 1877.

Cesalpinus is due the merit of having first partially proved the circulation of the blood; to Harvey of having afterwards proved the whole truth. Servetus, Realdus Columbus, and Cesalpinus, paved the way for Harvey, to whom alone belongs the glory of having discovered, demonstrated, and proved for ever the circulation of the blood.

About the time of which we are speaking, chemistry was beginning to develope into the dignity of a science, when it was applied in another direction. Some physicians, among whom the most prominent was Sylvius de la Boe, pursued their investigations in tracing diseases to chemical actions in the body.

Sylvius de la Boe, a Frenchman, was the most celebrated representative of the medical chemists and the supporter of the chemical theory. He was born in Flanders, 1614. He studied medicine in the university of Basil, where he took his degree. He then left that city to practise in Amsterdam. In the year 1658 he was appointed to the chair of medicine at Leyden.

Sylvius ascribed the phenomena of life to chemical agencies, and diseases to acidities, alkalinities, fermentations, &c. If a disease arose from an excess of acid in the system, his method of cure consisted in administering alkalies, and *vice versá*. He traced fever to an excess of acid in the blood, and gave alkalies largely to neutralize it. Such was the supposed curative system of Sylvius and the chemical physicians—a system notwithstanding the attacks of its antagonists that existed for many years and attracted many adherents. Sylvius was a man of learning and ingenuity who obtained a considerable degree of popularity by his professional attainments, but in his zeal to upset old theories in medicine he founded and defended a new but absurd theory of his own.

Willis, one of the great anatomists of his age, and who made some discoveries in the structure of the brain, was another defender of the chemical doctrine who maintained that each organ had its special fermentation, and that the deterioration of these ferments gave rise to diseases. In 1659 appeared his work containing dissertations on fevers, fermentations, &c. in which he defends his theories of diseases with considerable ingenuity.

While the iatro-chemical school was thus becoming developed, the iatro-mathematical sect arose in Italy, represented first by Borelli and later by Bellini. Borelli was one of the disciples of Galileo and a member of the " Academy of Experiments" at Florence. He was a great mathematician, and the mechanical theory started by him attracted many adherents. One of the most zealous followers of the mathematical school, termed also the iatro-mechanical school, was Bellini, the pupil of Borelli, and Professor of the university of Pisa. The physicians of the iatro-mechanical school explained the various operations of the living body on mechanical principles. "The body was regarded," says Dr. Bostock, " simply as a machine composed of a certain system of tubes, and calculations were formed of their diameters, of the friction of the fluids in passing along them, of the size of the particles and the pores, the amount of retardation arising from friction and other mechanical causes, while the doctrines of derivation, revulsion, lentor, obstruction, and resolution, with others of an analogous kind, all founded upon mechanical principles, were the almost universal language of both physicians and physiologists towards the close of the seventeenth century."

Among the writers of this age Thomas Sydenham has acquired considerable fame by his labours in improving the art of medicine:—

> "Sydenham a great, a mighty genius came,
> Who founded medicine on the noblest frame:
> He studied Nature through, and Nature's laws,
> Nor blindly puzzled for the peccant cause.
> Father of Physic He—Immortal Name
> Who leaves the Grecian but a second fame.
> Sing forth, ye Muses, in sublimer strains,
> A new Hippocrates in Britain reigns:
> With every healing plant his grave adorns
> Saviour of many millions yet unborn."

Thomas Sydenham was born in the year 1624 in Dorsetshire. At the age of eighteen he entered Magdalen Hall in Oxford. It is probable that he had a commission in the Parliamentary forces at the time when England was plunged in civil war. He found nothing to his taste in the army. His own inclinations and the persuasion of an eminent London physician prompted him to follow the profession of physic. He retired from military service, and in 1646 returned to Oxford to pursue his medical studies. In 1648 he obtained the degree of Bachelor of Medicine, but took his degree of Doctor of Medicine at Cambridge. He was also made a Fellow of All Souls' College. For the acquisition of further knowledge he visited the celebrated Montpellier school of medicine, and after a course of medical studies, returned to his native country, and successfully practised medicine in Westminster. In 1663 he was elected a member of the College of Physicians of London. Sydenham was a martyr to gout during the greater part of his life. He died on the 29th of December 1689, and was buried in the church of St. James in Westminster. As a faithful and accurate observer of the phenomena of diseases he had deservedly attained the appellation of the English Hippocrates. The symptoms of diseases which he has so graphically delineated, he learnt by a series of most diligent and judicious observations. We shall go over his interesting writings.

Nearly half of his writings is occupied with a clear account of the various epidemics which had come under his own observation; the rest contains a few short treatises on acute and chronic diseases and their treatment. "The improvement of physic," says he in his preface, "depends (1) upon collecting as genuine and natural a description or history of all diseases as can be procured; and (2) laying down a fixed and complete method of cure." He then makes the important remark that the third and best way of improving medicine is by discovering *specific* remedies, and laments that the Peruvian bark was the only specific he knew of:—

"But if it be objected that we have long been possessed of a sufficient number of *specifics*, I answer that the contrary will soon appear, provided a strict search be made in this particular: the *Peruvian* bark being the only one we have, for there is a wide difference between medicines that *specifically* answer some certain curative indication, which being effectually performed, perfects the cure, and those that specifically and immediately cure a disease without regarding any particular intention or curative indication. To exemplify this: *mercury* and *sarsaparilla* are usually reckoned specifics in the venereal disease, though they ought not to be deemed proper and immediate specifics, unless it could be demonstrated undeniably that *mercury* had cured the patient without causing a *salivation*, and *sarsaparilla* without raising a *sweat*. For other diseases are cured in the same way by other evacuations, and nevertheless the medicines exhibited for this purpose do no more immediately contribute to the cure of diseases than do those evacuations, which these medicines are principally designed to promote, than a lancet does towards the cure of a *pleurisy*; which nobody, I imagine, will call a specific in this disorder."

Sydenham apologises for any error in point of theory in his writings, but shows the utility of observation and experience towards the further improvement of the healing art. He observes:—

"I have contributed, to the utmost of my abilities, that the cure of diseases might, if possible, be prosecuted with greater certainty after my decease; being of opinion that any accession to this kind of knowledge, though it should teach nothing more pompous than the cure of the tooth-ache, or corns, is of much greater value than all the vain parade of refinements in theory, and a knowledge of trifles which are perhaps of as little service to a physician in removing diseases, as skill in music is to an architect in building."*

Sydenham was partly a follower of the views of chemical physicians, and agreed with them that diseases originated in an unhealthy fermentation or ebullition in the fluids of the body. Intermittent fevers he divides into three stages,—1st, the *shaking* stage; 2nd, the stage of *fermentation* or *ebullition*; 3rd, the stage of *despumation* or *depuration*. "I judge," he says, "the *shaking* from this cause, that the febrile matter, which being not yet turgid, was in

---

* Swan's *Sydenham*. Fifth Edition, p. 97.

some measure assimilated by the blood, becomes at length not only useless, but prejudicial to nature, raises a kind of violent motion in the mass, and endeavours, as it were, to escape, causes a chilness and shaking. . . . .

" Nature, therefore, being by these means irritated, raises a *fermentation* in order to expel the enemy with less difficulty, this being the common instrument she uses to free the blood of its morbid particles, as well in fevers as in some other acute diseases. For by means of the fermentation, the separated parts of the peccant matter, that were equally mixed with the blood, begin to be united together in some measure, and consequently may be more easily moulded so as to be fitted for despumation. . . . . . But these stages are severe, but in the third, namely, the *despumation*, all the symptoms first grow milder and afterwards go off entirely. *By despumation I mean no more than the expulsion, or separation, of the febrile matter, now in a manner overcome, when what is thrown off partly resembles yeast, and partly lees, as may be seen in other liquors.*"*

With regard to fevers and other acute diseases his indications of treatment were to keep the fermentation raised by nature in the blood in order to expel the morbific matter within bounds. In short he neither unseasonably checked nor promoted but duly regulated it. "But when the fermentation," says he, "neither rises too high, nor sinks too low, I leave it in that state without prescribing any medicine, unless forced to it by the importunity of the patient or his

---

* Swan's *Sydenham*, pp. 47, 48.

friends: and then I direct such only as may please without prejudicing."* For the treatment of intermittent fevers he cautions us not to give the Peruvian bark too early, for the following reason :—" The greatest caution must be had not to give it too early, namely, before the disease be in some measure spontaneously abated, unless the extreme weakness of the patient requires it to be given sooner; for the giving it too soon may render it ineffectual, and even fatal, if a sudden stop be thus put to the vigorous fermentation raised in the blood in order to its despumation."†

Let us now examine how much Sydenham resembled Hippocrates in his method of practice. Sydenham, like Hippocrates, remarks that nature does not always require the help of art. Speaking of the continued fever he observes :—" And in reality I have sometimes thought that we do not proceed slowly enough, and ought to use less expedition in removing distempers, and that more is frequently to be left to nature than is usual in the present practice. For it is a grand mistake to conclude that nature always wants the assistance of art."‡ Again he writes that children and young persons often recover from intermittents without medicines :—" I think it is best to forbear the use of medicines, and make no change as to air and diet; having hitherto found no inconveniency in leaving the cure wholly to nature, at which I have often been surprized, especially in infants; for the depuration of the blood being finished, these distempers go off spontaneously."§

---

* Swan's *Sydenham*, pp. 31, 32.　† Ibid., p. 61.
‡ Ibid., p. 214.　§ Ibid., p. 63.

Hippocrates bled and purged to evacuate the vitiated humours, Sydenham to evacuate the morbid fermentations. But to the credit of the latter it should be mentioned that he pursued the sanguinary plan sometimes with a feeling of regret in the absence of specifics, which he in vain struggled to discover. In pleurisy it was his practice to bleed four times from the arm, and draw blood not less than forty ounces without the least injury, as he says, to his patients, and yet our English Hippocrates was earnestly in search for another method of treatment as appears from the following :—

"I have indeed frequently endeavoured to discover some other method that might prove equally effectual without bleeding so copiously."

In rheumatism, Sydenham likewise recommends bleeding four times, because the blood in rheumatism " exactly resembles that of persons in a pleurisy." He however soon found out the mischief of this practice, and thus wrote to Dr. Brady :—

" As to the cure of the *rheumatism*, which you likewise desire to be informed of, I have frequently regretted, as well as you, that it could not be accomplished without the loss of a large quantity of blood by repeated bleeding ; whereby the strength is not only lost for a time, but weak persons become usually more disposed to other diseases for some years; when the matter occasioning the rheumatism afterwards falls upon the lungs, the latent indisposition in the blood being put into action, by taking cold, or some other slight cause. These reasons induced me to search after some other method of curing this disease than such repeated bleeding. And having well considered that it seemed to proceed from an inflammation, as appears from the other symptoms, but especially from the colour of the blood, which exactly resembles that of pleurisies, I judged it might probably be as successfully cured by a plain, cooling, and moderately nourishing diet, as by repeated bleeding ; and the inconveniencies likewise attending that method avoided. Accordingly, I found that a diet of *whey* used instead of bleeding had the desired effect."*

After giving a case in illustration he thus exclaims in favour of therapeutics of the simplest kind, for combating disease :—

"If any one should lightly esteem this method, by reason of its inelegance and plainness, I must tell him, that only weak minds slight things because they are common and simple ; and that I am ready to serve mankind, even at the expense of my reputation. And I must add, that were it not for the prejudice of the vulgar, I am certain that this method might be suited to other diseases, which I shall not now enumerate. And in reality, it would be much more serviceable than the pompous garlands of medicines, with which such as are ready to expire are crowned, as if they were to be sacrificed like beasts."†

From all this it would appear that Sydenham was forced as it were to follow the sanguinary plan in the absence of specifics; but he was at the same time in search after milder and better means which he discovered and applied for the cure of certain diseases. For the simplicity of his prescriptions he apologizes thus :—

"But if it be objected, that in some cases I have not only renounced the pompous part of prescription, but likewise recommended such medicines, as, by reason of their simplicity, have little or no affinity with the *materia medica* ; I answer, that I conceive that this procedure will offend none but persons of little understanding and less benevolence ; for the wise know that everything is good which is useful. And that Hippocrates in advising the use of bellows in *iliac passion*, and the total disuse of all medicines in a *cancer*, with other articles of a like nature, which occur in almost every page of his writings, deserves to be esteemed as able a physician as if he had filled them with the most pompous prescriptions."

Sydenham was a free thinker and a candid and

---

* Swan's *Sydenham*, p. 327.   † Ibid., p. 328.

impartial writer. Simplicity, clearness, acuteness of observation, and strictest attachment to truth, characterize every page of his writings. He did not blindly attach himself to the practices of the ancients, or to vain speculations, as will appear from the following passages:—

"I am persuaded the judicious part of mankind will not condemn me, who cannot but know that the improvement of medicine is alike obstructed by two sorts of men. The first are those who do not at all contribute to improve the art they profess, but hold those in contempt who do so in the smallest degree; and these men screen their ignorance and idleness under the specious pretence of an extraordinary respect for the ancients, from whom, they contend, we ought not in the least to depart."*

"There is likewise another kind of men, who, out of vain affectation to pass for persons of a superior understanding, plague the world with speculations that do not at all contribute towards the cure of diseases, but rather tend to mislead, than to direct, the physician."†

Sydenham was the first regular practitioner in England who investigated the properties of the Peruvian bark, and employed it largely in fevers. Peruvian bark, called also Cinchona bark, which is now sold from 3s. to 5s. per lb., was in the seventeenth century sometimes sold for by its weight in gold or silver. At other times it had not a single purchaser, for we learn that in the year 1690 " several thousand pounds lay at Piura and Payta for want of a purchaser." In short its price fluctuated with the fluctuating opinions of its admirers or detractors, and had opened a new field for the speculators of the period.

The American Indians were first acquainted with the virtues of the bark in curing malarious fevers.

---
* Swan's *Sydenham*, p. 535. † Ibid., p. 537.

They called it *Yara-Chuccu* and *Cava-Chuccu*, meaning the shivering tree or bark. Its properties were discovered by an accident. It is said that an American Indian suffering from fever, and becoming thirsty, drank some water from a pool which had been highly impregnated with the bark, and was consequently cured.

The term chinchona was derived from the Countess of Chinchon, the vice-regent of Peru, who was cured of her fever by taking the bark. The Jesuits learned from her the properties of this drug, and distributed it among the poor who were afflicted with the ague. From that period it also became known by the name of "Jesuits' powder." It was first introduced by the Jesuit missionaries into Spain, and was tried upon an ecclesiastic of Alcala. Its introduction met with much opposition from the medical profession, and it was in danger of falling into utter oblivion, when Pope Innocent X., by the solicitations of Cardinal de Lugo, a Spanish Jesuit, ordered a further trial of it. It was favourably reported upon, and was again received as a remedy for ague. But an unfortunate circumstance occurred which nearly put a stop to its use in Spain. In the year 1652 it failed to cure Leopold, Archduke of Austria, of a quartan fever. His chief physician Chifletius, who was always opposed to the use of bark, taking a base advantage of this failure, wrote a book against its virtues, denouncing it not only as useless but injurious.

Peruvian bark was introduced into England in the year 1653. The Members of the Royal College of Physicians, who should have been most forward in giving it a trial at a period when ague was sweeping off its victims by thousands in Britain, ridiculed, opposed and condemned its use. In 1658, the death of Mr. Underwood, an alderman of London, and of Captain Potter, an apothecary in Blackfriars, who were treated with cinchona, created a great sensation in London, "as if an alderman," remarks Dr. Russell, "had never died of ague before!" The drug now fell totally into disrepute. In the same year Oliver Cromwell died of an intermittent fever. Probably his life could have been saved by the timely administration of an ounce or two of the bark by his attending physician Dr. Bates. But this timid gentleman, blinded by prejudice and *usual routine*, treated him in his own way, and so brought about the death of the "Lord Protector of the three kingdoms."

Sydenham was the only practitioner in England who differed from those who attributed the death of Mr. Underwood and Captain Potter to the bark, without which, he emphatically says, "intermittents could not be better cured." But he is equally mistaken when he assigns the cause of the death to the exhibition of the bark "only a few hours before the coming of the fit." According to him "the danger proceeds less from the *bark* itself than from the unseasonable use thereof; for when a large quantity of febrile matter is collected in the body on the well days, the bark if taken immediately before the fit obstructs the expulsion of the morbific matter in the natural way (namely, by the violence of the fit), which being hereby improperly detained usually endangers life."*

---

* Swan's *Sydenham*, p. 307.

For this reason he invariably gave it directly after the fit in intermittent fevers. "When I am called," says he, "to a person afflicted with a *quartan*, suppose on a *Monday*, if the fit is expected the same day, I refrain from doing anything, and only give the patient hopes that he shall be freed from the next fit. And, in order to effect this, I exhibit the *bark* upon the two intermediate or well days, namely *Tuesday* and *Wednesday*."* On these days he administered an ounce of bark divided into twelve parts, one of which he gave every fourth hour. In fevers of a quotidian and tertian type, instead of giving bark in a few and larger doses, he gave it in the same dose and interval as in the quartan. "It must further be observed," says he, "that the intervals between the fits in *tertians* and *quotidians* are so short, that there is not sufficient time to impregnate the blood thoroughly with the febrifuge virtue of the bark; so that it is not possible that the patient should so certainly miss the next fit the first time of taking it, as it commonly happens in a *quartan*, for the medicine in these cases will frequently not perform the expected cure in less than two days."† When the intermittent approaches to a continued fever, it would not yield, he adds, to less than an ounce and a half or two ounces of the bark.

We have already remarked that to Sydenham is due the credit of having been the first, among the physicians of his period, who boldly re-introduced the bark into practice in England. But after an attentive perusal of that portion of his work which treats of

---

* Swan's *Sydenham*, pp. 307, 308. † Ibid., p. 311.

intermittent fever, we come to the conclusion that the way in which he used the drug was faulty. Richard Talbot, an English empiric, was more successful in curing agues than Sydenham. He must have been bold in the use of bark either before, during, or after the fit, in a large single dose or small oft-repeated doses. Richard Talbot or Talbor served as an apprentice to an apothecary. He was a scholar of St. John's College, Cambridge, but whether he obtained his degree is not known. Talbot acquired a considerable amount of wealth and reputation by his successful cures of ague. His fame spread abroad, and during his stay in Paris he cured the Dauphin of France (afterwards Louis XV.) of a fever which had resisted the treatment of his household physicians. Louis XIV. purchased his secret remedy (bark) for sixteen hundred pounds sterling, and allowed him a yearly pension of eighty pounds. He was knighted by king Charles II. Sir Richard was looked upon with jealousy by his less successful rivals. Even Sydenham seems to have had a feeling against him, and thus writes to a friend in a letter dated October 1677:—" I have had but few trials, but I am sure that an ounce of *bark*, given between the two fits, cures, while the *physicians* in *London*, not being pleased to take notice of my book, or not believing me, have given an opportunity to a fellow, that was but an apothecary's man, to go away with all the practice on *agues*, by which he has got an estate in two months, and brought great reproach on the faculty."*

---

* Swan's *Sydenham*, note to p. 308.

Sydenham was not knighted, Talbot was. "Kings and princes can indeed make professors and privy-councillors, and hang upon them titles, but great men they cannot make." The fame of the latter was short-lived, that of the former is unshaken and immortal. Sydenham, indifferent to his own bodily ailments, worked for the welfare of mankind up to the last, with hopes of success and not of reward. Sydenham was a man of liberal and enlightened spirits. He was an independent thinker, a zealous explorer of truth, self-relying, honest and religious. Among the English physicians of that period none stood so high in point of professional reputation and literary merits as Sydenham.

CHAPTER XV.

Stahl—His reputation as a teacher—Rejects the doctrines of the Chemical and Mechanical Physicians—His Anima—Expectant treatment—Hoffmann—Nervous fluid—Theory of Spasm—Flee doctors and drugs—Boerhaave—His reputation as a successful lecturer and practitioner—His system of cure—Power of Attenuated Medicines—Van Swieten—Haller—His early acquirements —Professor at Gottingen—His fame as a Physiologist—Doctrine of Irritability and Sensibility—Glisson—Whitt—His notions of the influence of Mind upon the Body.

At a time when the chemical and mathematical physicians were defending their respective theories and accusing each other of errors, another revolutionist entered the field of controversy, and originated a new theory. We allude to George Ernest Stahl, surnamed the Medical Plato, who was born at Anspach in the year 1660. At an early age he applied himself to the study of medicine. In 1683 he became M. D. of the university of Jena, and obtained great reputation as a teacher and practitioner. For some time he was physician to the court at Weimar. In 1694 he occupied the chair of medicine at Halle. In addition to a course of lectures on the institutes of medicine, he lectured on botany, materia medica and physiology. Trained as a chemical physician, he pursued with great zeal the study of chemistry, and began to entertain doubts about the correctness of the prevailing theories. He boldly rejected the chemical and mechanical doctrines which assigned vital manifestations to the laws of chemistry and mechanics, as erroneous. Stahl maintained that there is in the body a spiritual principle which he denominated *anima*. He believed it to be identical with the soul (which differed only in name from the Archæus of Van Helmont), and explained all the vital actions of the system to its presence. He taught that every part of the living economy is under the direct control of this dominating force; that this great agent presides over every tissue and organ of the body; and that it has control over assimilation and secretion. He also pointed out that it restrains or guards every part of the body from the effects of noxious causes, but when they have already invaded the animal economy, it tends to destroy them. In short, he supposed that the anima governed the body both in health and disease. Such was the famous theory of Stahl, in defence of which he wrote several dissertations. He supposed spontaneous evacuations to be the efforts of anima to relieve the *vena portæ*, which, according to him, was the seat of all distempers. In conformity with these views he occasionally made use of blood-letting and evacuant remedies, but only when the wisdom of anima failed.

Trusting much to the intelligence of anima, his system of rational medication consisted, for the most part, in the art of curing by *expectation*. Cullen condemns his practice as "inert and frivolous." Regarding this Dr. Thomson, the biographer of Cullen, justly observes:—" It being a matter of extreme difficulty to say at what point a cautious and prudent abstinence from interference passes into ignorant and careless negligence." Stahl totally discarded the use of opium and cinchona bark, and was very sparing in his use of blood-letting, emetics, purgatives, &c.

Stahl merits our particular attention, not as the founder of a new sect, but as an exposer of the errors of the prevailing theories which for a long time had divided the medical schools of Europe. Dr. Thomson, speaking of the *animism* of Stahl, makes the following observations:—" It is but just to Stahl, however, to acknowledge that he had the merit of directing the attention of medical practitioners in a more particular manner than had been done before his time, to that resistance to putrefaction which exists in the solid and fluid parts of the body during life,—to the vital activities by which the state of health is preserved, and its functions duly performed,—to the influence which the mind indirectly exercises over the different functions of the body,—to the effects of the different passions in exciting diseases,—and especially to those powers of the animal economy by which diseases are spontaneously cured or relieved."* Stahl was too presumptuous, and valued himself highly as the discoverer of a new theory which he upheld as correct, without any regard for the opinions and arguments of his learned colleagues and contemporaries. He even asserted that the study of the allied branches of medicine was of very little value, and boasted that " he had had no time to saunter through class rooms and wriggle through

---

* Thomson's *Cullen*, p. 181.

antiquarian libraries." Stahl was unpopular with the most distinguished teachers of his age. His unpopularity, however, was undoubtedly owing to his arrogant pretensions. His theory was embraced and followed by many learned physicians of the age, among whom the names of Juncker and Alberti, professors in the university of Halle, are prominent.

Another great ornament of the university of Halle, and one of the most famous teachers of his time, was Frederick Hoffmann. He was born at Halle in the year 1660. After a regular course of instruction he became M. D. of the university of Jena in 1681, and was elected a professor in the university of Halle in 1694. Stahl was his only colleague in the university. Both of them were born in the same year, took their degree of M. D. in the same university, and were appointed professors in the same year in the university of Halle. Both were men of learning and ingenuity. Stahl was stern, intolerant, arrogant, and self-willed, Hoffmann frank and communicative, and therefore more popular. There was also a striking dissimilarity in their medical opinions. Both taught and defended their own doctrines with equal zeal and emulation, and created a great agitation in the medical world.

The physiology and pathology of Hoffmann differed from those of his colleague Stahl. Hoffmann disputed that the moving power ascribed by Stahl to anima was in reality produced by a nervous influence. "Not the soul," he said, "but a material substance of extreme subtlety, something like æther— whatever that is,—something of a gaseous nature, secreted in the brain, and poured into the blood, which it vivifies. This something, finer than all other matter, but not exactly spirit, or soul, or mind, is the moving principle of the animal organization,— also called the nervous fluid. It is upon this that the contractility of the muscles depends; it is this in excess that gives rise to spasm; and a defective supply of this induces atony."*

He pointed out that the phenomena of life and the seat of disease originated in the solids of the body and not in the fluids. He conceived that the moving fibre is naturally endowed with a certain amount of tone for the healthy performance of its functions, and that any augmentation or diminution in its tone gives rise to spasm or atony. General spasms give rise to fever, inflammation, &c., particular spasms to diseases in particular organs of the body, and atony to most chronic diseases. He classified his remedies accordingly, and administered sedatives in diseases which arose from spasm, and stimulants when from atony. He advises us to suspend the administration of medicines in long standing diseases for a time, in order to maintain the susceptibility of the system.

Hoffmann rejected humorism, and was not an advocate of the heroic treatment. He recommended the use of fewer medicines in his practice rather than the abuse of a considerable number, and approved his favourite maxim, " Flee doctors and drugs if you wish to be well."

Another great man, perhaps the most distinguished

---

* Hoffmann, *Anweisung zur Gesundheit*, quoted by Russell.

of his age, was Herman Boerhaave, born in the neighbourhood of Leyden in 1668. Hutchinson describes him thus :—" He was of a robust and athletic constitution of body, so hardened by early severities and wholesome fatigue that he was insensible to any sharpness of the air or inclemency of weather. He was tall and remarkable for extraordinary strength. There was in his air and motion something rough and artless, but so majestic and great at the same time that no man looked upon him without veneration, and a kind of tacit submission to the superiority of his genius. He was always cheerful and desirous of promoting mirth by a facetious and humorous conversation. He was never soured by calumny and detraction, nor ever thought it necessary to confute them, 'for they are sparks,' said he, 'which if you do not blow them will go out of themselves.'" He was designed by his father to follow the profession of theology, and was sent to Leyden to prosecute his studies. Here he evinced much ability and diligence in mastering the ancient languages and history. Changing his mind he quitted theological studies for medicine. He began his medical studies with much zeal and assiduity, and so rapid was his progress that he soon rose to high station and great honour. In 1701 he was appointed lecturer on the theory of medicine. Eight years later he was appointed professor to the chair of practical medicine. In addition to these he lectured on chemistry and botany. In 1715 he was elected physician to St. Augustine's Hospital, where he also gave clinical lectures. The reputation which he enjoyed as a successful and eloquent lecturer was undisputed. His lectures were read with great admiration in Europe, and his fame and influence spread through every part of the civilised world. He was more than usually successful in his practice, and on his death, which took place in 1738, left a large fortune of £200,000. A Chinese mandarin hearing of his fame is said to have consulted him by letter addressed " To the illustrious Boerhaave physician in Europe." Again: " The Czar Peter is reported to have lain all night in his pleasure-barge, against Boerhaave's house, to have the advantage of two hours' conversation with him on various points of learning, the next morning before college time."

The name of Boerhaave is not celebrated for any improvement in the practice of medicine. Properly speaking, he was an eclectic or a system-builder. He did not belong to any particular sect, but chose from the tenets of each what he considered most valuable and true. He based his system upon the combined opinions of others, with a few observations of his own. He supported the mechanical theory of Borelli and Bellini, believed in humorism, and agreed in some points with the opinions of Hoffmann. In fact he believed in crudity, coction, and evacuation; acidities, alkalinities, and the supposed mechanical condition of the solids and fluids of the body. His principal works, the " Institutions" and " Aphorisms" are valued for the varied and accurate information they contain on interesting topics connected, with medicine, but are seldom referred to by modern writers. As a chemist he was unrivalled in his age. His pathology is meaningless, and therefore of no value to the pathologists of the present day. The following two passages from his work show that he knew before Hahnemann the power of attenuated medicines:—

"Medicines may preserve their virtue although divided into such minute parts that the imagination can no longer follow them."

"It is evident from what follows that medicines may be so much attenuated that they evade our search, but although these particles are no longer appreciable to our senses, they do not the less produce very marked effects on our organization."

We are not informed whether he largely used attenuated medicines in his practice, and with what results. The homœopathists assert that it was reserved for Hahnemann to demonstrate their action.

Boerhaave was a man of erudition, learning, and practical skill. His acquirements were varied, his powers versatile, and his reputation brilliant. Possessed of an active mind, combined with unceasing industry, he became well skilled in medical literature. He read much and learned much. He was a man of such great renown that after his recovery from a serious illness in 1722, there was a general illumination in Leyden.

One of the most zealous adherents and propagators of the system of Boerhaave was his pupil Van Swieten. He was a man of considerable attainments. His professional reputation gained for him a professorship in the university of Leyden, where he was accounted one of its brightest ornaments. The fame of his learning obtained him an invitation from Maria Theresa. At Vienna he was appointed lecturer on materia medica and the practice of physic. The Empress bestowed on him special marks of favour by appointing him her physician and librarian. His Commentary on the Aphorisms of Boerhaave was considered a work of great research and observation.

Another writer of importance who deserves to be noticed on this occasion was Albert Haller. He was born in the year 1708 of a noble family at Berne. From early years he had a strong predilection for literature. At the age of ten he distinguished himself by his acquirements in the ancient languages and poetry. When about fifteen years of age he left to study medicine in the university of Tubingen, and at seventeen went to the famous university of Leyden, where his promising talents early recommended him to his illustrious teacher Boerhaave. Although only eighteen years of age, young Haller took his doctor's degree in that university. Such was his thirst after knowledge that he went to Paris, London, &c. for improvement, and on his return to Berne was appointed physician to the hospital. The fame of his learning soon gained for him the chair of medicine, anatomy, and botany in the recently established Hanoverian university at Gottingen. This post he occupied for many years with great distinction and success. He had the honour of being raised to the dignity of a baronet by the Emperor Francis I., and was chosen a member of many literary societies. After several years of patient and unwearied labour in the field of medicine at Gottingen, he returned to his native city to pass the remnant of his life and energies in pursuits of a literary character. Here he had been chosen a member of the Grand Council. His death took place on the 12th of December 1777.

Haller was a versatile and voluminous writer. Few employed their pens upon so many and such varied subjects. He enriched science by the publication of a great many works. But his fame principally rests upon his physiological writings, which were long held in high estimation. Haller ranks high among the distinguished physiologists, and is deservedly called the Father of Physiology. He maintained that all the actions of the living system are not, as Stahl affirmed, under the control of the soul, but depend upon the property of irritability or *vis insita* and sensibility or *vis nervosa*, both of which he regarded as co-ordinate principles; and that stimulating agents, chemical, mechanical, or thermal, which he called irritants, produced muscular contraction. Depressants or stimulants were indicated in acute diseases in accordance to increased or diminished irritability.

The term "muscular irritability" was first applied by Glisson to that power in virtue of which a muscle contracted on the application of a stimulus. According to him there are three degrees of irritability—the moderate, the sluggish, and the excessive; and all diseases were regarded as arising either from excessive or defective irritability of the living fibres. His opinions did not attract the attention of medical men. The subject was more fully investigated by Haller, and his experiments on irritability and sensibility have ever since had a great share in directing the attention of physiologists to the necessity of entering deeper into the study and investigation of the nervous system.

The theory of Haller met with much opposition from Dr. Whitt, a professor and colleague of Dr.

Cullen, in the university of Edinburgh. The following are his notions of the influence of mind upon the body:—" The mind in carrying on the vital and other involuntary motions, does not act as a rational but as a sentient principle, which without reasoning is as certainly determined by an ungrateful sensation or stimulus affecting the organs, to exert its power in bringing about these motions, as is a scale which, by mechanical laws, turns with the greatest weight."

CHAPTER XVI.

Cullen—His early education—Visits Glasgow and Edinburgh—His fame as a Lecturer—His notion of Life—Experience without Reasoning fallacious—His theory of Fever—Cinchona Bark not a specific—Its action in curing fevers explained—Blood-letting in Pneumonia and Measles—Blisters in Small-pox—John Brown—His early career—Theory of Excitability—The Brunonians—Their fanaticism—Brown's disorderly behaviour and death.

Among the great men of the eighteenth century Cullen deserves prominent mention. William Cullen was born at Hamilton in Scotland in the year 1720. His parents were of humble descent. His early education was obtained at the grammar school of his native town. He was afterwards sent to study in the university of Glasgow, and was subsequently apprenticed to an eminent surgeon of that city. In his twentieth year young Cullen went to London, and received an appointment as surgeon to a trading vessel. After an absence of three years he returned to London. Thence he went to Shotts and Northumberland, where he assiduously applied himself to the study of general literature, philosophy, and medicine; and finished his medical education by attending two sessions in the university of Edinburgh. At the age of twenty-six he started in practice at Hamilton, where he became acquainted with the celebrated William Hunter. After a stay of seven years in his native city, he revisited Glasgow, and took a conspicuous part in the formation of its medical school. In the university of Glasgow no lectures were delivered with the exception of those on anatomy. Cullen soon obtained permission to deliver a course of lectures on the theory and practice of physic, materia medica, chemistry, and botany, not in the Latin language, as was the established practice at that period, but in English. Under his auspices the school acquired considerable celebrity. The reputation of Cullen as a lecturer and practitioner was fast rising. In 1755 he went to Edinburgh, and was appointed to deliver lectures on chemistry along with Dr. Plummer, in the university, and also gave clinical lectures at the royal infirmary. His success and reputation soon gained for him the professorship of materia medica on the death of Dr. Alston. To these appointments was added the chair of theoretical medicine on the decease of Dr. Whyte. In 1765 Cullen failed to succeed Dr. Rutherford in the chair of practical medicine, as that gentleman only resigned in favour of Dr. John Gregory of Aberdeen. But such was Cullen's fame as a lecturer, that in the year 1768 Dr. Gregory, complying with the desire of the students and professors, permitted him to lecture alternately with himself on the theory and on the practice of medicine, and in the year 1773 he was solely appointed to the chair of practical medicine vacant by the death of Dr. Gregory. From this period he rose to a foremost position in the profession in his own country, and his works rendered his name known all over Europe.

The works of Cullen are of considerable merit, and contain much interesting information. His "Synopsis Nosologæ Methodicæ" is treated at length and with much clearness. His "Materia Medica" betrays an intimate acquaintance with this branch of the art, and marks a state of considerable advancement. It was translated into German by Samuel Hahnemann. Our limits will not permit us to enter into an analysis of the above works. His " Physiology" is fairly written. The subject is treated with great clearness and simplicity; and the chapters devoted to the nervous system are excellent. The following passages express his notion of life :—

"There is seemingly diffused over the whole of nature a quantity of electric matter, which, however, in the ordinary state of most bodies, shows no disposition to a particular mobility in passing from one body to another, so that though it is present, it does not show any disposition to motion; but we can, by certain artifices, accumulate this electric matter in more considerable quantity upon the surface of certain bodies, in consequence of which it can be put in motion from one body to another, exhibiting the various phenomena of electricity; and it is agreed upon by philosophers to call this *excitement*, and to say that electricity is excited, and that such bodies are excited electrics; and all bodies may be so either by being excited themselves, or by having such bodies applied to them as are. So, in our medullary fibre, there is a fluid which was present in the germ, but was not excited; and it is in the excited state of this that I suppose life to consist, and when it is no longer excited in any degree, we call it the state of death; and I can suppose, as in electricity, that it may exist in different degrees. Thus, sometimes I can take a stroke at a yard's distance from the surface of the body that is excited, and show that the electric fluid extends to such a distance ; at other times we must come within a quarter of a yard, and at other times we must come still nearer ; and so it can pass through various degrees till it is collapsed altogether."*

---

* *Cullen's Works*, by Thomson, vol. I., p. 130.

"From what is now said of the excitement and collapse of the brain, it will appear that we suppose LIFE, so far as it is corporeal, to consist in the excitement of the nervous system, and especially of the brain, which unites the different parts, and forms them into a whole. But, as certain other functions of the body are necessary to the support of this excitement, we thence learn that the causes of death may be of two kinds; one that acts directly on the nervous system, destroying its excitement; and another that indirectly produces the same effect, by destroying the organs and functions necessary to its support."*

It is not, however, our intention to deal with his "Physiology," as a great and important change has taken place in the knowledge of this department of science.

The greatest and most interesting of all his works, entitled "First Lines of the Practice of Physic," has always been held in enthusiastic admiration in Great Britain. Dr. Cullen in his introduction to the "First Lines" says :—

" The knowledge of the circulation did indeed necessarily lead to the consideration as well as to a clearer view of the organic system in animal bodies; which again led to the application of the mechanical philosophy towards explaining the phenomena of the animal economy; and it was applied accordingly, and continued, till very lately, to be the fashionable mode of reasoning on the subject. Such reasoning, indeed, must still in several respects continue to be applied: but it would be easy to show that it neither could, nor ever can be, applied to in explaining the animal economy, and we must therefore look for other circumstances which had a greater share in modelling the system of physic."†

He next forcibly impresses upon us the importance and utility of studying physic upon a dogmatic plan, and states that experience without reasoning is " dif-

---
* *Cullen's Works*, by Thomson, vol. I., p. 135.   † Ibid., p. 398.

ficult, fallacious and insufficient." In support of this statement he produces the three following arguments:

"The *first* is, that reasoning in physic is unavoidable, and that, to render it safe, it is necessary to cultivate theory in its full extent.

"The *second* argument is, that supposing the chief object of our study to be the acquiring of facts, the study of a dogmatic system has been the chief means of obtaining those which we have already acquired, and is also the most certain means of acquiring those we still want; it is therefore useful and necessary.

"Our *third* argument is, that there is no tolerable foundation for the study of physic upon an empiric plan, and that all attempts hitherto made towards delivering it upon that footing have been not only fruitless but pernicious."*

Fevers are next brought into notice. The account given of their phenomena, causes and prognosis is full and clear. His theory of fever is this. The most remote causes of fever, he says, are contagion, malaria, fear, anxiety, cold, &c. These act as sedatives to the nervous system, and induce a state of debility. The *vis medicatrix naturæ*, to prevent the noxious power from hurting or destroying the system, intervenes, and induces a cold fit and a spasm of the extreme vessels. The heart and arteries become irritated, and act with increased force, and produce the hot stage. Such a force has the effect of resolving the spasm, dilating the extreme vessels, and consequently terminating the fever by spontaneous sweating. Therefore, one of his indications for the cure of fever was to remove the supposed spasm of the extreme vessels, which he believed to be the cause of subsequent reaction. "During the whole course of the fever," he says, "there is an atony subsisting in the extreme

---

* *Cullen's Works*, by Thomson, vol. I., p. 417.

vessels, and the relaxation of the spasm requires the restoring of the tone and action of these."

Cullen ascribes the operation of cinchona bark in curing agues to its tonic power. Let us hear of his own explanation of its action:—

"This bark has been commonly considered as a specific, or as a remedy of which the operation was not understood. But it is certainly allowable to inquire into the matter, and I apprehend it may be explained.

"To this purpose it is to be remarked, that as, in many cases, the effects of the bark are perceived soon after its being taken into the stomach, and before it can possibly be conveyed to the mass of blood, we may conclude that its effects do not arise from its operating on the fluids; and must, therefore, depend upon its operating on the nerves of the stomach, and being thereby communicated to the rest of the nervous system. This operation seems to be a tonic power, the bark being a remedy in many cases of debility, particularly in gangrene: and, as the recurrence of the paroxysms of intermittent fevers depends upon a recurrence of atony, so probably the bark, by its tonic power, prevents the recurrence of these paroxysms; and this is greatly confirmed by observing, that many other tonic medicines answer the same purpose.*

The subject of treatment in fevers, inflammatory diseases, and exanthemata, is the only really defective portion of this book. His erroneous theory of fevers in general led him to the use of—or properly speaking the abuse of—bleeding, purgatives, emetics, blisters, &c., in these diseases. The utility of such a practice is very doubtful, and the use of such strong means is now abandoned by the most eminent practitioners in Europe. As a sample of his treatment we shall only quote a few. Pneumonia he be-

---

* *Cullen's Works*, by Thomson, vol. I., pp. 639, 640.

lieves to be spasm of the pulmonary arterioles, and was invariably treated by bleeding:—

"A quantity of from four to five pounds, in the course of two or three days, is generally as much as such patients will safely bear; but if the intervals between the bleeding and the whole of the time during which the bleedings have been employed have been long, the quantity taken, upon the whole, may be greater.

"When a large quantity of blood has been already taken from the arm, and when it is doubtful if more can with safety be drawn in that manner, some blood may still be taken by cupping and scarifying."*

In the treatment of measles he in like manner seems to be free with the blood of his little patients, and recommends bleeding even after the desquamation takes place:—

"The expectation of an eruption should never prevent us from bleeding. I have hinted, once and again, how much certain practitioners were adverse to it, from the consideration that the fever is necessary for the eruption; but in the measles it is agreed that if the fever or dyspnœa give any suspicion of a high degree of inflammation, bleeding is necessary, safe and proper, at every period in the course of the disease." †

"When the desquamation of the measles is finished, though there should then be no disorder remaining, physicians have thought it necessary to purge the patients several times, with a view to draw off the dregs of this disease, that is, a portion of the morbific matter which is supposed to remain long in the body. I cannot reject this supposition; but, at the same time, cannot believe that the remains of the morbific matter, diffused over the whole mass of blood, can be entirely drawn off by purging; and it appears to me that to avoid the consequences of the measles, it is not the drawing of the morbific matter which we need to study so much, as the obviating and removing the inflammatory state of the system which had been induced by the disease. With this last view indeed, purging may still be a proper remedy; but bleeding, in proportion to the symptoms of inflammatory disposition, is yet more so." ‡

---

* *Cullen's Works*, by Thomson, vol. II., p. 58.
† Ibid., vol. II., p. 172. ‡ Ibid., vol. II., p. 173.

For the treatment of small-pox, in addition to bleeding and purging, he says:—" It will be always proper to give a vomit, as useful in the commencement of all fevers, and more especially in this, where a determination to the stomach appears, from pain and spontaneous vomiting."* And what are we to think of the following passage:—

" In a violent disease," meaning the small-pox, "from the eighth to the eleventh day, it is proper to lay on blisters successively on different parts of the body, and that without regard to the parts being covered with pustules."†

We repeat that such a practice has been attended with mischievous consequences. The old-fashioned practice of bleeding, blistering, and administering emetics in acute diseases has happily died out. In chronic diseases he seems to have wisely disapproved of the practice of preceding physicians.

That Cullen had a great genius as a writer is unquestionable. He was a man of great natural sagacity and considerable learning. By the exertion of his own faculties he obtained a high degree of celebrity, and his merit in his own country was unrivalled. His writings give us a correct idea of the state of medicine in the eighteenth century. They also give proof of the fine genius and extraordinary powers of this great man.

We now pass on to the history of one who became the founder of a new medical system which created a great sensation in Europe. We allude to John

---
* *Cullen's Works*, by Thomson, vol. II., pp. 163, 164.
† Ibid., vol. II., p. 165.

Brown. He was descended from a poor Scotch family who resided in Berwickshire. In his early years he became a tolerable scholar, and entered the family of a laird of that city as tutor. He was originally designed for the church, but having a taste for medical studies he resolved to make medicine his profession. This ingenious and eloquent though not deeply accomplished youth, on his quitting Berwickshire, went to Edinburgh, where he obtained great reputation by his lectures in opposition to the doctrines of Cullen, his former friend and patron, and produced a number of works which gained him some distinction. Brown was one of those who endeavour to bring themselves into notice by assailing the character of their superiors. He distinguished himself by his force of style, eloquence, and ready wit, but chiefly by his determined opposition to the doctrines of Cullen and by the promulgation of a new theory, the production of his own unaided genius. The simplicity and novelty of his theory attracted many adherents in his own country and abroad.

Brown accounts for all diseases by excessive or diminished *excitability*. He divided all diseases into sthenic and asthenic, the former was induced by excessive excitability, which produced direct debility or exhaustion, and is to be treated by bleeding, purging, &c., the latter arose from exhausted excitability, which was characterized by indirect debility or accumulation of excitement, and is to be combated by stimulating substances. " He assumed," says Dr. Bostock, " that the living body possesses a specific property or power, termed excitability ; that everything which in any way affects the living body acts upon this power as an excitant or stimulant, that the effect of this operation, or excitement, when in its ordinary state, is to produce the natural and healthy condition of the functions; when excessive it causes exhaustion, termed direct debility, when defective, it produces an accumulation of excitement, or what is termed indirect debility. All morbid action is conceived to depend upon one or other of these states of direct or indirect debility, and diseases are accordingly arranged in two great corresponding classes of sthenic or asthenic; while the treatment is solely directed to the general means for increasing or diminishing the excitement, without any regard to specific symptoms, or any consideration but that of degree, or any measure but that of quality."*

This simple doctrine of excitability attracted many young and inexperienced followers, and agitated the medical schools of Europe. It was received with a considerable degree of popularity in the university of Edinburgh and in Italy, and had even some followers of great celebrity. Among the followers of Brown, known as the "Brunonians," the young and inexperienced always betrayed a want of temper in hearing the arguments of their opponents. "In the famous university of Gottingen, the Brunonians, as they were called, to the number of four hundred, headed by a young professor, made so furious an attack with cudgels upon their opponents, that the police had to be called in, who with difficulty dis-

---
* *History of Medicine*, prefixed to the Cyclopædia of Practical Medicine.

persed the young zealots. Indignant at being defeated, they collected again the next day, carried the guard-house of police by assault, and remained masters of the situation, from which it required a regiment of Hanoverian horse to dislodge them. Had they been trained and armed, as our students happily are, with rifles, even this *ultima ratio* would have failed; and who knows whether the jewel of Hanover might not have been prematurely lost to the British Crown, and a Brunonian dynasty established! As it was, a regular *émeute* of all the students took place, to the number of 1,500. They marched out of Gottingen to show their sense of the insult done to their body by the interference of the military, and nothing but the removal of the dragoons from the town could pacify them."*

On the other hand, the theory of Brown was opposed and unfavourably regarded by a majority of men of medical erudition and experience; and he himself was exposed to ridicule. Enraged at such treatment, he held the learning of these men in contempt, and attributed their opposition more to envy and jealousy than to the defect of his own system, or to the want of ripe judgment, discrimination, and prudence in disseminating and forcing it upon the profession as true. From Edinburgh Brown went up to London as the place of making a fortune, still bent on preaching his own doctrine as true. Provoked by the incessant attacks of the critics, and deluded by his own powers of argument, he there showed great eccentricity of character, and plunged into dis-

---

* Russell's *History and Heroes of Medicine*, pp. 335, 336.

sipation. It is said of him that for several years he was never free from the influence of liquor.

Brown was a man of moderate attainments, dissipated habits, and overbearing temper, but of great natural acuteness and ingenuity. His theory was noticed more on account of its novelty than from any intrinsic merits, and like all other theories based upon slender foundation, maintained its celebrity in a few medical schools only for a short time after the age in which it was produced. Brown died in London of apoplexy at the age of fifty-two, in great penury, caused by his own excesses.

CHAPTER XVII.

Birth and education of Jenner.—The peasantry of Gloucestershire and the reputed power of Cow-pox—Jenner investigates the subject—Meets with various obstacles—True and Spurious Cow-pox—The *grease* in horses—Identity of Cow-pox and Small-pox—Birthday of Vaccination—Small-pox after Cow-pox—Revaccination—Ravages of Small-pox—Honours paid to Jenner—Parliament votes him £30,000—India transmits a present of £7,383—The Peculiar People—History of Small-pox Inoculation.

Among the most eminent of British physicians Jenner holds a prominent place. Edward Jenner, the chief ornament of the age in which he flourished, and who has acquired immortal fame by his discovery of vaccination, was born at Berkley in Gloucestershire on the 17th of May 1749. He was the third son of a vicar in Gloucestershire. From an early age he evinced a capacity for the study of natural history. After going through the usual course of study in Cirencester under Dr. Washbourn, he received his professional education from Mr. Ludlow, a surgeon at Sudbury, near Bristol. Thence he removed in 1770 to London, and entered as a pupil in St. George's Hospital. For two years he resided as a pupil in the house of the celebrated John Hunter, who soon admitted him to his friendship. The genius of Jenner early displayed itself, and the situation of naturalist to accompany Captain Cook in his second voyage was offered to him, but he declined it. On his return to Berkley in 1775 he immediately started in practice, and his reputation increased rapidly. Here he devoted his time and energies to the pursuits of a literary character, and became an active member of several learned societies. Jenner knew that there was a common belief among the peasantry of Gloucestershire that the milkers who had had the cow-pox were secure against the small-pox. While an apprentice at Sudbury he had heard the remark from a country woman, in whose presence the subject of small-pox was casually introduced, "I cannot take that disease, for I have had cow-pox." During his residence in London, Jenner mentioned the popular notion of the people inhabiting the dairy-farming districts of Gloucestershire to John Hunter, but he received little satisfaction or encouragement for his opinion on the interesting subject. It also excited no interest, and met with no support from the profession. Though discouraged he continued his industry, and on his return to Berkley, pursued his labours with increased assiduity and ardour. Hitherto his great passion seems to have been to investigate the prophylactic virtues of cow-pox. Many difficulties presented themselves, but they retired before his perseverance. Jenner remarked that some persons not previously attacked by small-pox could not be inoculated with matter taken from the pustules of those suffering from the natural disease, while others who considered themselves protected by the cow-pox, took small-pox by inoculation. By diligent attention and perseverance he found that the teats of cows were liable to several eruptions, all of which were indiscriminately called the cow-pox. He also ascertained that only one variety possessed the power of protection against small-pox, which he called the *true*, the others the *spurious* cow-pox, and that it was only at a certain period of its progress that the true cow-pox possessed antivariolous properties. "During the investigation of the casual small-pox," he says, "I was struck with the idea that it might be practicable to propagate the disease by inoculation, first from the cow and finally from one human being to another." In prosecuting his studies into the nature of cow-pox he came to the conclusion that the true cow-pox did not originate with the cow itself, but was at all times communicated to that animal by persons who had dressed the heels of horses affected with a disorder known to farriers by the name of the *grease*. This observation of Jenner is right to some extent. Later researches have shown that it may sometimes originate in the cow independently of any contagion from the grease; and on the other hand the vaccine virus can be easily conveyed to the horse with the result of reproducing it in a pure state. It has been also proved that the disease is directly communicated to man without the medium of the cow. Dr. de Carro of Vienna states that "the matter in use at Vienna from 1799 to 1825 was partly British vaccine and partly originated from the grease of a horse at Milan without the intervention of a cow. The effect was so similar in every respect, that they were soon mixed; that is to say, after several generations, and in the hands of innumerable practitioners, it was impossible to distinguish what was vaccine and what was equine." And adds: "The whole British settlement in India were *equinated*; for the first liquid drop sent thither was the second generation of Milanese equine, or greasy matter transplanted at Vienna."*

Jenner next hints that the variolous and vaccine poisons were identical, and derivable from one common source; that small-pox itself may have been a virus of the nature of cow-pox, but that it had after a lapse of time become contagious and malignant, and that small-pox in passing through the system of the animal had assumed a milder form of the malady, that is to say, was merely a modified small-pox. Very conflicting views are held regarding this theory of Dr. Jenner. Early in the history of vaccination it was inferred that " the infection of small-pox may by inoculation be communicated from man to the cow; that its result is an eruption of vesicles presenting the physical characters of cow-pox; that the lymph from these vesicles, if implanted in the skin of the human subject, produces the ordinary local phenomena of vaccination; that the person so vaccinated diffuses no atmospheric infection; that the lymph generated by him may be transferred, with reproductive powers, to other unprotected persons; and that, on the conclusion of this artificial disorder, neither renewed vaccination, nor inoculation with small-pox, nor the closest contact and cohabitation with small-pox patients, will occasion him to betray any remnant of susceptibility to infection." Such views have of late been abandoned by many men experienced in vaccination, who strongly

---
* Edinburgh *Journal of Medical Science*, vol. I.

suspect that this mode has given rise to outbreaks of true small-pox. Dr. Jenner also believed that the cow-pox was generally a local disease affecting the udder of the cow. Later observations have however shown this opinion to be erroneous. It is sufficient to observe that it is a constitutional disorder attended by febrile symptoms.

Although Jenner conceived the magnificent thought of propagating the cow-pox, first from the cow by inoculation, and successively from one individual to another, probably in 1780, no opportunity presented itself to him for several years to put to test the truth of his speculations by actual experiments, so that not being convinced he even inoculated his own son with small-pox matter in 1789. At length the cow-pox disease, which was absent for several years in the dairies of Gloucestershire, broke out with unusual violence in 1796. The 14th of May 1796 is a memorable day in the annals of medicine, as that in which Dr. Jenner for the first time vaccinated James Phipps, a boy of eight years of age, with matter taken from the hands of a milker named Sarah Nelmes, who had accidentally taken the disease from a cow. The disorder ran its course regularly and satisfactorily. The next step was to ascertain whether the boy was susceptible to small-pox contagion. On the 1st of July following Jenner engrafted the matter of small-pox pustule under the cuticle of the boy, and no disorder manifested itself in any form. Growing bold by his success, he subsequently vaccinated a number of children from each other. Success attended every effort, and Jenner after a delay of several months announced in June 1798 the discovery of cow-pox inoculation as affording protection against exposure to small-pox. The result of all his researches and the unremitting application of several years appeared in a treatise entitled " Enquiry into the Causes of Variola Vaccinæ."

At the commencement of the present century vaccination made rapid progress, and was almost universally adopted by the civilized nations of the world. Successful experiments were made with cow-pox matter in London by Mr. Cline, an eminent surgeon and intimate friend of Jenner. Dr. Gregory deserves the merit of introducing vaccination into Scotland. In 1799 the practice of vaccination was first introduced into America, and in 1800 into France. De Carro of Vienna and Dr. Sacco of Milan were the advocates who deserve credit for their exertions in propagating it over the Continent of Europe. In June 1802 vaccine lymph reached Bombay.

The cows in India are occasionally subject to an epidemic disease, attended with various eruptions, which the natives call *matta*, but the matter taken from such pustules is not known to possess anti-variolous properties. We learn that on two occasions true Jennerian cow-pox did prevail among cattle in India in 1832. Dr. McPherson discovered genuine cow-pox among some cattle in Moorsheedabad, and Messrs. Brown and Furnell in Assam. All of them inoculated children with the crusts removed from the animals. Fine pustules resembling vaccinia appeared, from which others were inoculated successfully.

In 1799 vaccination received a sudden check, and

was in danger of falling into discredit and neglect in England by the carelessness and ill-success of its two advocates, Drs. Woodville and Pearson, of the Small-pox Hospital. Many cases terminated unfavourably, and parents refused to vaccinate their children. Jenner went to London to detect any source of error. His prompt genius soon discovered that they had by mistake mixed the small-pox and vaccine poisons. The explanation was favourably received, and vaccination again became popular. In his second publication, which appeared in 1799, Jenner unassumingly recommends "that the investigations should be conducted with that calmness and moderation which should for ever accompany a philosophical research." But, elated by the success that everywhere attended the practice of vaccination, he, in his third publication, dated 1800, expressed his belief that "the cow-pox is capable of extirpating small-pox from the earth." And in his fourth publication in the following year he injudiciously gave out as his opinion that "it now becomes too manifest to admit of controversy that the annihilation of the small-pox, the most dreadful scourge of the human species, must be the final result of this practice." In 1801, Dr. Jenner stated that vaccination had been performed on upwards of six thousand persons, the greater part of whom were not attacked by small-pox either upon exposure to its influence or when tested by the mode of inoculation. There can be no doubt that vaccination gives permanent security during the whole life in most cases. It must also be admitted that small-pox does sometimes attack vaccinated persons, the greater number of whom pass through a mild form of the disease termed *modified* small-pox; only a very few who after vaccination receive small-pox in after-life are carried off.

Abundant evidence has been afforded to show that the protective influence of vaccination is impaired or lost in the course of years; and the practice of re-vaccination has been adopted in many countries as the only means of affording permanent security against small-pox. The Prussian Government was the first to give a strong impulse to the practice of re-vaccination. No vaccination can be held efficient which does not include re-vaccination at the period of puberty, or at shorter intervals when small-pox prevails epidemically. The advantages of re-vaccination are really very great, but it must be confessed that the idea of entirely eradicating small-pox from the earth, as Jenner imagined, has not, up to this time, been realized. It has been lately maintained by some, and not without good reason, that arm-to-arm vaccination has the danger of transmitting in a very few cases other diseases than cow-pox, and should therefore be abandoned as soon as a sufficient supply of pure lymph could be obtained, either directly from the heifers vaccinated by lymph taken from the vesicles of *true* animal cow-pox, or from the stock kept up by a long series of vaccinations practised on animals from the same source.

We repeat that since this extraordinary discovery, the saving of human life from this terribly fatal and disfiguring malady has been great beyond belief. "On one occasion, the capital of Thibet was deserted for three years by all its inhabitants, except the victims of this disease, who, of course, were left to perish. Similar scenes took place in Ceylon and in Russia. In one year *two million persons* are reported to have died of small-pox. In Iceland, in 1707, it destroyed sixteen thousand persons—one-fourth of the whole population. It is calculated that there perished of this disease annually in Europe alone 210,000," a small number indeed when we learn that in a severe epidemic of small-pox in the Russian empire *two million persons* perished in a single year. Before the introduction of vaccination in England the number of deaths by small-pox exceeded forty thousand annually. The average mortality from small-pox in London alone was two thousand a year. During the severe epidemic of 1796 the loss in this city was 2,549. When the disease raged throughout Mexico in the year 1520, it has been computed that *three millions and a half* of inhabitants fell victims to it. The disorder was brought to them by a negro, who had arrived on the Mexican coast.

The services which Jenner rendered to mankind began to be appreciated soon after his announcement of the discovery of vaccination. In the year 1800 Jenner had personal interviews with the King, the Queen, the Prince of Wales, and the luminaries of England, and was honoured with letters and presents from foreign princes. He also received several marks of distinction from learned societies. The German nation presented him with three medals, the surgeons of the British navy with one, and the London Medical Society with another. Parliament was petitioned to consider the claims of Jenner, and a committee of the House of Commons, after a careful and attentive investigation, having reported favourably of the merit of his discovery, a sum of £10,000 was voted to him in 1802, and in 1807 an additional grant of £20,000 was awarded to him. We have great pleasure in stating that India was not wanting in liberality and gratitude towards this benefactor of mankind. The friends of vaccination in Calcutta, Bombay, and Madras, transmitted to Dr. Jenner £4,000, £2,000, and £1,383 respectively. To use the words of Dr. Russell: " Surely the man who succeeded in subduing this terrible dragon, had he been a Greek, and lived in the age of mythology, would have come down to us as one of the demi-gods; but times are changed, and the life of the Englishman was sufficiently prosaic." It is impossible for any one to read the life of this philanthropic man without a feeling of surprise that he had not the honour of being raised to the dignity of a Knight or a Baronet. Nothing could have been more unjust. Even when it was proposed to place the statue of Jenner by the side of the hero of Scindh, an outcry was raised against it in the House of Commons. There is no better specimen than this of the ingratitude of a thankless world towards a man who rendered his name immortal by saving millions of lives, and to whom earthly rewards were as nothing. Surely times are changed. But let it be remembered that the services which Jenner rendered to mankind have transmitted his name to posterity ; immortal fame is his reward, the gratitude of posterity his everlasting title of honour. He died full of years, crowned with honour and success.

The opposition which great reformers had always met with was also expected in the case of Jenner; but fortunately his discovery was opposed only by the suspicious from the medical ranks and a few superstitious clergymen, not to mention the " peculiar people" who are always to be found among the poorer classes in every quarter of the world. Our space will not permit us to recall the names of those who were against his inestimable discovery, suffice it to say, that the anti-vaccinators in Europe have on many occasions suffered fine or imprisonment rather than vaccinate their children. Even in civilized England the friends of vaccination have still to encounter the inveterate prejudice of their countrymen. The following is an instance of the fanatic proceedings of the " peculiar people" :—

" One night last week a second torch-light demonstration of anti-vaccinators was held in one of our respectable country towns, in which several hundred persons took part, and the proceedings were terminated by burning the effigy of Dr. Jenner, which had been carried in the procession, in a field near the town."*

Let us now proceed to the history of small-pox inoculation, or the artificial production of small-pox by engrafting a minute quantity of lymph from a small-pox pustule beneath the cuticle of a person not previously attacked by the natural disease. It was employed at a remote period by the Chinese, Arabs, and Hindoos in order to afford protection from small-pox. We are surprised to learn that at the begin-

---

* *Medical Times and Gazette*, March 10, 1877.

ning of the present century small-pox inoculation was practised in Calcutta by the native inhabitants, although vaccination had been introduced there some time before. It had been used in Turkey in the seventeenth century. In 1713 Dr. Emanuel Timoni, a Greek physician and an Oxford graduate, who upon obtaining his qualifications had settled as a surgeon at Constantinople, first communicated to Dr. Woodward in London an account of the important discovery, and a description of the process appeared in the "Transactions of the Royal Society of London" in the following year. In 1715 Dr. James Pylarini, the Venetian consul at Smyrna, having heard of the success which attended the practice, published an account of it at Venice, which was noticed in the "Philosophical Transactions" for 1716. In the year 1715 the new process had also become known to the English public on the publication by Mr. Kennedy of his "Essay on External Remedies." The facts however were by no means received with favour by the British physicians. To Lady Mary Wortley Montague, wife of the English ambassador at Constantinople, is due the honour of being the first to introduce the practice in England. She gives the following description of the process in a letter dated Adrianople, April 1st, 1718:—

"The small-pox, so fatal and so general amongst us, is here entirely harmless by the invention of *engrafting*, which is the term they give it. Every year thousands undergo the operation; and the French ambassador says, pleasantly, that they take the small-pox here by way of diversion, as they take the waters in other countries. There is no example of any one who has died in it, and you may believe I am well satisfied of the safety of this experiment since I intend to try it on my dear little son. I am patriot enough to take pains to bring this useful invention into fashion in England."

Lady Mary was the first in England who had her daughter inoculated, in April 1721. In the same year inoculation was introduced in America. In the following year, satisfactory experiments having been made on six condemned criminals in Newgate, the Princess of Wales had her daughters Amelia and Caroline inoculated, with happy results. In 1727 Voltaire gave in France his testimony in favour of the protective power of inoculation. In England the operation was conducted by inexperienced men, and on account of several marked failures a general outcry was raised against it. It was not till the middle of the eighteenth century that the confidence of the people was restored by favourable reports from abroad; by the publication of a work by Dr. Mead entitled " De Variolis et Morbillis"; by the skill and success of the Suttons and their successor Baron Dimsdale; and by the foundation of a Small-pox and Inoculation Hospital and Dispensary. From the success which attended the practice, the Royal College of Physicians of London sanctioned its employment in 1754. In short, the public and the profession appreciated the amount of benefit and protection it afforded. In 1798 Jenner announced the discovery of vaccination, from which time the practice of inoculation gradually declined and disappeared. In England in the year 1840 an Act of Parliament was passed, which declared inoculation of small-pox illegal, and all offenders were accordingly punished by law.

The greatest of all objections urged against inoculation is that it contributes to spread the variolous poison ; in other words, infection from the inoculated exposes to danger the lives of the unprotected. In the words of Dr. Baron, the biographer of Jenner, " The practice of inoculation, the greatest improvement ever introduced in the treatment of small-pox, although beneficial to the person inoculated, has been detrimental to mankind in general ; it has kept up a constant source of noxious infection, which has more than counterbalanced the advantages of individual security." There can be no doubt that this mode of protection has its drawbacks, but the evil pointed out by Dr. Baron and others could be remedied to a certain extent. Our limits prevent us from entering into a discussion on the merits or demerits of inoculation. Suffice it to say, that the method, if carried out with due skill, discrimination, and precaution, is far preferable to leaving mankind exposed to the contagion of such a frightful and destructive disease as small-pox ; and if Jenner had not announced his discovery of vaccination, it might surely have been universally adopted up to the present day as a great blessing. Even now, when small-pox breaks out in an isolated district, or in a vessel out at sea where no vaccine virus is to be procured, inoculation is perfectly safe and justifiable.

CHAPTER XVIII.

Abuse of drugs and wholesale destruction of life—Vulgar physicians—Recent advances of Medicine—Uncertainty of medical practice—Mischievous experiments on the sick—Allopathy—Homœopathy—Outline of the life and labours of Hahnemann—*Vis medicatrix Naturæ.*

What we write in this chapter may probably be misunderstood or misrepresented, but we have felt it our duty in the interests of the public and the profession to speak with freedom and independence. History teaches us that too much self-complacency and want of humility have in all ages retarded progress, and it is on account of this that we venture to point out our own defects. It must not be understood that in giving credit due to the present, we forget reverence due to the past, and *vice versâ*. Dissent from great authorities does not necessarily lessen our respect for them. In the art of war the old paths are forsaken. Men do not now-a-days fight armed with the spear and the sword and buckler, and yet the conquests achieved by Alexander and Cæsar were as splendid as those of the First Napoleon. The naval victories of Trafalgar and the Nile have not diminished the glories of those of Salamis and Mycale. Has Napoleon's defeat at Waterloo at all impaired his extraordinary military reputation? With our increased knowledge of medicine, is our respect for the names of Hippocrates, Galen, and Celsus lessened? Is our respect for our teachers diminished because they were formerly guilty of errors? By no means.

From the earliest ages up to the present time, and in all tribes, savage and civilized, man, through fear of suffering or death, has always looked for medical assistance. The beneficent Creator never designed that His creatures should be oppressed, without remedies, by innumerable sufferings. He provided remedies for the multitude of diseases that flesh is heir to. Every drug is created for the lofty purpose of alleviating bodily suffering, and intended only to neutralize disease, but when used in its absence, is absolutely injurious, and shortens life. The wise enjoy the gifts of God, but the evils the foolish and imaginary sufferers bring upon themselves are great. Even lower animals are endowed with certain instincts by the aid of which they go into fields and forests, seek and select the suitable remedy, and cure themselves of their ailments, but will never swallow other than their legitimate food in the absence of disease. But men, endowed with reason, are often wilfully blind, and cannot be prevailed upon to believe that every drug is created for relieving suffering humanity, and not for the purpose of inflicting pain and misery. "The nurse welcomes the new-born infant with a dose of castor oil, as a foretaste of what it will have to endure in its course through life, and till its latest breath it lives up to its destiny." Is not the Government aware of the wholesale infanticide in its vast Indian empire, caused by poor mothers narcotizing their infants with opium, and shutting them up in a wretched den the whole day, while they themselves go to work for their miserable maintenance? How many have been ruined both in body and mind by freely indulging in drugs for imaginary complaints? How many deaths have resulted from the ignorant administration of patent drugs? How many from the habitual use of opium, bhang, ganja, spirituous liquors, &c.? How many suicidal and how many homicidal deaths from poisonous drugs? And lastly, how many from the ignorance of quacks, and the very dregs of the profession? We have no hesitation in expressing our opinion that each and all have had a share in the destruction of millions of human beings. Medicine, instead of proving a blessing in every instance, has entailed more misery and a greater amount of suffering upon the world than war, plague, or famine. It has become thus injurious in the hands of the ignorant, presumptuous and over-officious, so that "things have arrived at such a pitch that they cannot be worse, and that they must mend or end."

The healing art was called by the ancients the "Divine Art of Medicine," and its teachers the "Divine Professors." It was attributed by the Greeks to Apollo and his son Æsculapius, and by the Egyptians to their god Thoth. The Hindoos impute the art of physic to Brahma, who is said to have instructed the other gods. The divine art was considered so sacred by the ancients that none but the ministers of religion were allowed to practise it. It was for the first time brought to its greatest eminence and perfection by Hippocrates, justly styled the "Father of Medicine." The venerable old man was worthy of the praise bestowed on a skilful physician in the sacred writings of the Christians. "The skill of the physician shall lift up his head, and in the sight of great men he shall be in admiration." But as Hippocrates had himself complained, "there are many physicians in name and reputation, few in reality and effect," so in our own times we have a few physicians whose malpractices caused a person to rhyme—

> "Most of the evils we poor mortals know,
> From doctors and imagination flow."

"It is truly lamentable," says Hoffmann, "that so few are completely skilled in this divine art, while the number is endless of persons vulgarly illiterate and destitute of all solid knowledge, who, for the sake of lucre, enter with reckless frivolity on its practice and profession." No other profession claims so large a portion of public respect as that of physic. There are of course black sheep in every flock, but their number in our own is very small. It must be confessed that in the ranks of the medical profession there will always be found many who are content to practise honourably. On the other hand, we have a few unprincipled men who have degraded themselves and their profession by cultivating medicine, not as a science, but as a trade. Every honest person knows that there exists an inferior class of men in every country who do not maintain the social position and honour of our profession, but who for the sake of lucre associate with quacks, who endorse testimonials to quacks, who recommend a patent medicine, who advertise their skill and qualifications in the local papers, who, on the death of a professional brother, ask for certificates of competency and recommendation from their own patients in order to be appointed in other families, and who, for the sake of obtaining a trifling appointment in a railway department, submit themselves to be examined by a railway clerk! We are of opinion that something should be done, if possible, either to exclude men who are known to be of low extraction, or to give them sound intellectual training before they begin to study medicine, so that after obtaining their qualifications they may not, on account of bad training, or the meanness of their circumstances, bring the profession into disrepute. How can a man of low birth and position, bred up in an atmosphere of loose morality, and without receiving a thorough and liberal education prior to the commencement of professional training, maintain a high professional character?

At the present time, when public attention has been called in England to the fact that many surgeons are deficient in sound and liberal education, and unskilled in the art they profess, and when the profession displays much anxiety for its elevation and for raising the general status of medical men, the Government of Bombay, according to the resolution of the Government of India, have established two medical schools, one at Poona and another at Ahmedabad, in both of which instruction is given in the vernacular. We are of opinion that the origin of these institutions was not the result of mature deliberation on the part of Government, and its medical advisers were not wise in giving their approval and encouragement to the measure, which, though adopted and carried out with the best intentions, is open to more or less of abuse, and will tend to produce men decidedly inferior intellectually. In one of these institutions a student without any knowledge of English may pass, and receive all the necessary certificates, in a period of something under three years, and the public must take these " inferior men" upon trust. It is derogatory to the character of the profession that the son of an individual in the lower ranks of life, badly trained by the constant influences of those by whom he is surrounded, without receiving a sound and liberal education, and deficient in practical knowledge and skill, should receive a certificate to practise the noble profession—a profession of extreme responsibility. We do not hate poverty. Many poor and obscure men have in all times risen to greatness and fame from comparative or even actual poverty. But these were exceptional men—the examples only of intellectual greatness. These were men of brilliant talents, extraordinary powers, great natural genius or profound attainments. "Poets are born, not made." Every right-minded man is conscious of the shortcomings of the medical art. The medical profession is one ever changing, and in the interest of the public, we ask, what opportunity will these medical men, who do not understand English, have of bringing their knowledge up to the level of the day? To them everything will be stationary; things will ever be as they are now. We have no wish to be narrow. By all means let Government give the necessary helping hand for the medical education of the poor by raising a class of men for the public service as subordinates, but not with the view of throwing upon the public any particular set of men with a smattering of medicine and surgery. With such an army of *Officiers de Santé* it would be powerless to attack and exterminate the race of quacks. "It is not cheapness," says Dr. Black, "that supports the impudent charlatan; it is the uncertainty of the healing art as practised by the educated practitioner." We are of opinion that with a rising standard of medical education the quacks would fade away. It is with surprise as well as with regret we may pause here to remark, that a Licentiate of Medicine of the Bombay University, instead of upholding the dignity of his profession, meanly consents to consult a quack whenever the whim or caprice of a patient demands it. Unworthy member of an honourable profession! "Let us not impute these evils," as Pliny says, "to the art, but to the men who practise it." Before leaving the subject we may observe that the practice of medicine requires education and high mental training, and it is on account of this that we have felt it our duty in the public interest to speak thus plainly.

We now return to our subject. During the long period of more than two thousand years that followed the death of Hippocrates, the medical art groped in the darkness of empiricism and dogmatism, and during more than fifteen centuries humoural therapeutics prevailed in medical treatment. History furnishes us with instances of ancient physicians having added something to their old stock of knowledge. The opinions of Galen were accepted in all the medical schools for more than thirteen centuries. Every year since the modern regeneration of our art we have advanced step by step in exploring its wide and complex field, and in improving it to the best of our power. There cannot be the shadow of a doubt that medicine has advanced with strides as rapid as any other science during the present century. The importance of studying preventive as well as curative medicine has not been neglected or overlooked. The discovery of the causes of diseases, such as scurvy, typhoid fever, cholera, &c. have thrown light upon the means of preventing them or limiting their spread when they have actually prevailed. As the art of medicine is powerless in controlling the morbid actions set up by zymotic diseases, there is of late a tendency to discover germicidal agents for their treatment. The necessity of a correct knowledge of anatomy, physiology, and pathology, as the groundwork of practical medicine and surgery, has been fully appreciated. Our treatment of diseases has of late been based upon our knowledge of pathology. We have acquired an increased knowledge of the nature and diagnosis of diseases, and we are enabled to treat them with greater precision. The causes and diagnosis of organic diseases, such as Bright's disease of the kidney, which were formerly obscure, and in which sometimes no symptoms manifest themselves for a length of time, have now been made out with precision. The influence of the nervous system on disease is beginning to be recognised. The use of the microscope and the thermometer for clinical investigation is attended with the happiest results. The value and importance of the discovery of percussion by Auenbrugger, and of mediate auscultation by Laennec in the diagnosis of diseases of the lungs, pleura, and heart, are fully recognised. The therapeutic uses of electricity in some diseases are attended with good results. The experiments of some Parisian surgeons have of late thrown light on the external use of metals in some nervous disorders.

"If we pass," says Sir John Forbes, "to that noble department of the labours of medical men termed SURGERY, the illustrations of the efficacy and power of the medical art are found in much greater number, of a much more positive kind, and of higher importance. Surgery, indeed, must always be admitted to exhibit the least equivocal successes and the most splendid triumphs of the art. When we see the life that is manifestly ebbing away from a bleeding wound, instantaneously saved by the ligature of an artery; when we see the displacement of an organ or limb, producing in the first place most distressing pain, and necessarily leading to permanent incapacity or death, removed at once by skilled manipulations or by the knife of the surgeon; when we see, in the case of a portion of the body crushed into hopeless disorganization by external violence, or smitten with a mortal gangrene that cannot be stayed, the dead or diseased portion severed at once from the organism it would have destroyed, and life so saved and health restored; we need no reasoning to prove to us the reality and potency and inestimable value of an art which can do such great and admirable things. It is, indeed, to such facts as these,—it is to surgery, even taken as a whole,—that the practitioner, conversant only with internal diseases, and possessing no other means of combating them but the feeble and uncertain armoury of drugs, must often look up for consolation in his difficulties, in his blind gropings, and amid the insignificant or dubious results of his labours. It is a perpetual comfort for him to know with certainty that, in one of the fields of its display, at least, the noble art he professes leaves no room for doubt as to its vast powers, or as to the incalculable good worked by these in the cause of humanity; and this knowledge yields, moreover, a perennial and lively stimulus to his exertions, by fostering the hope that the time may yet come when the treatment of internal diseases may attain something of the like certainty and power."

Of all the sister sciences, surgery has no doubt made the most prodigious strides during the last few years. The free use of anæsthetics in surgical injuries and operations is the crowning triumph of surgery. The operation of ovariotomy, lately performed with such good results, is without question a proof of the greatest triumph achieved by our art, and of which every modern surgeon ought to be proud. The method of arresting hæmorrhage during an operation, introduced by Professor Esmarch of Kiel, and known as " bloodless surgery," and the introduction into practice of late of a valuable instrument, called the " aspirator," for the purpose of evacuating effusions from inner cavities of the body, have proved of great service. The extirpation of the larynx, occasionally performed by some surgeons with success, is admitted to be one of the greatest triumphs of modern surgery. The occasional success of transfusion of human blood into persons exhausted by excessive hæmorrhage cannot be denied. The advances made in orthopædic and conservative surgery deserve mention. Lithotrity is superseding the operation of lithotomy, and a limb may be saved by the excision of a diseased or wounded joint. Of the enormous progress that has been made in plastic surgery during the last few years, no surgeon will doubt. Lister's antiseptic method of dressing wounds, and the drainage tube invented by Chassaignac in the treatment of large chronic abscesses and surgical wounds, have been used with success. The value of the ophthalmoscope in diseases of the eye is admitted by all, and the laryngoscope plays an important part for the recognition and treatment of diseases of the air passages.

Although no doubt can be entertained of the great power of the medical art in curing diseases and saving life, yet when we compare our practice with those of the Egyptians and Greeks, we are astonished at the paucity of our present knowledge of the therapeutic treatment of diseases after a lapse of more than twenty centuries. We honestly confess that with the great advances in anatomical, physiological, and pathological knowledge, we cannot boast of having made a steady and triumphant progress in the treatment of diseases since the time of Hippocrates. "Although it is undeniable," says Dr. Moore, "that the science of medicine has made rapid advances during the last half century, still these advances have been in a great measure *confined to the art of diagnosis*. The means of cure which the physician of the present day is enabled to call to his aid are scarcely, with the exception of quinine, larger than his predecessors enjoyed at the commencement of 1800."* But, let us ask, who discovered the properties of cinchona bark, from which quinine is obtained? who wrote a book against its virtues? and who were the early persecutors of those who used it in fevers? The answer is humiliating. 1. The properties of cinchona bark were discovered by an American Indian. 2. Chifletius, physician to Leopold, archduke of Austria, wrote a book against its virtues. 3. The members of the Royal College of Physicians were the early persecutors of those who used it in fevers. Besides quinine, many of the valued drugs of which we boast have been discovered by accident. However, we give credit to Dr. Moore for his modesty and frankness.

From very early times up to the present day the want of a guiding principle in therapeutics, as well as the various conflicting theories adopted by some and rejected by others, each theory appearing in one age, forsaken again for a time, and slowly resumed, has given rise to confusion in the treatment of diseases. Many theories were started and as many exploded; remedies have been at various times extolled and at various times neglected; then a reaction comes on, and they are again introduced

---

* Moore's *Health in the Tropics*, p. 58.

by a medical upstart into general favour as his own discoveries. "There exists," says Dr. Paris, "a fashion in medicine, as in the other affairs of life, regulated by the caprice and supported by the authority of a few leading practitioners, which has been frequently the occasion of dismissing from practice valuable medicines, and of substituting others less certain in their effects and more questionable in their nature. As years and fashion revolve, so have these neglected remedies, each in its turn, risen again into favour and notice, whilst old receipts, like old almanacks, are abandoned until the period may arrive that will once more adopt them to the spirit and fashion of the times."*

Sir William Hamilton says:—"The history of medicine, on the one hand, is nothing more than a marvellous history of variations, and, on the other, only a still more marvellous history of how every successive variation has, by medical bodies, been first furiously denounced, and then (though always laughed at by the wiser wits) bigotedly adopted." The representatives of the various sects and schools, instead of working and assisting mutually in the same field of research, have always persecuted each other with reproaches of killing their patients. The views of many distinguished teachers have differed and still differ. Each one endeavours to put down the opinions of his antagonist. The dissatisfaction felt with the uncertainty of the action of drugs has given rise to schisms in our profession. Dr. Gregory, of Edinburgh, says that he "did not know of any one

---

* Paris's *Pharmacologia*, 7th edition, pp. 56, 57.

disease or of any one remedy that has not been the subject of obstinate controversy." There are many drugs in use whose *modus operandi* we can in no way explain. Medicines strongly advocated by some are as strongly deprecated by others. To what circumstances are we to attribute this diversity of opinion amongst men equally eminent? With a feeling of regret we confess that we have no unerring law, no principle, no method, to guide us at the bedside of our patient; hence the uncertainty, bewilderment and inconsistency which we see in our daily practice, as well as the gross contradictions found in books on practical medicine. Dr. B. W. Richardson, in his lecture delivered before the Faculty of Physicians and Surgeons of Glasgow in the Session 1878, says:—

"It is when we come to the question of remedies that the solemn signs of failure in positive knowledge begin. A leading provincial physician brought to London a sick man for consultation. It had been arranged that six physicians should see the sick man independently of each other, and should diagnose and prescribe independently. The case was a clear one and comparatively simple. In diagnosis there was practically no real difference of opinion . . . . Altogether, in fact, the six minds were as one mind, until the all-important subject of use of remedies came into question. To say that now there were not two minds alike is to tell but half the story. The fact is that the prescriptions were as opposed the one to the other, as any kind of opposition could possibly be. If the six prescriptions had been placed in the hands of a physician who knew nothing of the facts of the case, he could not from them have made a guess as to the precise nature of the case. One prescription suggested a mere placebo; a second, what some would call a nervous tonic; a third, an alterative medicine; a fourth, a warm stomachic mixture; a fifth, cod-liver oil and iron; the sixth, an antiphlogistic with a counter-irritant. In perfect bewilderment, the physician who had personal charge of the sick man asked, what should be done? Whose direction should be followed? And this is the question daily before us all—What shall be done? Upon the answer to that question, our fate, as a practising physician, in whom the people shall have and retain confidence, will soon depend. It is the fact that people care very little for our most positive knowledge of disease unless we can engraft upon it such knowledge of cure as shall lead to removal of disease. 'Wherein,' say the people, 'do you learned men differ from the ignorant quack, if you know and yet cannot do? Perchance the quack may, by doing and not knowing, drop upon something which shall be for our good. Any way, our case being desperate, let us give even the quack's nostrum a trial rather than try nothing at all.'"*

Mr. Jones, a medical practitioner, who had long suffered from hay fever, had on several occasions consulted eminent men of the profession. Let us hear their opinions of the causes of the disease and its remedies as given by Mr. Jones in a letter addressed to the *Lancet* of July 1864. It shows something of the conflicts of scientific opinions amongst physicians:—

Consulted.	Opinion of Cause.	Recommended.
Dr. A....	A predisposition to phthisis.	Quinine and sea voyage.
Dr. B....	Disease of pneumogastric nerve.	Arsen., bell., and cinchona.
Dr. C....	Disease of the caruncula...	To apply bell. and zinc.
Dr. D....	Inflammation of the schneiderian membrane.	To paint with nitrate of silver.
Dr. E....	Strumous diathesis	Quinine, cod-liver oil, and wine.
Dr. F....	Dyspepsia	Kreasote, henbane, quinine.
Dr. G....	Vapour of chlorophyll	Remain in a room from 11 A.M. to 6 P.M.
Dr. H....	Light, debility, haypollen...	Ditto, port wine, snuff salt and opium, and wear blue glasses.

* *The Lancet*, Aug. 17, 1878.

THE MEDICAL ART. 361

Consulted.	Opinion of Cause.	Recommended.
Dr. L. ...	From large doses of iodine *(never took any iodine)*...	Try quinine and opium.
Dr. M....	Disease of iris	Avoid the sun's rays from 11 A.M. to 6 P.M.
Dr. N....	Want of red corpuscles ...	Try iron, port wine and soups.
Dr. O. ...	Disease of optic nerve......	Phosph. ac. and quinine.
Dr. P. ...	Asthma from haypollen ...	Chlorodyne and quinine.
Dr. Q....	Phrenitis	Small doses of opium.
Dr. R. ...	Nervous debility from heat.	Turkish bath.

"We admire," says Dr. Russell, "the magnanimity of Mr. Jones; for after having been told that he had a 'predisposition to phthisis;' that he was of a 'strumous diathesis;' that he had 'disease of the pneumogastric nerve;' 'dyspepsia;' 'disease of the iris;' 'disease of the optic nerve;' 'disease of the olfactory nerve;' that he had had 'phrenitis;' and was 'poisoned by iodine;' and that in order to better his condition he was to take quinine, arsenic, belladonna, cod-liver oil, kreosote, henbane, opium, phosphoric acid, chlorodyne, soups and port wine; to paint his nostrils with lunar caustic, and snuff salt and opium; to wear blue glasses; to remain at home all day and take Turkish baths; we are surprised that he was restrained from taking all the revenge in his power upon his formidable friends."*

Again, the conflicts of scientific opinions amongst physicians and surgeons in courts of law are of daily occurrence. The surgeons of the Bombay Medical Service were not unanimous in deciding the nature of a fever that prevailed in Bombay in the year 1877.

---

* *Rheumatism, Epilepsy, &c.*, by R. Russell, pp. 9, 10.

Some stated that the fever was an ordinary intermittent fever, and was non-contagious; others contended that it was a relapsing or spirillum fever, epidemic and contagious in its nature. Nobody can deny that in a majority of cases, when our diagnosis is wrong, our treatment proves mischievous, and sometimes even fatal. "When doctors disagree, who shall decide?" Are all the patients treated on rational principles even after the nature of a disease is ascertained? We fear not. We have a dozen opposite modes of treating a disease; one treats it in one way, another in another way, and so on. On what principles do we treat cancer, cholera, typhus, tetanus, &c.? Dr. Gaston of Brazil, having published in the New Orleans *Medical and Surgical Journal* a case of tetanus successfully treated, the *Practitioner* for April 1874 notices it as *interesting*. It is a fair sample of a contribution to the curiosities of medical literature in the year 1874:—

"Dr. Gaston of Sao Paulo, Brazil, gives the detail of an interesting case of traumatic tetanus resulting in recovery. The patient was an able-bodied negro, who had received a blow upon the left side of the head, traversing the parieto-occipital suture, and about 2½ inches in length. He continued to work for several days. Dr. Gaston was called in on the sixth day after the accident. He had then slight opisthotonos and lockjaw. The wound was found in a state permitting it to be readily opened to the bone, but the bone was uninjured. The edges had a dark sanious appearance, without any indication of suppuration. A piece of lint saturated with spirits of turpentine was placed in the wound, and a poultice of corn-meal with flax-seed was applied over it. One grain of tartar emetic was then given every fifteen minutes for ninety minutes, and the patient was placed in a hot bath. On removal from the bath a marked improvement was observed, and the patient fell asleep; on awaking, spasmodic rigidity of the muscles recurred. A combination of calomel, gr. v; tartar emetic, gr. i; nitrate of potash, gr. x; and morphia gr. $\frac{1}{2}$, was now given every two hours, until six hours had elapsed, and afterwards three table-spoonfuls of castor-oil with a table-spoonful of turpentine were administered, which procured evacuation, without, however, inducing free purgation. The spasms were now milder, and recurred with milder intervals, yet were still of a distinct tetanic nature. Frictions with camphorated spirits of wine were made frequently throughout the entire extent of the spinal column and over the epigastric region; and a flannel moistened with this was kept constantly applied over the abdomen. In the mean time a blister was applied to the occiput and neck. At the end of the second day's treatment one grain of morphine was administered at night, and repeated within four hours, and after the second dose the patient slept several hours; but the morning of the third day of treatment, and the fourth of the disorder, found him still labouring under rigidity of the entire muscular system, with occasional attacks of opisthotonos and trismus, accompanied by spasmodic action of the diaphragm, that gave rise to a sound closely resembling hiccough. Regarding this stage of the disease as involving chiefly the nervous system, a wineglassful of lac assafœtida was given every three hours, and an enema of half a pint of the infusion of tobacco with a teaspoonful of laudanum, was ordered to be given and repeated in six hours. The attacks became still more moderate, but the disease did not yield entirely. On the following day, which was the fifth day of continued tetanus, 10 grains of sulphate of quinine, with half a teacupful of infusion of valerian, was administered every three hours, until a drachm of quinine was taken. At the same time injections of lac assafœtida with laudanum were given every six hours. The sixth day did not find him free from spasmodic rigidity and recurrence of the convulsive attack; but considering the dangerous violence of the disease as having been subdued, he was ordered simply to use the infusion of valerian and an occasional injection of lac assafœtida with generous diet. On the eighth day, strychnia in doses of $\frac{1}{16}$ grain was administered every two hours, but the tetanic rigidity being intensified, it was abandoned in twenty-four hours. Subsequent to this a combination of two grains of ipecacuanha, one grain of opium, and half a grain of calomel, was repeated every four hours during the day, till slight ptyalism supervened. A full dose of castor-oil now produced a most salutary effect; and the treatment from that time (twelfth day) was simply addressed to building up the exhausted frame of the patient and without any recurrence of the tetanic symptoms."

It is difficult to make head or tail of this treatment. Dr. Gaston gives the details of this case to show success; we give it to show the recklessness with which drugs are selected and prescribed. Surely the case is *interesting* as illustrating the want of certain principles in therapeutics, as well as the numerous prescriptions employed without consistency and clearness. However, we congratulate Dr. Gaston of Sao Paulo that in spite of such treatment the thick-skinned and tenacious negro recovered. Such has been the practice of many pretentious men described by Liston as "hitting here and there like a blind man interfering with a combat."

Not only are doctors opposed to each other concerning the use of a certain remedy, but they always disagree with themselves. The celebrated John Hunter used to say to his pupils when they took notes of his lectures: "Don't take notes of this; I dare say I shall change it all next year." Compare the first edition of a work on Practical Medicine with the succeeding ones by the same author, and you will find remarkable alterations in the treatment of diseases. May this not be owing to a change of type in disease?

Sir John Forbes in his article against homœopathy is forced to complain of the instability of orthodox practice in the following terms:—"What difference of opinion! What an array of alleged facts directly at variance with each other! What contradictions! What opposite results of a like experience! What ups and downs! What glorification and degradation of the same remedy! What confidence now, what despair anon, in encountering the same disease, with the very same weapons! What horror and intolerance at one time, of the very opinions and practices which, previously and subsequently, are cherished and admired!"—(*British and Foreign Journal*, 1846.) Such is the confession of "Sir John Forbes, M.D., D.C.L. (Oxon), F.R.S., Fellow of the Royal College of Physicians, Physician to the Queen's Household," etc., etc. Moreover, the confession is the result of fifty years of active practice. Poor Forbes! The very weapon with which he assailed his antagonists soon recoiled upon his own head, and he incurred the odium of his professional brethren, who instead of admiring his frankness exclaimed : "Oh, save us from our friend!" Twenty years rolled on, and behold!—the opinions once formed of him are subsequently reversed, and the *Medical Times* publishes the following announcement:—" None can forget the outburst of wrath which fell upon the head of that accomplished physician Dr. Forbes, when he published the startling article on 'Homœopathy, Allopathy, and Young Physic.' The seed he then sowed has germinated; the young plant has grown vigorously, and its fruit is seen in the daily increasing dependence of British practitioners upon the *restorative powers of Nature.*"

How unsettled is the character of medicine! How doubtful is the practice of its professors! Some have gone so far as to confess their scepticism in medicine. Dr. Moore, in his work entitled *Health in the Tropics*, modestly states: "It has been remarked that the practice of physicians, whether good or bad, according to orthodox medical views, does not materially influence the ultimate mortality of an hospital. Of this I was afforded a striking proof during the three years I was resident surgeon at the Queen's Hospital. To this institution three physicians were attached, of whom one treated his patients with stimulants scarcely in less quantity than the late Dr. Todd; a second had a decided preference for the Hamiltonian system of blue pill at night and black draught in the morning; the third treated his patients without any peculiar bias. On examining the records, I found there was very little difference between the mortality and cured among the patients of the three doctors, who, I trust, will pardon me this mention of their practice."

Professor Skoda, one of the most eminent physicians in Europe, being sceptical of every system of medication, at one time experimented on the sick who were admitted into the wards of the Vienna Hospital with any method of treatment, trusting more to chance than to the treatment he adopted. If the patient came under him during the appointed season of bleeding, he was bled; if he entered during the period of blistering, he was blistered, and so on. For instance, a robust man is admitted into the Hospital suffering from inflammation of the lung: he gives him infusion of foxglove for experiment; a day or two after follows the period of bleeding, and the poor man is bled. A marked falling of the pulse is observed, and the cause of the change is thus explained by the sceptical professor in a loose and doubtful tone to his class at the bedside of the sick: —" Perhaps it is the effect of the bleeding—such things have been; perhaps, too, it may have been the effect of the foxglove—that has been seen too; it may also be considered as connected with the natural evolution of the disease—that has been seen too."

Of all the cases of acute rheumatism admitted into St. George's Hospital during the five years ending December 31st, 1861, the heart was unaffected on admission in 161, as Mr. Dickinson frankly admits, in a paper read before the Medical and Chirurgical Society. We cannot for a moment doubt the accuracy of Mr. Dickinson's statement, as stethoscopic examination seldom or never fails to discover any disease of the heart. A series of experiments were then performed upon the poor sufferers. Every physician seems to have treated a certain number according to his own fashion, for we are distinctly told that "the method adopted in any case depended very much upon the *chance* of the patient coming under one physician rather than another." And what was the result of the different weapons employed? Affections of the heart! The startling facts are here honestly confessed :—

Bleeding produced heart-disease in every 2nd case.
Opium ,, ,, ,, 3rd ,,
Mercury ,, ,, ,, 4th ,,
Nitre ,, ,, ,, 10th ,,
Alkalies (carbonate of potass, etc.) ,, 48th ,,

Of the 161 cases of rheumatism admitted without

cardiac affection, 48 were subjected to the alkaline treatment, and 3 were treated with salts of ammonia. Out of the remaining 110 cases treated with bleeding, opium, calomel, &c., 35 gave signs of heart complications—*i. e.*, little more than twenty-five per cent; while of 48 cases treated with alkalisation, only one had the heart affected, or little more than two per cent. The treatment adopted was purely experimental, and could hardly be called scientific. Such practices have caused a writer to sarcastically style us "a murderous profession." We could give many other specimens of a similar kind, but our space will not permit dealing further with this disagreeable subject. It is sufficient to state that the action of remedial agents should, as far as possible, be discovered according to the suggestions of Hahnemann, Störck, and others, from experiments made upon ourselves and others in health. Experiments upon the sick and lower animals are sometimes erroneous and objectionable.

There are two distinct and principal modes of cure prevalent at the present day—Allopathic and Homœopathic. Before discussing these opposite methods of curing diseases adopted by physicians, we would wish to say a word on the subject of hydropathy, or the "water-cure." Hydropathy, formerly denounced as a system of quackery, is now recognised by the profession as one useful mode of treatment. Even in the middle part of this century, Dr. Simpson, in his work on *Homœopathy: its Tenets and Tendencies*, denounces it a quack system of medicine. If we compare the prejudiced judgment of Dr. Simpson with the liberal opinion of that very acute and lucid writer, Sir W. Hamilton, we perceive a striking difference. Sir W. Hamilton says:— " Homœopathy and the water cure are, now and here, blindly anathematised as heretical; in the next generation it is not improbable that these same doctrines may be no less blindly preached as exclusively orthodox—such is poor human nature! such is corporate, such is medical authority!" The predictions of Sir W. Hamilton have been to a great extent verified in a shorter time. Water cure, once denounced as heretical, is now preached as deserving a place in *scientific* medicine; and homœopathy, though not openly preached as orthodox, is slowly gaining ground, and has produced a salutary influence on the minds of heroic and meddling practitioners of our own school. "It is very pleasing to learn," says Dr. Lees, a disciple of the old school, "that the Homœopaths and the Allopaths approximate at one particular point. The first affirm, as we have seen, that drugs beyond a *minim* dose, well attenuated, aggravate disease; the second are fast finding out, through their theoretical expositors, that the less drugs are dispensed the better!" Hydropathy was discovered by Vincent Priessnitz, a Silesian peasant. As a system of therapeutics it cannot be regarded as a panacea in every case of curable disease, but an auxiliary to drug-medication or a part of the treatment of a limited number of acute cases. For example, the wet-sheet packing as an invaluable mode of applying water in specific fevers and acute imflammatory diseases is admitted by all. The systematic use of water administered internally and externally in a number of chronic disorders is highly beneficial. It is not the less true, however, that change of air, exercise, regulation of the diet, and freedom from mental care and excitement, form a very important part of the water treatment in hydropathic establishments.

Allopathy.—This term was applied by Hahnemann, the founder of homœopathy, to the ordinary system of medicine. The term is derived from *alloios pathos*, meaning a dissimilar affection. Allopathy is the growth of remotest ages, and its utility and value have been acknowledged with gratitude at all times. The allopathic practice is divided into the heteropathic and antipathic. The heteropathic or revulsive method is that in which one disease is substituted for another. The allopaths employ remedies after this method to remove natural disease from its original seat by exciting artificial disease of less intensity in a sound but less important part. Thus cathartics are administered to cause revulsion, or counter-irritation is applied to the external surface with the view of curing inflammation of the internal membranes. "The metastasis of disease from one organ to another has given rise to the practice of attempting to remove disease from important organs by exciting disease in other less important parts." The idea is plausible, but the remedies employed do not always operate in the right direction, though success often attends the revulsive method of treatment.

Antipathy is a branch of allopathy—a part of the ordinary old-school practice. The antipathic law *contraria contrariis curantur* is that in which a medicine produces symptoms directly antagonistic to those of the disease. The antipathic method of treatment is inferior to other therapeutic methods, in fact it does not deserve the name of curative. The action of antipathic medicines is palliative, not curative. Thus cathartics are given to remove constipation, and opium is prescribed to relieve pain. When their operation is over, the constipation and pain return again and again to be combated by the same means, but always at the expense of the patient, the cathartic doing nothing towards a cure, but acting otherwise, and creating a number of other disorders, such as dyspepsia, piles, chronic inflammation of the mucous coat of the intestines, and more or less paralysis of its muscular coat; while opium and other narcotic drugs, when frequently repeated, in addition to removing pain, produce disagreeable symptoms of their own, such as loss of appetite, headache, giddiness, constipation, acidity in the stomach, etc. Though the first duty of a physician is to cure, he frequently meets with cases of an incurable nature, where relief from pain and sleep are absolutely necessary. In these, as well as in relieving pain attendant upon spasmodic affections, such as the passage of biliary and renal calculi, anodynes play an important part. The exhibition of anæsthetics for the prevention of pain in surgical operations is a beautiful instance of the occasional success of antipathy, and their use is justifiable as affording relief for a time by paralysing the nerves of sensation.

Homœopathy.—The term homœopathy is derived from *homoiospathos*, meaning similar affection—that is, medicines tend to cure symptoms similar (not the same) to those they tend to produce. The homœopathist relies mainly on this principle. He takes a group of symptoms as the guide of a disease, and in order to remove them selects a medicine which, when given in large doses to a healthy person, is capable of producing a similar group. For example, cinchona bark when taken largely in health produces, according to Hahnemann and his followers, all the symptoms of ague which it is known to cure.

The fearful amount of mortality that prevailed in Europe by the malpractices of physicians,—in other words, the constant use of the lancet for all acute and most chronic diseases; the abuse of purgatives, emetics, blisters, cautery, etc.; the injuries inflicted by polypharmacy; and lastly, the dissatisfaction felt with the uncertainty of drugs, gave rise to homœopathy. People were bled and physicked to death. For instance, Louis XIII. was bled forty times and was dosed with a hundred drastic purgatives within a single year. We cannot forbear giving an instance of the plan of treatment practised by one of the disciples of the old school in the early part of this century. The celebrated Italian physician Rasori treated his patients affected with pneumonia by bleeding them morning and evening, for days in succession. " A robust man was admitted into the hospital the second day of his illness. He had considerable fever, and sharp pain in the right side of the chest; the pulse was strong, the breathing short. *Prescription :—Two pounds* of blood to be drawn from the arm, and 18 *grains of digitalis* to be taken. On the third day, the pain continued, pulse 112 : 18 *ounces of blood* to be drawn, and 24 *grains of digitalis* to be taken. The same evening, another 18 *ounces of blood* to be drawn. On the fourth day, the *same symptoms:* 18 *ounces of blood* morning and evening, and 36 *grains of digitalis*. On the fifth day, *no change:* to be twice bled, and to have two scruples of digitalis. On the sixth day, all the symptoms were worse; pulse 100; great weakness: *a pound of blood* to be drawn, and two scruples of digitalis to be taken. On the seventh day, no change. Repeat the bloodletting and the digitalis. On the eighth and ninth day, worse: repeat the bloodletting to one pound. After this operation the patient—*died.*"* This is a specimen of saguinary treatment of a disorder not necessarily fatal. The patient would have most probably recovered under a simple and judicious treatment.

When called to the bedside of a patient, the physician of half a century ago had a number of indications of treatment, such as to check inflammatory action, to relieve the bowels when constipated, to allay pain, to procure sleep, to check any tendency to vomit, etc. etc. Now, to meet each and all of these indications or symptoms, they as well as a few of us, even at the present day, prescribe a number of ingredients sometimes contrary in their actions, in a single prescription. In this respect we are no better than physicians of the remotest ages. " In former times," says Dr. Russell, " medicines were selected in accordance with purely arbitrary assumptions of their being in their nature either hot or cold, or moist or dry, and the confidence in a composition was, for the

---
* Vide Russell's *History of Medicine*, p. 459.

most part, in direct ratio to the number, variety, and, what we may call, the out-of-the-wayness of its ingredients. The more difficult any substance was to get, the more good it was sure to do. Like barbaric kings, the trust of physicians was in the multitude of their forces, however motley, confused, and unknown." Take, for example, Theriacum, a favourite remedy of a former period, which contained more than sixty ingredients in one prescription:—Squills, hedychroum, cinnamon, common pepper, juice of poppies, dried roses, water-germander, rapeseed, Illyrian iris, agaric, liquorice, opobalsam, myrrh, saffron, ginger, rhaponticum, cinque-foil, calamint, horehound, stone-parsley, cassidony, costus, white and long pepper, dittany, flowers of sweet rush, male frankincense, turpentine, mastich, black cassia, spikenard, flowers of poley, storax, parsley seed, seseli, shepherd's pouch, bishop's weed, germander, ground pine, juice of hypocistis, Indian leaf, Celtic nard, spignel, gentian, anise, fennel-seed, Lemnian earth, roasted chalcites, ammomum, sweet flag, balsamum, Pontic valerian, St. John's wort, acacia, gum, cardamom, carrot-seed, galbanum, sagapen bitumen, oposonax, castor, centaury, clematis, attic honey, Falernian wine.

1. It was to be taken twice a day, for seven years, by those bitten by venomous animals, or who had taken poison. 2. It was to be taken by people in a dangerous state from some obscure cause resembling poisoning. 3. For coughs and pains in the chest. 4. In hæmoptysis. 5. For flatulence, tormina and cæliac affections. 6. It removes rigors, coldness, and vomiting of bile. 7. It promotes

menstruation. 8. For loss of voice. 9. For diseases of the liver. 10. For diseases of the spleen. 11. For cancerous affections of these organs. 12. For nephritic complaints. 13. For dysenteric attacks. 14. For dimness of vision. 15. It is also used as a dentifrice, and many take it at new moon after digestion for the sake of prophylaxis.*

"I remember at Montpellier," says Dr. Granier, " our professor when speaking of theriaca, weary of quoting the substances that enter into its composition, summed up by saying—' Take a little of every remedy that you can find at a chemist's, mix all together, and you will have theriaca.' And yet this strange compound is in daily use." The great number and variety of medicines used for the treatment of diseases, is a sufficient proof of itself that the highest department of our art, therapeutics, is in an unsatisfactory condition.

Heroic practice, and monstrous polypharmacy, " the disgrace of our art," as stated by Dr. Forbes, prevailed in full force as late as the beginning of the present century. Physicians imitated each other in the fashionable practice of the time. There was no one who had the courage and power to show dissent. The revolution, however, came at last. Hahnemann appeared. He shook off the yoke of authority which for centuries had weighed on mankind, and had the moral courage and intellect to denounce the practice as mischievous. An outline of the life and labours of this reformer and the discoverer of the homœopathic system, would not be out of place in these pages.

Paulus Ægineta.

Samuel Hahnemann was born on the 10th of April 1755 at the little town of Meissen on the Elbe, in Saxony. He was the son of Christian Gottfried Hahnemann, who was a painter on porcelain. He was sent to the parish school at an early age, and as he showed great promise from his childhood, he attracted the particular notice of Dr. Müller. " My instructor in classics and German composition," says he, " the present rector of the college, Müller, whose integrity and diligence have rarely been surpassed, loved me as his own child, and granted me many privileges to facilitate my studies, for which I am grateful to this day, and which materially influenced my future pursuits. In my twelfth year he wished me to instruct others in the rudiments of the Greek language. Afterwards he listened patiently to my criticisms when construing the classical writers privately with his boarders, and frequently preferred my opinion to his own."*

Hahnemann was intended by his father for some lucrative trade, and in vain endeavoured to draw his attention from the pursuits of study by frequently removing him from school. This did not prevent young Hahnemann from prosecuting his studies with considerable zeal and diligence. Müller also perceiving that Hahnemann had a decided taste, and bent for superior studies, undertook to pay the school fees, and persuaded his father not to oppose the turn of his son's mind. After going through the usual course of school education, Hahnemann attended, at the age of sixteen, a high-school for superior studies, and at

---

* *Biographical Monument to Hahnemann*, p. 2.

the age of twenty he excelled as a Greek, Latin, French and English scholar. After finishing his studies at the school he was induced to study medicine, for which he evinced a decided predilection, and resolved to make it his profession. In the year 1755 he left Meissen for Leipsic to pursue his medical studies with twenty thalers given him by his father, which was his all, and the last he ever received from him, as he himself says. A disheartening prospect lay before him. What could he do with twenty thalers without either a profession or a patron? The unhappy thought preyed upon his mind. Necessity compelled him to resort to his pen. On reaching Leipsic he began his medical studies, and earned his livelihood by teaching English and French, and translating foreign works into German; so that he acted the part of a pupil, a teacher, and a translator. Herculean labour for a student of medicine possessing twenty thalers *minus* the expenses of a journey from Meissen to Leipsic! The works translated into German during his residence at Leipsic were "Steadman's Physiological Essays," "Nugent's Essay on Hydrophobia," "Falconer on the Waters of Bath," and "Ball's Modern Practice of Physic." After a stay of two years in Leipsic he went to Vienna to enlarge the bounds of his knowledge. As he had been robbed of a sum of money, he was obliged at the end of nine months to accept the post of librarian and private physician to Baron Bruckenthal at Hermanstadt. In less than two years he resigned his appointment, and went to Erlangen, and took the degree of Doctor of Medicine on the 10th of August 1779. He forthwith returned to Saxony, and settled to practise in the small town of Hettstadt. Here he found nothing to his literary taste, and left it for Dessau. In 1781 he received the appointment of district physician at Gommern, and in 1784 went to Dresden, where his talents soon introduced him to the notice of Dr. Wagner, who during his long illness entrusted to his charge all the infirmaries to which he was the chief physician.

"Thus in the bosom of my increasing family," says he, "four years passed at Dresden or its neighbourhood, more speedily than to the unexpected inheritor of a large fortune. In order to be near the centre of science, I removed about Michaelmas 1789 to Leipsic, in full confidence that Providence would guide whatever the lot of my daily life might be." In 1791 the Economical Society of Leipsic and the Academy of Sciences at Mayence elected him a member. Prior to 1792 his contributions to medical literature were varied and extensive, and he had translated no less than eighteen works from the English, French, and Italian.

About the year 1790, Hahnemann became dissatisfied with the ordinary method of treating disease, and abandoned practice in the hope of discovering another and a better system. He had already exhausted the medical literature of the day, and too well felt the want of principles and methods. He had lost faith in medicine, but this did not prevent him from prosecuting his inquiries with diligent attention and perseverance in search for some new guiding principle. One day, while translating the materia medica of Cullen from the English into German, Hahnemann was struck and perplexed with the efforts made by the author to explain the action of cinchona bark in curing ague, and resolved to try it upon himself when in health. He took the bark for several successive days, when, to his astonishment, symptoms of ague manifested themselves. It is certainly true " one swallow does not make a summer." Hahnemann did not arrive at his conclusion from a single experiment, but to prevent the possibility of a mistake repeated the experiment upon himself and friends with similar results. The thought then struck upon his mind, " Can it be that this property, which I have ascertained to belong to bark, is common to medical remedies of all kinds—have I now discovered the great law of healing by drugs ?" Convinced that bark when taken in health produces symptoms similar to those of ague, he made a series of experiments on healthy persons with other drugs, such as sulphur, belladonna, mercury, &c. in order to ascertain their effects. This being done, he administered them to the sick in whom symptoms showed themselves similar to those which they produced in health, and with similar results. Emboldened by success, he after six long years made known the result of his researches and labours—that diseases are to be cured by the use of those medicines which, when given in larger doses to a healthy person, produce symptoms similar to those of the diseases themselves. To this law of therapeutics Hahnemann gave the name of Homœopathy. Many ancient and modern authors had a glimpse of this law, but Hahnemann was the first to propound and propagate it. This law has been either misunderstood or misrepresented by many eminent men of the profession, who confound it with the Isopathic law *aequalia aequalibus curantur*, "the same is cured by the same," as for instance, giving opium to a person poisoned with opium, or spirits to counteract intoxication, which is simply absurd. The therapeutic law discovered by Hahnemann was the law of *similia similibus;* and the absurd Isopathic principle *aequalia aequalibus* was invented by Luz. That Hahnemann neither adopted nor believed in the law "the same is cured by the same," can be seen from his own writings. He, in various parts of his writings, warns his critics to learn the difference between "identical" (the same) and "similar" before discussing the homœopathic doctrine. A few examples of reputed homœopathic cures will suffice. Belladonna is the proper medicine for scarlatina, because it has the power of producing all the symptoms of that disease when given in large doses to a healthy individual. White hellebore and arsenic are capable of effecting an homœopathic cure of cholera by the power which they possess of exciting symptoms analogous to those of cholera itself. Ipecacuanha has been found efficacious in asthmatic fits by the power it possesses of creating an analogous state in health. Cantharides is given for the cure of inflammation of the bladder because it is capable of exciting a similar malady in health. Mercury is given for the cure of dysentery, evidently because this metal is known to possess the faculty of exciting symptoms analogous to that disease. We give no opinion. "Refute," says Hahnemann, "these truths if you can, by pointing out a still more efficacious, sure and agreeable mode of treatment than mine, and do not combat them with mere words, of which we had already *too* many.. But should experience show you, as it has me, that mine is the best, then make use of it for the benefit, for the deliverance of humanity, and give God the glory!" It may naturally be asked,—homœopathy is but fifty years old, and how can its practitioners account for all the brilliant cures effected throughout the course of two thousand years and upwards? The followers of Hahnemann do not deny, but attribute the successful cures in allopathic practice to the homœopathicity of the means employed empirically by the allopaths and to the curative powers of nature. Hahnemann was indiscreet in boldly and unhesitatingly laying down the therapeutic law *similia similibus curantur* as "the only therapeutic law conformable to nature,"—" the great sole therapeutic law," —"a mode of cure founded on an eternal, infallible law of nature." It is necessary, however, to remark that, although admitted to a certain extent by some disinterested men of the old but advancing school of medicine, it is far from being an "infallible," "unerring," and "universal" law of cure.

Hahnemann when he commenced to practise homœopathy observed that, although a homœopathically selected remedy, when employed in ordinary doses, cures, yet it produces severe and often dangerous aggravation of the existing symptoms of the disease, which induced him to the administration of small doses as most safe and efficacious. Had he been at this period content with a mere announcement of his discoveries of the law of *similia similibus curantur*, and the efficacy of a small dose, and left the medical world to follow him step by step in his method of inquiry and of reasoning thereon, instead of inventing globules and defending the possible curative action of infinitesimal doses of drugs, there could be no objection made to the principles and practice inculcated by him. But it may be observed that he was carried away too far by his zeal when he attributed successful cures in his practice to the use of infinitesimal quantities only. Now, granting, for argument sake, his assertion to be true, we are still left in doubt as to whether his cases may not have tended to a favourable issue naturally. It is but just to remark, that his conclusion is not supported by a comparison of cases treated by imponderable doses with those left to the unaided efforts of nature alone, and without the institution of such comparison between their claims it is difficult to decide which effected the cure.

In 1792 Hahnemann, at the request of the Duke of Saxe-Gotha, took charge of a lunatic asylum at Georgenthal, and after a temporary residence in Pyrmont, Brunswick, &c. removed to Königslutter in 1795. Here he experienced some trouble from the jealousy and attacks of his professional brethren, who at length compelled him to leave it. Hahnemann's discoveries were considered so extraordinary, that he was persecuted and driven from one place to another. He became a wanderer, and his life was one of extreme poverty and struggle. Persecution pursued him to Hamburg, Eilenburg, and Machern, when in 1810 he, for the third time, went to Leipsic, where his practice increased with most unusual rapidity, and he found himself surrounded by followers of great celebrity. In 1820, Hahnemann drew upon himself the abuse of the Leipsic apothecaries, who, dreading that homœopathy might injure their trade, prosecuted him for infringing on their right of compounding medicinal substances, and succeeded in obtaining an order of the Government prohibiting him to prepare and dispense his own medicines. Unwilling to entrust his prescriptions to the apothecaries, and tired of persecution, he with a broken heart was compelled to leave Leipsic and repair to Anhalt Cœthen under the protection and patronage of Duke Ferdinand, who granted him privilege to make up his own prescriptions, and honoured him with the title of Councillor of State. Here he pursued his labours with increasing assiduity, and continued to disseminate his doctrines.

Persecution has been the fate of great men and new discoveries in all ages. Christ suffered to save sinners, Zoroaster was stabbed by an idolater, and Mahomed had to flee from city to city, for preaching a belief in one God before their superstitious countrymen. Socrates, the Greek philosopher, was condemned to die by poison because he exposed the superstitious teachings of the sophists, and preached monotheism. Anaxagoras, the tutor of Socrates, was tried for impiety, and condemned to death for calling the sun a mass of glowing iron. Columbus was treated at first as a madman, and after his magnificent discovery, was put in irons and imprisoned. After his acquittal "he always had his chains hung up in his sight wherever he lived; and in his will, he ordered them to be placed with him in his coffin, as if he had desired to appeal to God against the injustice of his contemporaries, and to take with him to heaven a material proof of the wickedness and cruelty with which he had been treated on earth." Luther, finding his liberty endangered, fled to Saxony. The Dominicans in Germany caused one of his works to be burnt publicly. The same opposition marked the invention of the art of printing. When Galileo announced to the world that the earth turns round the sun, people rose against him. From fear of persecution and excommunication he was obliged to acknowledge his penitence, but immediately after whispered, stamping his foot, "*e pur si mouve*"—"*with all that, it turns.*" M. Lesseps was looked upon at first as insane, and the Suez Canal a chimera and a delusion. In the sixteenth century Servetus was burnt as a heretic chiefly for his new discoveries in anatomy. The stethoscope and its inventor M. Laennec were ridiculed by a few of the best teachers of his day. 'Harvey was persecuted for his discovery of the circulation of the blood, and was called "circulator" or quack. And what was the treatment Jenner, the discoverer of vaccination, experienced at the hands of his professional brethren? "The medical men of that day said that 'the king ought to suppress the destructive practice of vaccination throughout his dominions'; that 'it ought to be prohibited by Act of Parliament'—that ' it destroyed a great number of lives'—that where life was not destroyed, the most terrible maladies followed, such as 'the loss of the finger-ends,' 'blindness,' 'various kinds of deformity,' 'enormous and hideous swellings,' making the 'human face divine' resemble ' the face of an ox'; that some, ' after vaccination, had been actually known to cough like cows, and to bellow like bulls'; and they even said that 'the inventors of vaccination ought to be hanged.'"

From 1810 to 1830 Hahnemann published several volumes of his principal works,—" The Organon of Rational Medicine" and " Pure Materia Medica," as well as his treatise on "Chronic Diseases." Besides the works abovementioned, he had composed several other treatises prior to 1810. Towards 1830 a great calamity befel him in the loss of his wife. In 1835 Hahnemann married a young and highly-accomplished French lady, who had come from Paris to consult him for a disorder which had been pronounced incurable by the French doctors. She was cured, and by her persuasion he left Cœthen for Paris, where he acquired a considerable degree of popularity and a large fortune by his practice. He spent the remainder of his days in that gay capital, surrounded by many professional disciples, and died in 1843 at the age of eighty-nine. In 1851 a statue was erected to his memory at Leipsic.

Hahnemann no doubt has founded a school, and his system has found many eminent supporters in the profession. In Europe and America there are thousands of educated medical men practising on

Hahnemann's method. Homœopathy is received with less opposition than when it was first introduced. The bitterness of feeling and the antagonism that existed, and still exists to some extent, between the disciples of the new and old school, is well known. It must be confessed that Hahnemann, in various parts of his writings, expresses hatred for the work of his predecessors and contemporaries, but not till he experienced annoyance from the jealousy and attacks of his bitterest opponents. He was exposed to severe persecution; his system met with a great deal of opposition and abuse from the disciples of the old school; and he knew that he had no mercy to expect from his opponents. When we think of all this, we have no hesitation in saying that he was forced into an indiscreet warmth of expression by those who differed from him in opinion. The odious quarrels between the two divergent schools of medicine we must necessarily pass over, and confine ourselves to the consideration of the operations of nature and art in the cure of diseases, as being more connected with our object.

Dissatisfaction felt with the uncertainty of drugs and " an active and perturbative system of medicine" gave rise to homœopathy; undeniable recoveries under homœopathic treatment gave rise to the revival of Naturalism. The healing powers of nature to cure many diseases, and the mischievous interference of art in every case, caused Butler to rhyme—

> "For men are brought to worse distresses
> By taking physic than diseases.
> And therefore commonly recover
> As soon as doctors give them over."

It must indeed be admitted that certain diseases, when left to themselves, often terminate in the restoration of health; in other words, nature has a curative power to throw off disease. No doubt, in a large proportion of patients the regulation of the diet alone is sufficient to remove diseases, and without any medicinal treatment whatever. In hæmorrhages, wounds, fractures, and contusions, the modes of reparation adopted by the natural conservative powers of the system need no explanation. Every medical man knows that simple catarrh will, under rest and proper diet, disappear without any drug at all. Even cases of acute inflammation of the lungs, treated by diet and regimen alone, terminate favourably. " Even in the instance of the most fatal of acute diseases," says Sir John Forbes, "as in Asiatic cholera, plague, and yellow fever, we find a considerable proportion of the sick recover, under every variety of treatment, and alike under nominal as real treatment. The half, the third, or fourth part of those attacked by such diseases, who recover, are, generally speaking, restored by the powers of nature alone. In less fatal diseases, as in ordinary inflammations of the viscera or membranes, as in inflammations of the lungs, liver, pleura, peritoneum, &c., whether left entirely to nature or treated by means incapable of controlling them in any way, we find a still larger proportion of cases terminating in recovery, more or less perfect. In the zymotic or poisonous eruptive fevers, as in small-pox, measles, scarlatina, &c., it is now universally admitted to be impossible to check their course; and all our most experienced and most enlightened practitioners agree that the terminations, whether favorable or unfavorable, are only very slightly modifiable by treatment; and yet we find a large proportion of such diseases always terminating in restoration of health."*

How often do we see a young and inexperienced practitioner, ignorant or regardless of nature's curative tendency, increase his patient's sufferings by the mischievous interference of his art? Instead of recommending rest and a suitable diet and regimen in a simple disorder, he, perhaps from excessive anxiety about his patient, jumps to the other extreme with the full strength of the armoury at his disposal. Let us suppose the disorder to be trifling bronchitis. It is by no means uncommon to meet with a young doctor who, with an erroneous appreciation of the power of art, will in such case write several mixed prescriptions in the course of the day, each prescription composed of a number of ingredients, such as diaphoretics, to promote perspiration, purgatives to open the bowels, nauseants and expectorants. Foolishly yielding to the desire of his patient, he will prescribe an anodyne mixture to cause sleep; or, if he complains of tightness or pain in the chest, a few leeches or a blister. Such treatment, no doubt, makes him worse, and the poor sufferer is often reminded of the *gravity* of his disease. On taking a dose or two of the mixture he feels nausea, and is of course disinclined to take food. His doctor sends him effervescing powders, or a sedative mixture, to remedy the evil caused by his own prescription. Again, the effect of his purgative is uncertain; sometimes it acts vio-

---

* *Nature and Art in Disease*, by Sir J. Forbes, pp. 108, 109.

lently, and opium and astringents are prescribed, which in their turn produce their baneful effects, to be combated again by other means; at other times, the purgative does not act, and the patient complains of uneasiness and distension of the abdomen, and another powerful one is administered, and so on, until another practitioner is consulted, or nature cures in spite of bad treatment. The unhappy patient, after his recovery from a long and tedious illness, will attribute the cure to the skill of the doctor instead of the *vis medicatrix naturæ*, and the young doctor, elated by his success, will fancy that he has performed a wonderful cure. Even some senior members of the profession, forgetful of the healing efficacy of nature, have, from over-appreciation of the medical art, fallen into the error of attributing cures to their own skill, rather than to the wonderful powers of nature. Sir John Forbes, in his *Nature and Art in Disease** (pp. 21, 22), says:—" In acute diseases, of short duration ore particularly, as in many fevers and inflamations, the abatement of the severe symptoms hich often ensues speedily after the administration of remedies, is invariably attributed to the active measures usually had recourse to in such cases: a conclusion which, however false, can hardly be wondered at under the circumstances. When the observer sees bleeding, blistering, vomiting, purging, and all the other heroic arms of Physic, brought into action against the disease, and with the avowed object

---

* We can recommend this excellent little book to the "whole band of heroes fresh from the schools," as the result of the experiences of a man of great talent and observation.—*Author*.

of curing it; and when the disease is seen to abate or disappear within a short period after their employment; the inference seems inevitable that the artificial treatment was the exclusive agent in effecting the cure."

From the above statement it must not be understood that nature always succeeds, if not assisted or controlled by art. Desperate diseases require desperate remedies, but the employment of desperate remedies in insignificant maladies makes them formidable, and much more difficult to remove. Though in a large number of common ailments the powers of nature will cure without any aid from medicine, they fail to do so in others. When disease invades the animal economy, a struggle ensues between it and nature; the latter uses all its endeavours to resist and expel the intruder. If nature unaided does not succeed, life is extinguished. It is therefore the duty of every medical man to watch nature's tendencies and aid her in her necessity. As to the comparative merits of nature and art in the cure of diseases, the conclusion which Sir John Forbes arrives at is this:—" That of all diseases that are curable and cured, the vast majority are cured by nature independently of art; and of the number of diseases that, according to our present mode of viewing things, may be fairly said to be curable by art, the far larger proportion, may be justly set down as cured by nature and art conjointly. The number of diseases cured entirely by art (of course, I omit in all these statements *surgical* art) and in spite of nature—in other words, the number of cases that recover and

www.ingramcontent.com/pod-product-compliance
Lightning Source LLC
Chambersburg PA
CBHW032019220426
43664CB00006B/305